The International Society of Business, Economics, and Ethics Book Series

Volume 1

Series Editors

Joanne Ciulla
Laura L. Spence

For further volumes:
http://www.springer.com/series/8074

Geoff Moore
Editor

Fairness in International Trade

 Springer

Editor
Prof. Geoff Moore
Durham University
Durham Business School
Mill Hill Lane
Durham
United Kingdom DH1 3LB
geoff.moore@durham.ac.uk

ISSN 1877-3176   e-ISSN 1877-3184
ISBN 978-90-481-8839-0   e-ISBN 978-90-481-8840-6
DOI 10.1007/978-90-481-8840-6
Springer Dordrecht Heidelberg London New York

Library of Congress Control Number: 2010924809

Printed on acid-free paper

Springer is part of Springer Science+Business Media (www.springer.com)

Contents

Contributors

Maria Cecilia Coutinho de Arruda Associate Professor, Fundacao Getulio Vargas, Sao Paulo, Brazil, maria.cecilia.arruda@fgv.br

Frederick Bird Research Professor, Department of Political Science, University of Waterloo, Waterloo, Ontario, Canada; Distinguished Professor Emeritus, Concordia University, Montreal, Quebec, Canada, fbird@uwaterloo.ca

Paul Collier Professor of Economics, Oxford University Economics Department, Oxford, UK; Director, Centre for the Study of African Economies, Oxford, UK, paul.collier@economics.ox.ac.uk

Georges Enderle Ryan Professor of International Business Ethics, Mendoza College of Business, University of Notre Dame, Notre Dame, IN, USA, genderle@nd.edu

Elio Ferrato Professor of Foreign Trade, Business and Production Administration and Ethics, São Paulo, Brazil, kandra@uol.com.br

Christine Wanjiru Gichure Associate Professor of Applied Ethics, Department of Philosophy and Religious Studies, Kenyatta University, Nairobi, Kenya, gichure.christine@ku.ac.ke

Geoff Moore Professor of Business Ethics, Durham Business School, Durham University, Durham, UK, geoff.moore@durham.ac.uk

Munyaradzi Felix Murove Senior Lecturer, School of Philosophy and Ethics, University of KwaZulu-Natal, Durban, South Africa, murovem@ukzn.ac.za

Piet J. Naudé Professor of Ethics and Director, Nelson Mandela University Business School, Port Elizabeth, South Africa, piet.naude@nmmu.ac.za

Symphorien Ntibagirirwa Doctoral Researcher, Philosophy Department, University of Pretoria, Pretoria, South Africa; Director, Revue Ethique et Société, South Africa, nsymphorien@yahoo.fr

Iwao Taka Professor of Business Ethics, Reitaku University, Kashiwa, Japan; Visiting Professor, Kyoto University, Kyoto, Japan, itaka@reitaku-ac.jp

Thomas Vance Assistant Professor of Accounting, School of Accounting and Finance, University of Waterloo, Waterloo, Ontario, Canada, twvance@artsservices.uwaterloo.ca

Peter Woolstencroft Associate Professor of Political Science, Department of Political Science, University of Waterloo, Waterloo, Ontario, Canada; Director, MA Global Governance Internship Program, University of Waterloo, Waterloo, Ontario, Canada, pwool@watarts.uwaterloo.ca

Introduction to Fairness in International Trade

The chapters in this book all have their origins in the International Society for Business, Economics and Ethics (ISBEE) World Congress that was held in Cape Town, South Africa in July 2008 (see www.isbee.org) under the title 'Global Fairness – Local Integrity'. ISBEE, as many will know, aims to be a truly global association which draws together scholars and practitioners from all continents. In doing so, it helps to counter the kind of parochialism that is all too often a temptation – to work with others and write for others that share similar cultural assumptions. South Africa in general, and Cape Town in particular, was a good venue to host such a conference with its history as a meeting place for the peoples of the world.

The World Congress of ISBEE is sometimes referred to as the Olympics of Business Ethics conferences because it meets every four years. A lot of work, however, takes place in between Congresses because one of the key contributions that ISBEE makes is to co-ordinate Global Research Projects. These are loose but global networks of academics working on related areas with the World Congress as the initial focal point for the dissemination of that research. I had the privilege of co-ordinating one of the two Global Research Projects for the 2008 World Congress – Fairness in International Trade and Investment – and the papers from that research project form the second part of the book. The first part of the book contains a careful selection of other papers from the World Congress.

Part I: Economic Development, Wealth Creation and Africa

Given that the World Congress was being held in Africa for the first time, there is a deliberate bias towards African scholarship here with three of the five chapters being by African authors. This part of the book begins, however, with a chapter based on an edited version of one of the keynote addresses given by **Paul Collier**. We were, indeed, privileged to have Prof. Collier with us. His work on development economics and African economics in particular is well known. In his speech he reviewed the economic divergence of the poorest one billion from the other five billion people in the world. These people, he argued, lack any credible hope of ever emerging from their poverty, and their position has been made worse by commodity booms and the recent rise in food prices. He criticised the 'bottom of the pyramid' solution which sees people in the developing world as consumers, but also criticised micro-credit which sees them as entrepreneurs. What these people need from business, he argued, is to become wage-earning producers in manufacturing industries. And to enable this solutions are needed to both restrictive World Trade Organisation (WTO) policies and the powerful agricultural lobby in developed countries. So here the WTO emerges as a key player in enabling the bottom billion to break free from the chains of poverty – an issue that is considered in much more detail in the second part of the book.

The chapter by **Georges Enderle** is a more reflective piece, but nonetheless is related both to Paul Collier's chapter which precedes it and to the three African chapters which follow. He considers the concepts of wealth and wealth creation which, as he argues, are often assumed in discussions of business ethics – we are all *for* wealth creation. But Enderle shows that this is often because we have either a simplistic understanding of wealth (as in making money), or a vague concept (as in adding value). Instead, he argues that the concept of wealth is a rich and varied one – one that includes physical, financial, human and social capital wealth, takes both private and public forms, involves a consideration of both wealth creation and distribution, and has both material and spiritual aspects. Sustainability, and therefore intergenerational considerations, are also essential elements of any serious consideration of wealth creation. Hence there are challenges here for business and business ethics in considering the purpose of business – what it is for, what kinds of goods it produces or services it provides – rather than just how it goes about its business. In relation to development economics, this raises a question about a single-minded concentration on material wealth measured in monetary terms, important as that clearly is. Perhaps a wider understanding of wealth, and a focus on well-being and quality of life measures rather than just GDP per head, would help to ensure that development is truly beneficial to those whose need is greatest.

Symphorien Ntibagirirwa's chapter links with the issues of wealth creation and economic development. He makes the argument that cultural values underpin the pursuit of self-interest and rational choice that have led to growth and development in western economies. That these cultural values are fundamental to economic growth is often an unstated assumption, and an assumption that then leads to the simplistic conclusion that self-interest and rational choice (*western* values) can and perhaps should be universalised. In showing that this is not the case, Ntibagiriwa derives a powerful explanation for the failure of economic development in sub-Saharan Africa and, by considering shared African values, he argues for the development of an 'Ubuntu economy' which is true to Africa's cultural heritage. The concept of Ubuntu has an ontological basis to do with the nature of our shared humanity but also normative implications in fostering harmony in both society and with the ecological environment. There may be challenges here for Collier's proposals which may seem to suggest, at best, the export of a western economic model and, at worst, western economic colonialism.

Munjaradzi Murove's chapter on Black Economic Empowerment (BEE) reviews the problems with both capitalism as applied in South Africa (that it had tamed Africans into being victims of expropriation) and colonisation (that it had expropriated African resources and was, therefore, a form of legalised robbery). He then moves on to the commonplace that political independence has not meant economic independence or control; the problem remains that western countries are in favour of economic decolonisation only in so far as it provides fertile ground for perpetuating western economic interests. This leads on to a consideration of the policy of BEE, an attempt to draw indigenous Africans into capitalist forms of business. But he argues that this has merely served to produce a partnership between an African ruling class and international capitalism and that its benefits have not been widely shared. Drawing on Veblen's Institutional Evolutionary Economics, he argues that BEE will merely create a class of African capitalists whose economic standing will make it impossible for them to be in solidarity with the majority of the African poor.

The first part of the book concludes with **Christine Gichure's** chapter in which we see the impact of economic colonialism very directly as she discusses the case of the Kenyan cut flower industry. Here the (quite possibly ignorant but nonetheless not innocent) demands of western consumers are mediated through western companies and have serious effects on Kenyan employees in the industry. She provides a summary of the issues to illustrate the deleterious knock-on effects down the supply chain. In support of Murove she argues that this has resulted in exploitation and the violation of some basic rights of some of the more vulnerable stakeholders.

In considering theoretical perspectives that might help to resolve these issues, she draws particularly on Pope Benedict's encyclical *Caritas in Veritate* to argue for the common good as the missing link between ethical sourcing and moral responsibility. This moves moral responsibility from satisfying minimal requirements or complying with regulation to meeting aspirations of an ethical ideal based in distributive justice and gratuitousness. There are links here with African Ubuntu philosophy (see Ntibagiriwa's chapter).

Part II: Fairness in International Trade – A Global Perspective

We move then to the second part of the book which, as noted above, contains the papers from the ISBEE Global Research Project on Fairness in International Trade and Investment. International trade and investment are, perhaps, the most visible form of globalisation and raise issues that touch on the lives of hundreds of millions of people across the world. One focal point for this activity is the WTO and this was taken as the starting point for the five regional projects – from Africa, Latin America, Japan, North America, and Europe – that made up the global project. The order in which these are presented is quite deliberate – to allow the perspectives from the developing world to speak first rather than, as so often, to find them speaking second and on an agenda that has already been set.

The questions that each regional project agreed to review were as follows:

1. To what extent are the workings and outcomes of the WTO perceived as fair in your region/continent?
2. What are the main ethical issues regarding international trade and investment (or alternatively the WTO) in your region/continent?
3. What developments are there in your region/continent to address the above ethical issues?

These questions have, perhaps inevitably, been interpreted broadly by the different regions, and here I summarise the contributions and then attempt a global overview from these five projects. We begin with **Piet Naude's** chapter on Africa. He identifies Africa's dire economic situation: that with 13% of the world's population it has only 1% of the world's GDP; that over 40% of the sub-Saharan population lives on less than US$1 per day. He then traces the historical development of Africa including the slave trade, colonisation, de-colonisation and the development of the current global financial system which, he argues, has always been centrally managed with a severe democratic deficit in decision-making power as a result. He notes a general Afro-pessimism – something similar to Paul Collier's idea that the bottom billion (of which many are in Africa) lack credible hope.

In turning to trade and the role of the WTO Naude notes Africa's lack of ability to participate, that the agenda is not pro-development, the inappropriateness of a 'one-size-fits-all' strategy for trade liberalisation, and the need for aid to meet adjustment costs. But he also notes Africa's need to regain its own sense of self-worth and, in a manner similar to Ntibagirirwa, the need to reconstruct Africa's own identity. This will require special and differential treatment (as agreed in principle by the WTO) and, more generally, a redefinition of distributive justice. But he also turns to Ubuntu philosophy as something that Africa may be able to offer not only as an appropriate underpinning philosophy for African economic development (see Ntibagirirwa's chapter again), but for the global trading system in general. The ancient wisdom of interconnectedness and reciprocity may be part of what Africa can contribute as we face the challenges of sustainable development.

Elio Ferrato and Cecilia Arruda's chapter reports on the Latin American perspective. In a similar fashion to the chapter on Africa, they provide evidence of the lack of economic progress that has been made across Latin America. The chapter then produces a litany of protectionist measures, operated under WTO sanction, against these countries. As a result, it seems that they may be condemned to being the suppliers of primary goods only, instead of gaining the economic benefits of adding value in-country and exporting higher value goods. About the only positive aspects that they are able to report on is the impulse for the development of an understanding of the benefits of free trade among Latin American countries and, more specifically, some benefits deriving from Trade-Related Aspects of Intellectual Property Rights (TRIPS).

With these kind of challenges from developing countries, how do the developed nations view the WTO? We look first at **Iwao Taka's** contribution from Japan. He identifies that, while broadly in agreement with WTO principles, Japan's history (particularly when it took protective measures during its own post-World War II development) has led Japan to be sympathetic to developing countries' needs for special treatment. Japan also recognizes, along with other countries, that WTO outcomes are not always fair and that the WTO does not always function as it should. In the light of the latter, Japan's strategy has moved from negotiating WTO-based multilateral agreements to bilateral Economic Partnership Agreements (EPAs), though still operating within WTO guidelines. But there is also evidence that, while fair in terms of process, the outcomes of EPAs are not always fair to the bilateral partners. Japan is also sensitive to its own continued protectionism in relation to food security in general and rice production in particular.

This leads Taka to consider the purposes of globalization and the WTO and, drawing on a Rawlsian analysis, he concludes that in both cases the purpose must be to share the benefits of globalization and improve the situation of the least advantaged countries. This leads him to show how Japan has taken its responsibilities in this regard, as the world's second largest economy, seriously. So he identifies Japan's contribution to investment in Asian countries, and its more recent work in solving food production and poverty problems in Africa, particularly through infrastructure investment. He also notes the private sector's contribution to such development through projects in education, healthcare and security. All in all, then, it seems Japan sees the benefits of globalization and of WTO-style processes to free up trade, but is both sensitive to developing countries' needs and prepared to make its contribution to ensure the benefits of globalization are shared.

The chapter by **Fred Bird, Thomas Vance and Peter Woolstencroft** takes a 'big picture' perspective on fairness in international trade, focusing particularly on North America (Mexico, Canada and USA). They begin by discussing the trading relations between these three countries, noting that Canada has used WTO dispute resolution procedures successfully against the USA, and claiming that multi-lateral trade relations like those embodied in the WTO can be used to serve the interests of economically weaker nations. They then note four typical and competing normative views of what represents fairness in trade, each of which is or has been evident in North American trade – protectionism, the hegemonic liberal fair play approach, a concern for outcomes under a distributive justice approach, and anti-globalization dissent in the name of the environment or the working classes.

They acknowledge that any universal resolution between these normative views is unlikely, but offer some common points of reference which might usefully be used to inform and help towards resolution in such debates. These comprise respect for flexibility, the importance of institutions, greater attention to the commutative justice principles for fair exchanges between nations with asymmetrical economic power, the need to find a fitting balance between local, national, regional and international trade, and finally more concern for the ways false pricing and abusive transfer pricing distort international trading relations. In particular, they focus on the way in which such transfer pricing can distort international trade relations and suggest that there may be a role here for the WTO in shaping transfer pricing policy.

Finally, we turn to my own chapter (**Moore**) which offers a critical perspective on European trade relations with African, Caribbean and Pacific (ACP) countries. The recent focus for these relations has been the negotiation of WTO-compatible bi-lateral Economic Partnership Agreements (EPAs – see also Taka's chapter above). These have given rise to concern for five main reasons: their detrimental effects on the ability of the individual ACP regions to achieve local integration; the need for reform in local institutional arrangements for EPAs to have beneficial effects; the estimated direct trade and fiscal effects, which are generally predicted to be poor (see again Taka's chapter on Japan in this respect); the introduction of 'Singapore' issues to do with investment, competition, government procurement and services which are not required for such an agreement to be WTO-compatible; and issues over the amount and conditionality of aid to support ACP countries by mitigating supply side constraints such as poor infrastructure, weak production facilities and low levels of human resource capacity.

The position with regard to signing these EPAs is summarized in the chapter as of December 2008. Since that time further interim EPAs have been signed, but the overall situation – developing countries generally signing because they have most to lose while Least Developed Countries (LDCs) tending not to sign – remains the case. In other words, the contentious nature of EPAs is still very much in evidence.

Assessing fairness in international trade is problematic, but I discuss conven-tional procedural and distributive approaches and suggest, from virtue ethics, that an Aristotelian, *teleological* question over the purpose of EPAs (how they will support and benefit community both within developing countries and between developing and developed countries) may be a helpful addition. Applying these principles to the case of EPAs leads to various conclusions: the EU has generally both prioritized and compromised on procedural fairness whereas the ACP countries have, unsur-prisingly, sought but failed to achieve distributive fairness. Asking questions about community and purpose, which the ACP countries have been better at doing than developed countries, may help to ensure that the necessary flexibility is built in to enable LDCs in particular to develop at their own pace and thus genuinely benefit from trade liberalization.

Taking these five chapters together, then, what key themes emerge? We can discern five:

1. The benefits of international trade have clearly not been fairly distributed to date, with developing countries lagging far behind and in danger of losing out even further by being condemned to be, at best, the providers of primary goods;
2. Protectionism has played a key part in developed countries' economic progress and hence the inappropriateness of a 'one-size-fits-all' approach to development becomes apparent. This leads to the need for flexibility of approach to allow developing countries to protect infant and fragile industries and to liberalise when the time is right;
3. The over-riding purpose of trade liberalisation should be pro-development and, though this came out to only a limited degree, increasingly pro-*sustainable* development;

4. There is an appropriate degree of critical analysis of developed countries'
   approaches, and some evidence of these countries taking their responsibilities seriously towards developing countries in terms of aid and technological
   assistance, but questions remain over self-interested motives;
5. Developing countries may well have something to offer in relation to their
   understanding of community, of interconnectedness and reciprocity, that will be
   important as we strive towards a greater degree of fairness in international trade.

One final but important point is that the WTO came in for repeated criticism
throughout these chapters. As the key organisation at the centre of international
trade agreements it is both a relatively easy target for criticism and a fundamentally
important organisation if trade is to be for the common good. This raises the question
about the role and purpose of the WTO – whether it should be concerned solely
with trade liberalisation or should take on a more development-oriented stance. Not
surprisingly the dividing line between the camps taking these alternative positions
is broadly defined by developing countries on one side of the line and developed
countries on the other. It seems that resolution of this issue is crucial if the concerns
expressed here over the observed unfairness in international trade are to be resolved.

The contribution of this book towards this debate, and more generally towards
fairness in international trade, then, is more than simply academic commentary and
critique. There is a practical edge to the various dissatisfactions expressed here. It is
certainly my hope, and a hope that is evidently shared by the other contributors, that
the future of international trade is, indeed, fairer. If this book makes even a small
contribution towards the goal of the common good for all, it will have served its
purpose.

Durham   Geoff Moore
November 2009

Part I
Economic Development, Wealth Creation and Africa

Chapter 1
The Bottom Billion and What We Can Do to Help

Paul Collier

1.1 Introduction

Paul Collier was introduced by Georges Enderle:

> Let me now introduce our first speaker, Professor Paul Collier. For people like me who are not experts in development economics but concerned about globalisation and development, Prof. Collier is best known for his recent book about why poor countries are failing and what can be done about it. He developed a perspective for overcoming poverty that lies between those who think development has failed completely and those who advocate the substantial increase of aid believing that the problem could be solved that way.

> Prof. Collier is from Oxford University where he is the Director of the Centre for the Study of African Economies. He has previously served as Director for Development Research at the World Bank from 1998 to 2003 and he was a senior advisor to the former Prime Minister of UK, Tony Blair, as part of his Commission for Africa. He is carrying out current research on the challenges facing low income countries including research on the economics of conflict, governance and macro-economic policy with a strong focus on the effect of AIDS, exchange rates, and trade policy. We are particularly grateful for Prof. Collier for interrupting his family vacation and flying to Cape Town last night to speak to us, so please give him a warm welcome.

1.2 Paul Collier

Well thank you very much for inviting me. I think the ethical discussion on globalisation is being horribly and dysfunctionally polarised. There are two camps, and there has been a dialogue to the death between them. The one camp, which is implacably hostile towards globalisation and business in all its forms, sees global capitalism as evil. And there is another bunch of denying optimists, which see globalisation and business as a panacea. I think both of these camps are seriously wrong.

P. Collier (✉)
Professor of Economics, Oxford University Economics Department, Oxford, UK;
Director, Centre for the Study of African Economies, Oxford, UK
e-mail: paul.collier@economics.ox.ac.uk

G. Moore (ed.), *Fairness in International Trade*, The International Society
of Business, Economics, and Ethics Book Series 1, DOI 10.1007/978-90-481-8840-6_1,
© Springer Science+Business Media B.V. 2010

My book, *The Bottom Billion* (2007), is about a divergence, a term for what we used to call developing countries. When I grew up the world looked rather stark where there were 1 billion people living in rich countries and 5 billion people in poor countries. And that is still how, for example, the United Nation's Millennium Development Goals rate the performance amongst the 5 billion people living in developing countries. The world has not been quite balanced and has not been so for quite a long time. But I think that the world is about the 5 billion versus the 1 billion, or perhaps better the 1 billion, 4 billion, 1 billion. And that's the shape of the world we need to look at.

Yes, there are 1 billion people living at the top in the rich countries that have comfortably "made it". Then there are 4 billion people that are living in countries that are converging on that 1 billion at the top, and that are converging at rates which have no historical precedence. But that means 1 billion people are left at the bottom. One billion people living in about 60 countries that probably for the last 40 years have stagnated. And because they have stagnated and everybody else is growing, what we have is a process of divergence, divergence between those billion at the bottom and everybody else. And a divergence especially between the 1 billion at the bottom and the next 4 billion.

Now there are still a lot of poor people amongst those 4 billion. There are many poor people in China. But the poorest people are in Chad. And there is a big difference between being poor in China and being poor in Chad, and that can be summed up in one word – and that word is hope. A poor family in China has a credible prospect that their children will grow up in a transformed society. The parents will stay poor for the rest of their lives, but their children are likely to grow up in an economy that is rich enough to make them fully participating members of a modern global society.

But a poor family in Chad does not have that credible hope. The last 40 years have been stagnant and the danger is that the next 40 years will be the same. So the big divergence between the bottom billion and the rest is that of credible hope and the absence of credible hope in those societies. And that is both a human tragedy on a massive scale and a nightmare globally because the world, although economically divergent, is socially integrated, and 1 billion people living in societies that cannot provide credible hope is quite a bill for the future world to pay off.

So, my book is about why that divergence has happened, what has gone wrong, what the four traps[1] are that have prevented the 60 now poorest countries from growing, and then more particularly what can be done about it. And I do not want to go through the book today. I wrote the book so that you could read it at your leisure on a beach. Sixty thousand people have bought it and I now know that

---

[1] The four traps are the conflict trap, the natural resource trap, being landlocked with bad neighbours and bad governance in a small country.

many people have indeed read it on a beach on their vacation, and that is what I recommend.

Now what I want to do first is move on a little bit from that process of divergence. That process of divergence is a very long slow process over the last 40 years and there are two reasons which we can now say have complicated it. One is commodity booms, and commodity booms have provided an enormous opportunity for some of the countries of the bottom billion. Take a country like Angola. Angola is getting oil revenues of something over $50 billion US per year and that is much more than the entire net inflow of revenue to the 60 countries at the bottom. So how Angola uses its oil money is a first order issue of opportunities for transformation, and rapid transformation at that. There were opportunities like this that happened before in the 1970s, and usually they became lost opportunities. They could have been used for transformation, but that would have turned the politics of the country very sour. So a country like Nigeria is actually poorer now than if it hadn't had the first barrel of oil. So that is the first problem with the recent phenomena of commodities.

And then the more recent issue in relation to commodity prices has been the rise in food prices. And just as the commodity booms are a big opportunity for some of the countries at the bottom, so the enormous increase in food prices are a real nightmare, not just a potential nightmare, but a current nightmare for a lot of countries at the bottom. Food price rises are hitting one segment of the population very hard indeed and that is the urban poor, the urban population, because they have to buy their food. The rural population is to some extent protected because they grow their own food. The urban population has to buy their food. For not only do the urban poor have less money, but as you get poorer, a higher share of your budget goes on food. So the urban poor are spending about half their budget on food. And that is a really big nightmare in itself, but then worse than that is that those at the bottom of the food chain are the children of the urban poor.

We now know from nutrition studies that when children are malnourished for a continuous period of more than 2 years, it causes stunting. The stunting causes not only irreparable, irreversible physical damage, it causes irreparable, irreversible mental damage. So unless we can bring global food prices down fast, the current generation of children will grow up and will have irreversible damage done to it and we will witness the problems that will arise from this for another 70 or 80 years.

So the slow crisis of economic divergence in the countries of the bottom billion has been made more complicated by the huge opportunities, the high risk opportunities that commodity booms have led to, coupled with the current crisis of exploding global food prices.

And now I want to turn to what businesses can and should be doing about it. And let me start off with this slow process of the economic divergence of the 60 countries at the bottom of the world economy and what could probably be done about it. There is a business discourse on this and I do not want to be disparaging about it, but I want to suggest that to an extent it is disappointing.

The business discourse which I hear most often, and even though I have written a book called *The Bottom Billion*, they termed it the "Bottom of the Pyramid",[2] and this idea is very fashionable in business. I am not the writer of the "Bottom of the Pyramid". The guys who wrote that missed the point. For there is basically an opportunity for business, but it is not an opportunity for the people at the bottom as consumers. In fact, really poor people are so poor that there is not much of a market at all. Treating these people as *consumers*, misses the point. The real opportunity is to harness them as *producers*, because the tragedy of these billion people is that they are so unproductive. That's why they are very poor. But we now know how to organise economic life so that they, ordinary people, are much more productive than they have ever been in history. That is what business does, it organises ordinary people to be productive. That is what the bottom billion need. They need to be treated as producers, not just as consumers. And business needs to work its magic and raise their productivity and hence their income.

Now to an extent business is focussed on people as producers, but then it flips over from what I regard as the obvious focus and it goes all the way to treat people as entrepreneurs. And that is this huge movement for micro-credit, for micro-finance. And again I do not want to be disparaging, but frankly this flip from treating people as consumers who are so poor that they do not represent a sensible market to target, to treating them as entrepreneurs, growing their own businesses, is also so silly. For some of them will be entrepreneurs, but the reality of these terribly poor countries in Africa is that far too many people are being forced into the role of entrepreneur.

Most people in most societies are not suited to be entrepreneurs. The success of an entrepreneur is about risk taking, of an obsessive concern for details, all these personal characteristic that most people just do not have. That is why in most societies where people are given the choice, most people prefer to participate in production as wage earners rather than to act as entrepreneurs. And that is very sensible. Those ordinary people are much better as wage earners, for they do not need to make the everyday decisions themselves as entrepreneurs. And in the societies of the bottom billion, they are thrust into the role of entrepreneurs because there are no jobs. So then the job of business is obvious – to teach ordinary people to become decent wage earners. These wage-based jobs that provide the organisation with what it needs also make ordinary people more productive.

Now, some of this is happening, and there is a new wave of *social* entrepreneurs, and I think it is a hugely exciting phenomenon. I have lived through three instances of public concern with developing economies. The first instance came after the war, where the big public enemy was the World Bank, the United Nations and the big democracies. And then about 20 years ago we got a new way which was the compassionate organisation, the compassionate NGOs. And they had huge energy, but they were not really very good at looking after business strategy. And now the new way of social entrepreneurship combines all the compassion of entrepreneurs with

---

[2] See the references for details.

all the business "savvy" and flexibility required. And there is only one thing that is missing at the moment, and that is any sense of being strategic, intervening, providing the businesses which in a particular environment can scale up and make an overall massive difference to these economies.

So, what I urge is to become more strategic and pursue those opportunities in particular environments which have the ability to scale up. The big thing that powered Asia's poverty was Asia breaking into global manufacturing. And that really happened only from the 1980s on. Until the 1980s global manufacturing was basically a developed country activity. But that has changed. Take the case of buttons. Two-thirds of all the buttons made in the world are now made in one city. This is as a result of what is known as clustering – the formation of clusters of mutually supporting firms (suppliers of various forms, manufacturers, distributors) which develop a combined technological expertise. This would be an ideal, scalable technology for the bottom billion, but the difficulty is in breaking in to that kind of cycle of economic development.

For the Least Developed Countries (LDCs) a system known as "Everything But Arms" (EBA) exists. This was originally adopted by the European Commission, granting duty-free access to imports of all products from all LDCs without any quantitative restrictions, except to arms and munitions. But in practice this is ineffective and is, in effect, no more than gesture politics. It might be better termed EBM – "Everything But Manufacturing"! What Africa needs is temporary access to developed markets in order to be able to break in to these markets and develop the kind of manufacturing base that would provide long-term economic development. We need a temporary waiver of World Trade Organisation trade laws, perhaps for a period of 2 years or so, for that to be possible.

However, one of the traps that I identified in my book is the problem of being landlocked with bad neighbours. This means that, even if a manufacturing base could be established in some of these countries, the problem of poor transport infrastructure in neighbouring countries would mean that the supply chain would be costly and difficult to maintain. For that reason the best place for manufacturing to be developed is in coastal areas. For that reason too, it may be that e-services may be part of the solution.

I want to return finally to the problem of the present food crisis and the need to bring world food prices down, in order to make one further point. Western societies have the solution to this problem. In the USA one third of grain is now grown for bio-fuels instead of for food. In the European Union there is a ban on production using genetically modified crops. Changes to either or both of these policies would make a huge difference to the quantity of food produced and hence to its price. But, as usual, there is another factor here and that is that both of these situations are being exploited by the greedy agricultural lobby. So, we need to find solutions to this kind of protectionism if we are to help solve the problem of the bottom billion.

As I said towards the end of my book, our approach toward the bottom billion has been failing. Unfortunately, many of these countries are heading down, not up, and they are collectively diverging from the rest of the world. But it does not have to be like that. If we could narrow the target onto these bottom billion and broaden the range of instruments that we bring to bear on the problem, we can solve it.

Thank you.

References

Collier, P.: 2007, *The Bottom Billion. Why the Poorest Countries Are Failing and What Can Be Done About It* (Oxford University Press, Oxford).
Prahalad, C.K.: 2006, *The Fortune at the Bottom of the Pyramid. Eradicating Poverty Through Profits* (Wharton School Publishing, Upper Saddle River (Pearson Education Inc.)).
Prahalad, C.K. & A. Hammond: 2002, 'Serving the world's poor, profitably', *Harvard Business Review* 80, 9: 48–57.

Chapter 2
A Rich Concept of Wealth Creation Beyond Profit Maximization and Adding Value

Georges Enderle

"Making money" can be destroying wealth while creating wealth can be losing money.
A thorough understanding of wealth creation enables us to sharpen our economic critique of fashionable and short-sighted management recipes and to bring the power of ethics to bear where it matters most.

2.1 Need for a Fresh Look at the Creation of Wealth

The purpose of this chapter is to take a fresh look at the concept of the creation of wealth. We need a fresh look because the notion of wealth creation we encounter is often very simple (as in "making money") or extremely vague (as in "adding value"). Moreover, the urgency for a fresh look becomes even more articulated and pressing when we envision the global importance of wealth creation and its widespread factual neglect. Not only need we better understand what wealth creation really is, but we also need to understand how it should be valued in the global context from moral, cultural and religious perspectives. Therefore, the search for the meaning of wealth creation can't be conducted but in both a critical and a constructive approach.[1,2]

G. Enderle (✉)
Ryan Professor of International Business Ethics, Mendoza College of Business, University of Notre Dame, Notre Dame, IN, USA
e-mail: genderle@nd.edu

[1] On a personal note, I may add my exposure to and my interest in the question of wealth creation, having taught and done research in China for many years.

"To be rich is glorious," a famous saying attributed to Deng Xiaoping in the mid 1980s (see note 2), marked a radical change of attitude towards wealth and prosperity, one that came to constitute a core value of the moral foundation for China's economic reform and open-door policy. It has been embraced by millions and millions of Chinese and proved, overall, to be quite successful. I personally have been fortunate, since 1994, to observe and study the remarkable economic development in China and particularly in Shanghai, to seek possible lessons applicable to other parts of the globe and to reconsider my own views with regard to poverty and wealth and business responsibility.

G. Moore (ed.), *Fairness in International Trade*, The International Society
of Business, Economics, and Ethics Book Series 1, DOI 10.1007/978-90-481-8840-6_2,
© Springer Science+Business Media B.V. 2010

In order to illustrate the huge gap between the global importance of wealth creation and the attention paid to it, I would like to point to three concerns about globalization and the roles and responsibilities of corporations.

2.1.1 Winners and Losers in the Process of Wealth Creation Over the Last 50 Years

The first concern is highlighted in the fascinating and powerful historical account "why some [nations] are so rich and some so poor," of David Landes (1999), who scrutinizes the winners and losers in the process of wealth creation over the last

---

These Chinese challenges are in stark contrast to what I had experienced before my involvement with China and in other regions of the world. Highly motivated by an eye-opening trip to India in summer 1970, I wanted to complement my education in theology with studies in economics, especially on poverty and income inequality. My focus was clearly on the poor, not the rich. How could the rich be "glorious" when, as Jesus said, "it is easier for a camel to go through the eye of a needle than for someone who is rich to enter the kingdom of God" (Luke 18: 25)? Although living in Europe, I was strongly influenced by the Latin American theology of liberation, the preferential option for the poor, and the debate on the pastoral letter *Economic Justice for All* of the U.S. Catholic bishops (Enderle, 2002b). To fight against poverty made sense. Jesus' saying that "you always have the poor with you" never meant to me to accept the fact of poverty in resignation and to give up the hope to essentially eradicate poverty. Thus I wrote my "habilitation" (Enderle, 1987) in business ethics on economic and ethical aspects of poverty in Switzerland and, by doing so, discovered how poverty research can open up a wide range of perspectives that are also of great relevance to business and economic ethics in general (see Enderle, 1991). But at that time I didn't realize the importance of the creation of wealth.

In the 1990s I was increasingly exposed to two very different types of continental experiences. I couldn't help comparing them on a continuous basis, although such comparisons are certainly incomplete and somewhat biased and unfair. My connections to and activities in Latin America, and particularly my involvement in the long preparation of the World Congress of Business, Economics, and Ethics in São Paulo (2000), helped me to understand more deeply the ethical challenges of business ethics on that continent and the presence of Catholicism in its multiple forms (see Enderle, 2003). My trips to East Asian countries and my studies of some of their core ethical issues opened my Western eyes to a very new and highly complex reality with which I still have difficulty coming to grips (see Enderle, 1995; Lu and Enderle, 2006).

In juxtaposing and comparing those countries' experiences, I'm beginning to understand how important a proper concept of and a determined focus on wealth creation are precisely for addressing the issues of poverty and inequality of income and wealth. Furthermore, these vital problems cannot be dealt with in a purely technical and value-free manner. Culture and religion obviously matter and their impact, for better or worse, needs to be investigated and evaluated.

[2]Remark about the saying "to be rich is glorious": This saying ("zhi fù guāng róng"), actually, was neither directly uttered nor denied by Deng Xiaoping. A journalist asked the leader in an interview on September 2, 1986: "How would Mao Zedong see the current situation?" and proposed the answer that remained uncontested by Deng Xiaoping: "In such a way as the current leaders maintain that to be rich is glorious...." (*Deng Xiaoping's Selected Works in Chinese*, vol.3, Beijing: People's Publishing House, 1993, p. 174). I acknowledge my gratitude to Xiaohe Lu for this information.

50 years. On the winners' side, in addition to "the thirty wonderful years from 1945 to 1975" of France and the "economic miracle" in Germany, he highlights the East Asian success stories of Japan, the four "Little Tigers" (South Korea, Taiwan, Singapore, and Hong Kong), and the regional followers such as Malaysia, Thailand, and Indonesia, referring, among others, to the World Bank's study *The East Asian Miracle* (1993), and adding China in his "Epilogue 1999" (Landes, 1999, pp. 524–531). The losers are the Middle East, Latin America, the countries of the Communist-Socialist bloc, and sub-Saharan Africa.

We may add some historical trends based on the World Bank's "World Development Indicators." The first set of charts (Tables 2.1, 2.2, 2.3 and 2.4; World Bank, 2007) depicts the annual growth rates in percent of the Gross Domestic Product (GDP) in different world regions (showing only the values of every third year and with varying scales of the vertical axis). It also contains the GDP growth rates in percent per capita, accounting for the changes of the respective populations over the years. Of course, these indicators can provide only a very rough picture of what might be called "creation of wealth."

Among others, it does not account for environmental degradation. Therefore, we supplement the growth rates with CO_2 emissions (metric tons per capita) as an indicator of this kind of degradation. It turns out that the "winners" over the last 15 years are East Asia and the Pacific as well as South Asia. Little economic growth with some negative annual growth rates can be found, in decreasing order,

Table 2.1 Strong economic growth: GDP growth, GDP per capita growth, CO_2 emissions

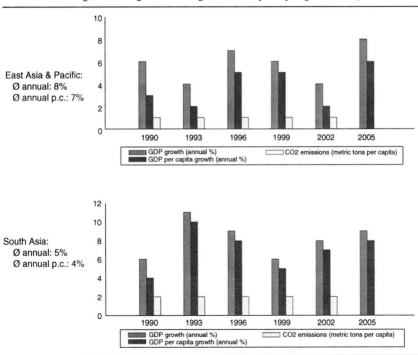

Table 2.2 Little economic growth: GDP growth, GDP per capita growth, CO_2 emissions

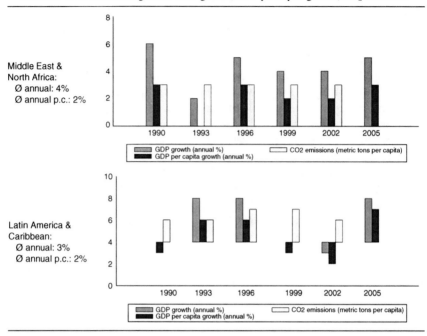

Table 2.3 Little economic growth: GDP growth, GDP per capita growth, CO_2 emissions

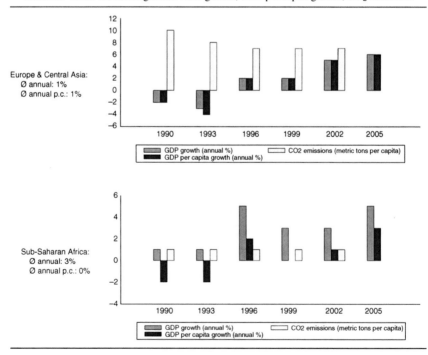

Table 2.4   GDP growth, GDP per capita growth, CO$_2$ emissions

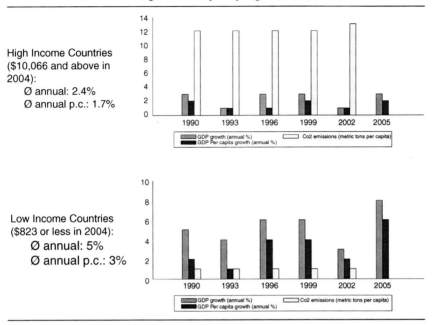

in the Middle East and North Africa, Latin America and the Caribbean, Europe and Central Asia, and Sub-Saharan Africa. Overall, High Income countries ($10,066 and above in 2004) showed low annual growth rates of GDP and GDP per capita (an average of 2.4% and 1.7% respectively), but very high levels of CO$_2$ emissions (12 and more metric tons per capita). In contrast, Low Income countries ($823 or less in 2004) had higher growth rates (i.e., 5% and 3% respectively) and very low levels of CO$_2$ emissions (1 metric ton per capita).

The second set of charts (Tables 2.5, 2.6 and 2.7; World Bank, 2007) shows the ratio of the poverty population as an important aspect of the unequal distribution of wealth, namely the poverty headcount ratio at $1 and $2 a day (in purchasing power parity) as percentage of the entire population in 1990 and 2002 (which are the only available data for that period of time). While the poverty ratios decreased dramatically in East Asia and the Pacific and considerably in South Asia, they declined only slightly in Latin America and the Caribbean and in the Middle East and North Africa, stagnated in Sub-Saharan Africa and even increased markedly in Europe and Central Asia.

Obviously, these very diverse developments have been caused by multiple factors which cannot be discussed at present. But these facts are enormous and provide paramount import to the question of how we may understand the creation of wealth with its environmental and distributional implications.

Table 2.5 Significant poverty reduction: Poverty headcount at $1 and $2 a day (PPP) (% in population in 1990 and 2002)

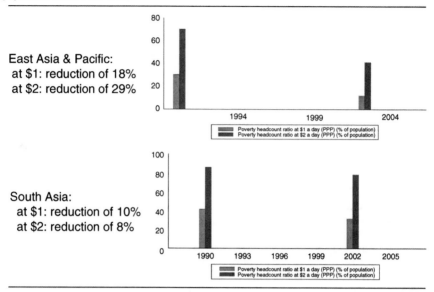

East Asia & Pacific:
at $1: reduction of 18%
at $2: reduction of 29%

South Asia:
   at $1: reduction of 10%
   at $2: reduction of 8%

Table 2.6 Modest or no poverty reduction: Poverty headcount at $1 and $2 a day (PPP) (% in population)

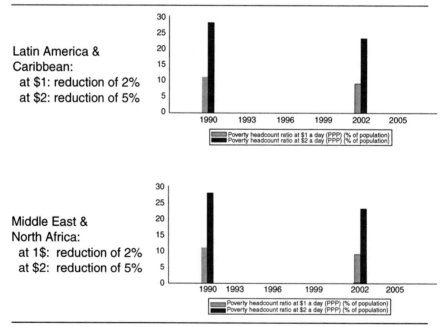

Latin America &
Caribbean:
   at $1: reduction of 2%
   at $2: reduction of 5%

Middle East &
North Africa:
   at 1$: reduction of 2%
   at $2: reduction of 5%

Table 2.7 Stagnation or poverty increase: Poverty headcount at $1 and $2 a day (PPP) (% in population)

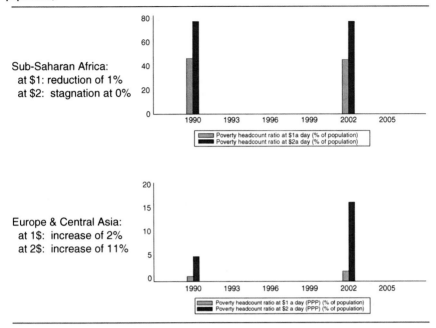

2.1.2 Wealth Creation: A Blind Spot of CSR?

A second concern relates to the worldwide discussions about "corporate social responsibility," or CSR, that have gained considerable momentum in the last 10 years. Corporations are expected to care about their environmental impact, to behave as corporate citizens, to defend freedom on the internet, to support cultural and sports events in their communities, to help the victims of natural disasters such as the tsunami and Katrina, to provide health care at reduced prices or for free to the needy who can't afford it, etc. Against the backdrop of this wealth of expectations, it is striking that, quite often, the financial and economic responsibilities of business organizations seem to be ignored, and, more specifically, no attention is paid to the questions of how companies can and should create wealth. In fact, creating wealth seems to have nothing to do with the social responsibility of companies.

2.1.3 What Is the Economic Underpinning of "Maximizing Shareholder Value" and "Adding Value"?

Finally, surveying the management literature, a third concern arises. It seems fair to say that a large part of this literature assumes the companies' objective of "maximizing shareholder value," giving it no critical examination in economic terms. A prime example is found in the survey "The Good Company" published by *The Economist* in January 2005. The authors present and criticize the almost irresistible rise of the CSR movement and conclude by falling back on Milton Friedman's catchy but poorly grounded slogan of 1970 "The business of business is business. Period." Moreover, when the broader objective of "adding value" is adopted, it is unfortunately often used as a black box that can be filled with any type of so-called value. Indeed, the notion of wealth creation is not seriously scrutinized even by prominent writers like J. Collins and J. Porras (Collins and Porras, 1994; Collins, 2001). Here again, in the management literature, we can often observe a strange phenomenon that the notion of wealth creation is taken for granted without critical reflection.

2.2 Conceptual Clarifications: What Is the Creation of Wealth?

Wealth can be defined in several ways. As Robert Heilbroner states (1987, p. 880), "wealth is a fundamental concept in economics indeed, perhaps the conceptual starting point for the discipline. Despite its centrality, however, the concept of wealth has never been a matter of general consensus." As for the term itself, it figures prominently in Adam Smith's work, *An Inquiry Into the Nature and Causes of the Wealth of Nations* (1776), but is conspicuously absent from Gunnar Myrdal's *Asian Drama: An Inquiry Into the Poverty of Nations* (1968) and is complemented with its opposite in David Landes's book title, *The Wealth and Poverty of Nations: Why Some Are So Rich and Some So Poor* (1999). It is noteworthy to see how Smith's "wealth" is translated into other languages: as *Wohlstand* prosperity (not as: *Reichtum* riches, *Wohlfahrt* welfare, *Vermögen* wealth) in German, *richesse* riches in French, *riqueza* riches in Spanish and *fù* rich in Chinese. Figure 2.1 offers an overview of the components of wealth creation as they are presented in the following. How this concept can be applied to wealth creation in China is discussed elsewhere (Enderle, 2010).

In order to discuss the concept of wealth, we first might concentrate on what is meant by the wealth of a single nation. While this approach may seem outmoded and inappropriate because of the "decline of the nation-state" in present times, the increasing number of pressing international challenges and the extraordinary power of many transnational corporations, however, it provides some advantages when compared to other approaches. When we ask for the "wealth of a nation," it is difficult to deny that wealth should encompass both private and public goods or assets, that is, endowments of two types: those that can be attributed to and controlled by individual actors, be they persons, groups or organizations, and those from which no actor inside the nation can be excluded. (In technical economic terms, "public goods" are defined by the characteristics of non-rivalry and non-exclusive consumption; see Enderle, 2000.) For instance, a SARS-free environment is a "public good" and a SARS-threatened environment a "public bad" that has clearly a material component, even though it might be difficult to put a price on it. It is obvious that the functioning of the markets and the production of private goods depend on such

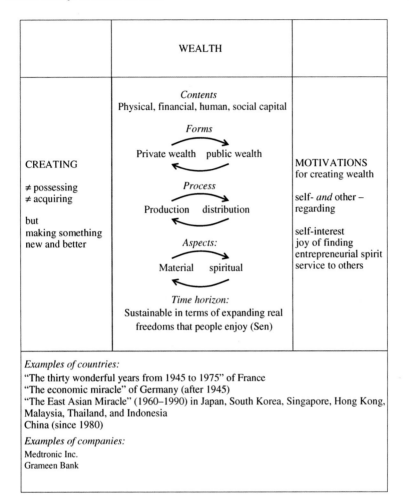

Fig. 2.1 A rich concept of wealth creation

public goods and public bads. In contrast, when speaking of the wealth of an individual or a company, we usually consider only the assets under its control while ignoring the public goods it also benefits (or suffers) from. In the international realm, public goods are only beginning to be discussed, although they are of increasing importance and often the driving force for transnational regimes and institutions (see, e.g., Kaul et al., 1999).

We may define the wealth of a nation as the total amount of economically relevant private and public assets including physical (i.e., natural and produced), financial, human, and "social" capital. Consequently, the creation of wealth includes the production of public as well as private assets, which indicates the important but limited role of the market and price mechanism. Wealth is primarily a stock (an economically relevant quantity at a certain point in time); but, in a broader sense, it also includes flows (increasing or decreasing quantities over a certain period of time). This basic distinction in economics is particularly relevant for our discussion on wealth because flows such as income per person, a commonly used indicator of the development of a country, express the economic situation of an economic actor only inadequately; the expected flows in the future are subject to a great deal of uncertainty and risk.

Another fundamental issue, fraught with multiple difficulties, is the question of how wealth as "economically relevant stocks and flows" can be properly expressed in monetary terms and added up to a total amount of money. From the recent experiences of the U.S. stock market, we all know that there might be huge gaps between the real economic and the monetary performances of companies, as the monetary indicators are only reliable if the markets function properly. Even then, this pertains only to private and not to public goods. In other words, sound economic thinking offers serious caveats against equating money with wealth. "Making money" can be destroying wealth while creating wealth can be losing money. It goes without saying that making money and creating wealth should go hand in hand.

What do we mean by the "creation" of wealth? Obviously, wealth creation is both more than possessing wealth and is only one form of increasing wealth. According to Jacob Viner, "Aristotle ... insisted that wealth was essential for nobility, but it must be inherited wealth. Wealth was also an essential need of the state, but it should be obtained by piracy or brigandage, and by war for the conquest of slaves, and should be maintained by slave works" (quotation in Novak, 1993, p. 105). In the course of history, the colonial powers acquired a great deal of wealth, usually with no regard for legal and ethical concerns, which, by and large, amounted to a redistribution rather than a creation of wealth. In the capitalistic system, the "acquisitive spirit," "the accumulation of capital," and the "acquisition of companies" do not necessarily entail the creation of wealth, properly speaking. It is, therefore, crucial to investigate precisely what this concept of "creation" means.

To create is to make something new and better. Take the example of Medtronic Inc., which is proud to be "the world's leading medical technology company, providing lifelong solutions to chronic disease" (http://www.medtronic.com). In its over 50-year history, it has developed a wide range of medical devices, from heart pacemakers to devices to alleviate neurological and spinal disorders and to manage diabetes, and it continues to be in the forefront of the industry (see *Financial Times,* "Medtronic shows off future of healthcare," February 8, 2002). Inspired to serve the customers, its innovative spirit has revolutionized not only its products and services but also its production processes, organization, culture, and identity, while yielding continuous financial success. As this company illustrates, while wealth creation has a lot to do with technological innovation, it is more than that, since the innovation is made feasible and successful in economic and financial terms. Aiming at material improvement for the benefit of human lives, wealth creation includes both a material and a spiritual side and goes beyond the mere acquisition and accumulation of wealth. It is a qualitative transformation of wealth.

On a national scale, the meaning of wealth creation can be easily understood against the backdrop of the debacle of a war. In the aftermath of the Second World

War, Germany and Japan had to create, to a large extent, new economies; and China, after the traumatic civil war of the Cultural Revolution (1966–1976), engaged in a transformation process from a centrally planned to a market-oriented economy. In those situations, creating wealth is a national objective that mobilizes a great many forces for a new and better future. In general, the state and companies operate on a broad consensus regarding the need for the creation of both public and private wealth. Without a doubt, the material side of these endeavors is essential, but the spiritual (or ideological) side is indispensable as well. As a good example for both the material and spiritual commitment of companies to participate in public wealth creation, we may recall Konosuke Matsushita's determination in 1954 to continue, despite serious financial difficulties, the joint venture with Philips. "I definitely do not think that the tie-up has been a failure.. . . I did not choose to form a technical tie-up with Philips in order to stimulate the growth of Matsushita Electric. I did not do it to gain personal publicity. I did it in order to bring the underdeveloped electronics industry in Japan up to world standards more quickly" (Yamaguchi, 1997, p. 6).[3]

In further exploring the notion of wealth, we may question its purpose and use, first in economic terms and then in noneconomic terms as well. Besides the fact that wealth creation can have intrinsic value (for instance, the hard and diligent work and great enjoyment of producing life-saving medical equipment), wealth has instrumental value, being usable for consumption or investment. If consumption is the sole purpose, the road to poverty is predetermined. For an historic example, we may recall the decline of Spain in the seventeenth century. As Landes writes (1999, p. 175), "Spain . . . became (or stayed) poor because it had too much money. The nations that did the work learned and kept good habits, while seeking new ways to do the job faster and better. The Spanish, on the other hand, indulged their penchant for status, leisure, and enjoyment, what Carlo Cipolla calls 'the prevalent *hidalgo* mentality'." And Landes offers a moral (relevant to the United States of today): "Easy money is bad for you. It represents short-run gain that will be paid for in immediate distortions and later regrets" (p. 173).

---

[3] One might ask whether this innovative spirit leading to wealth creation is one or even the essential feature of capitalism? Different scholars offer a variety of answers. David Landes argues that it was already in the Europe of the Middle Ages when the division of labor and widening of the market encouraged technological innovation (Landes, 1999, p. 45). For the peculiarly European cultivation of invention, as distinct from the Chinese attitude, he stresses the importance of the market. "Enterprise was free in Europe. Innovation worked and paid, and rulers and vested interests were limited in their ability to prevent or discourage innovation. Success bred imitation and emulation; also a sense of power that would in the long run raise men almost to the level of gods" (p. 59).

For Michael Novak, the innovative spirit becomes the hallmark of capitalism. Criticizing Max Weber who holds "economic rationality" to be the essence of capitalism and drawing on Hayek, Schumpeter, Kirzner and others, Novak states: "The heart of capitalism . . . lies in discovery, innovation, and invention. Its fundamental activity is insight into what needs to be done to provide a new good or service. The distinctive materials of capitalism are not numbers already assembled for calculation by the logic of the past. On the contrary, its distinctive materials are new possibilities glimpsed by surprise through enterprising imagination" (Novak, 1993, p. 10).

Investment is necessary for both wealth maintenance and growth. Of course, if the investment rate is very high, the present generation may carry an undue burden of reduced consumption for the benefit of future generations. However, today's consumer society tends to move in the opposite direction with a high preference for consumption to the detriment of investment. This trend becomes particularly clear when we take into serious account not only "the nature of wealth" but also "the wealth of nature."[4] One can reasonably argue that humankind at present is over-exploiting nature, the costs of which future generations will have to pay. It is therefore imperative to include the concept of sustainability in our notions of consumption, investment, and wealth. Wealth creation must be "sustainable," fulfilling the demand "to meet the needs of the present without compromising the ability of future generations to meet their own needs" (as defined by the World Commission on Environment and Development, see WCED, 1987, p. 8).

While this definition clearly presupposes a wide, intergenerational time horizon, it does not specify "the needs" of the present generation and "the ability" of future generations to meet their own needs. I therefore suggest adopting Amartya Sen's "capability approach," masterfully crafted in *Development as Freedom* (1999), in order to substantiate the concepts of needs and capabilities in this definition of sustainability. Development is defined as "a process of expanding the real freedoms that people enjoy" (Sen, 1999, p. 3). Although Sen does not directly refer to the WCED definition, from the outset he mentions "worsening threats to our environment and to the sustainability of our economic and social lives." He argues that:

> individual agency is, ultimately, central to addressing these deprivations. On the other hand, the freedom of agency that we individually have is inescapably qualified and constrained by the social, political and economic opportunities that are available to us . . . It is important to give simultaneous recognition to the centrality of individual freedom *and* to the force of social influence on the extent and reach of individual freedom. To counter the problems that we face, we have to see individual freedom as a social commitment. (Sen, 1999, pp. xi–xii)

In addition, it is easily ignored that wealth creation involves a distributive dimension, permeating all of its stages from the preconditions to the generation process, the outcome, and the use for and allocation within consumption and investment. In fact, the productive and the distributive dimensions of wealth creation are intrinsically interrelated. However, the separation between "producing the pie" and "sharing the pie" has marked for too long the ideological struggle between "the right" and "the left," despite its flawed economic underpinning. The time has now come to correct this misleading separation and to take the interrelations between the two dimensions (again) into account.

Having clarified different aspects of the concept of wealth creation, we now turn to the question of motivation. What motivates people, companies, and countries to engage in wealth creation? Common answers in the economic and sociological

---

[4] An interesting attempt to take nature into account has been made in the report to the Club of Rome by Wouter Van Dieren (1995).

literature are self-interest, greed, the will to survive, the desire for power aggrandizement, the enjoyment of riches, and the glory, honor, and well-being of nations. However, these motivations, taken individually or in mixed combinations, are rarely related specifically to the creation of wealth, but instead drive economic activities in general and, most often, incite merely the acquisition and possession of wealth. When economic activities clearly focus on wealth creation, other motivations such as the entrepreneurial spirit, the desire to serve others, and the *joie de trouver* (or the "joy of finding" that, in Landes's judgment [1999, p. 58], was the distinctive motivation in medieval Europe as compared to Islamic countries and China) become more important. At the same time, the purpose of business and consequently its role in society gets elevated. Business is no longer just about making money and acquiring wealth, relegated to the role of the ugly, yet indispensable servant that provides others with the material means to pursue higher, i.e., spiritual ends. Accordingly, it does not deserve a low reputation that is, unfortunately, even reinforced by those who stress the purely material and instrumental view. Rather, it is a creative and thus noble activity including both material and spiritual aspects, driven by a mix of motivations that are self- and other-regarding.

We may ask why, in history, wealth creation has often been ignored, disregarded or even treated with contempt. It seems to me that these attitudes depend on the valuation of the material world and the "bodiliness" of the human person as well as on the notion of creation. If the material world is considered inferior or even evil and if hostility towards the human body prevails, wealth cannot but share these qualities and is likely to be denigrated. Operating under those assumptions, it becomes nonsensical to produce such wealth, were it not for another, really valuable purpose. Moreover, without proper understanding, the creation of wealth cannot be really appreciated for its capacity to serve as a purpose of economic activity that matters more than the possession and acquisition of wealth. In sum, the determined affirmation that wealth creation is both good and necessary constitutes an essential prerequisite for thriving business in the long run. This necessarily includes, as mentioned above, a distributive dimension that permeates the entire creation process. It deeply affects the motivation for wealth creation as this motivation, in turn, strongly impacts wealth distribution.

What has been developed in the previous conceptual clarifications of wealth creation can be substantiated with Benjamin Friedman's work on *The Moral Consequences of Economic Growth* (2005). A prominent economist, he provides the facts and the analyses of how economic growth or stagnation may interact with the moral character of society and its social and political development over time. Carefully researching the histories of the United States, Britain, France, and Germany as well as the economics and politics in the developing world, he develops a deep understanding of "economic growth," similar to our notion of wealth creation. Economic growth is the production of a combination of private and public goods by both market forces and public policy. It should be broadly based and sustainable, thus involving necessarily a distributional and an environmental dimension. Economic growth has not only negative side-effects but also bears moral benefits in terms of openness of opportunities, tolerance of diversity, economic and social mobility, commitment to fairness, and dedication to democracy. In turn, the moral quality of society affects economic activity and policy. Consequently, Friedman conceives economic growth in both material and moral terms and rejects opposing material versus moral considerations as a deeply flawed and false choice.

2.3 Challenges for Business Ethics

After exploring the meaning of wealth creation, we now try to relate it to business ethics. But, by doing so, aren't we sending owls to Athens? Isn't this relationship so obvious that any thought would be superfluous?[5] After all, business is about producing wealth and ethics has to make sure that this is done properly. Nevertheless, I would like to argue that we need to pay serious attention to this relationship because, without this focus, business ethics becomes a superficial undertaking, evading the struggle with arguably the central issue of economic activity while expanding its reach far beyond what it can and should deliver.

In my view, a thorough understanding of wealth creation enables us to sharpen our economic critique of fashionable and short-sighted management recipes and to bring the power of ethics to bear where it matters most. From the conceptual analysis in the previous section we can draw a number of lessons for a sound, comprehensive, and differentiated understanding of business ethics. To equate business with just making money is not only questionable from the ethical perspective, one that asks for the ethical quality of both its means and its ends, but also from the economic perspective. Without adequate economic underpinning, making a lot of money can entail the destruction of much wealth, as the recent debacles of Enron and the like have demonstrated.[6]

It is relatively easy, though necessary as well, to criticize scandalous business behavior. But from the perspective of wealth creation, examples of an innovative spirit and best practices of "making things new and better" are more inspiring and should play a more prominent role in business ethics research and teaching. They would also highlight the fact that wealth creation forces the economic actor to look beyond the short term and definitively adopt a long-term perspective as well, in which "sustainability" is the key. As examples we may mention Medtronic Inc. (see above), Rohner Textil AG (www.climatex.com), and the Grameen Bank (www.grameen-info.org; the latter two companies being featured in Enderle, 2004).

---

[5] One might wonder if this is the reason why an entry on "wealth" (and on "poverty" as well) is missing in the *Encyclopedic Dictionary of Business Ethics* (Werhane and Freeman, 1997, 2005).

[6] With the benefit of hindsight we wouldn't qualify Enron as a company that created enormous wealth in the late 1990s despite its spectacular published financial results: its operating results, for instance, increased from $515 million in 1997 to $698 million in 1998, $957 million in 1999, and $1.266 billion in 2000. The bankruptcy filing lists $31.2 billion of debt, later revised to $40 billion and the asset values estimated at $62 billion in the Chapter 11 filing were later revised to $38 billion (Tonge et al., 2003, p. 5).

When exploring the concept of the wealth of nations, we concluded that it should encompass both private and public wealth. As we know from economic theory, properly functioning markets are powerful instruments to create private wealth, but they fail in creating public wealth. This involves far-reaching implications for business ethics. Business ethics should not be limited to the creation of private wealth and reduced to corporate ethics, that is, the ethics of business organizations, because the economy is bigger than the realm of markets and companies. Rather, business ethics should include the ethics of the economic system (and therefore go beyond "market morality"). It is only in this context that the creation of wealth with its productive and distributive dimension and, we may add, the re-distribution of wealth, can be treated in a proper and comprehensive manner.

With regard to globalization, wealth creation provides a focus for business ethics, the importance of which cannot be overestimated. As long as globalization is the acquisition of wealth, most often by the rich from the poor, it does not create but only reshuffles and redistributes wealth, although accumulated wealth may masquerade as created wealth. The creation of sustainable wealth is a highly complex and demanding process and cannot be achieved without paying serious attention to its distributional preconditions and consequences. Moreover, if it is true at the national level that the creation of private wealth necessitates a certain amount of public wealth, the same is likely to hold at the international and global levels. Given the difficulties in creating public wealth at the local and national levels, one can easily imagine the almost insurmountable problems to do so at the global level.

These difficulties in creating wealth call for a thorough examination of motivations. They should be strong and effective, providing the driving force necessary not simply for acquiring and possessing wealth but, more importantly, for creating wealth. Furthermore, they should aim not only at private, but also at public wealth at all levels, from the local to the global. Recalling the array of motivations indicated above, I suggest considering a mix of motivations that are self- as well as other-regarding. Certainly, self-interest and the honor of the country remain powerful driving forces and, properly understood, are ethically legitimate. But if they are purported as the sole important motivations (for economic activity), they are questionable on empirical grounds and can involve grave inconsistencies (for instance, the self-interest of the manager may conflict with the self-interest of his company, or the honor of the country may require the sacrifice of the individual's interests). For the very creation of wealth, as mentioned above, other motivations such as the entrepreneurial spirit, service to others, and the joy of finding (that might be combined with the will to make a decent living for oneself and one's family) assume more importance and are indispensable to producing public wealth. Generally speaking, the enormous challenges of creating wealth require a shift in motivations that shape the cultures of companies, countries and the world. But such a shift cannot take place unless it is internalized and advanced by individuals.

The motivation for wealth creation can be further strengthened to the extent that the production of economic wealth is intrinsically coupled with the production of non-economic, e.g., social and environmental, wealth, thus designed "to hit two birds with one stone." No doubt, to achieve this is an even bigger challenge to the entrepreneurial spirit, but the gain is bigger as well. At the organizational level, companies can employ strategies that simultaneously fulfill both economic and also social and environmental responsibilities so that the different dimensions of corporate activities reinforce rather than weaken each other. To give a few examples: Activities such as feeding hungry workers in poor areas will improve their productivity. Empowerment of workers on the shop floor will have a similar wealth-enhancing effect. Extending a plantation's water system into the local squatter community or investing in a hospital will improve worker health and motivation with a resulting productivity and positive cash-flow impact. In the environmental realm, programs to reduce energy consumption can enhance economic wealth. In other words, economic growth not only generates the means for social and environmental progress, but also social and environmental advances can enhance the economic performance of companies. As Benjamin Friedman points out for the societal level, there is also interaction between economic, social, and environmental activities at the corporate level. To account for this interrelationship, we may speak of a "balanced concept of the firm," which, in my view, is one of the top challenges for corporate ethics in the twenty-first century (see Enderle and Tavis, 1998; Enderle, 2002a).

Having said this, we should not forget that wealth creation at the national as well as the international level is a combined production of private and public wealth. This means that companies cannot generate wealth without benefiting from public wealth, and public wealth cannot be created without profiting from companies. In addition, this implies that companies should not be held responsible for nearly everything as many champions of CSR seem to demand; however, they do bear responsibility (shared with other social actors) for creating public wealth, which those deny who claim that profit maximization be the sole responsibility of business.

2.4 Conclusion

In this essay we have tried to show the need for taking a fresh look at the creation of wealth. From a global perspective it is crucially important to understand why some countries are so rich and some are so poor. From a business perspective and in the wake of the financial and economic crisis it seems necessary to better calibrate the purpose of the corporation. We suggest adopting a multifaceted concept of wealth and a genuine understanding of its creation. Wealth is more than financial capital by including physical, human, and social capital. Wealth is not only private wealth but also encompasses public wealth, both influencing each other in multiple ways. Because the process of wealth production inescapably involves a distributive pattern, wealth creation and wealth distribution, strictly speaking, cannot be separated (often "wealth distribution" actually meaning wealth re-distribution.) Wealth is not merely material but also has a spiritual side, which ennobles its creation to a truly human activity. By placing wealth creation in the time horizon of sustainability enriched by Sen's capability approach, one overcomes an exclusively short-term view and integrates an intergenerational fairness perspective. The emphasis on creating as distinct from possessing and acquiring highlights the need for innovation in both private and public wealth creation and requires "mixed" motivations (that is self- *and* other regarding) in order to overcome the exclusive and thus insufficient motivations of either self-interest or collective interests.

Such a rich concept of wealth creation involves far-reaching consequences for business ethics. It brings the power of ethics to bear where it matters most: the proper understanding of wealth, its creation and the motivations thereof. The purpose of business becomes a noble and sustainable goal that diligently serves customers, attracts talented and committed employees, provides decent returns to investors and protects the environment. Because the wealth of a nation (and of similar entities from the local to the global level) results from the combination of private and public wealth, business ethics should include the ethics of economic systems and deal with the proper roles the various social actors should play in this systemic context. With regard to globalization, business ethics should not content itself with the acquisition and/or redistribution of wealth; rather it should focus on genuine wealth creation, particularly among the losers of globalization.

References

Collins, J. C. 2001, *Good to Great. Why Some Companies Make the Leap – and Others Don't* (HarperBusiness, New York).

Collins, J. C. and Porras, J. I. 1994, *Built to Last. Successful Habits of Visionary Companies* (HarperBusiness, New York).

Enderle, G. 1987, *Sicherung des Existenzminimums im nationalen und internationalen Kontext. Eine wirtschaftsethische Studie* [Securing the Minimal Standard of Living in the National and International Context: A Business Ethics Perspective] (Haupt, Bern).

Enderle, G. 1991, 'La pauvreté, paradigme de l'éthique économique', in R. Rémond (ed.), *Démocratie et pauvreté. Du quatrième ordre au quart monde* (Editions Quart Monde/Albin Michel, Paris), pp. 453–469. [In German: 'Das Armutsproblem als Paradigma der Wirtschaftsethik', in P. Eicher (ed.): 1989, *Neue Summe Theologie*, Vol. 2 (Herder, Freiburg), pp. 340–373.]

Enderle, G. 1995, 'An Outsider's View of the East Asian Miracle: Lessons and Questions', in S. Stewart and G. Donleavy (eds.), *Whose Business Values? Some Asian and Cross-Cultural Perspectives* (Hong Kong University Press, Hong Kong), pp. 87–120.

Enderle, G. 2000, 'Whose Ethos for Public Goods in a Global Economy? An Exploration in International Business Ethics,' *Business Ethics Quarterly* 10 (1), 131–144.

Enderle, G. 2002a, 'Algunos vinculos entre la ética corporativa y los *estudios* de desarrollo,' in B. Kliksberg (ed.), *Ética y Desarrollo. La Relación Marginada* (El Ateneo: Buenos Aires), pp. 345–372 [English title:'Corporate Ethics at the Beginning of the 21st Century'].

Enderle, G. 2002b, 'The Option for the Poor and Business Ethics', paper presented at the conference *The Option for the Poor in Christian Theology* on November 10–13, 2002, at the University of Notre Dame. Manuscript available from the author.

Enderle, G. (ed.) 2003, 'Special Section: Religious Resources for Business Ethics in Latin America,' *Latin American Business Review* 4 (4), 87–134.

Enderle, G. 2004, 'Global Competition and Corporate Responsibilities of Small and Medium-Sized Enterprises,' *Business Ethics: A European Review* 13 (1), 51–63.

Enderle, G. 2010, 'Wealth Creation in China and Some Lessons for Development Ethics,' *Journal of Business Ethics*, doi: 10.1007/s10551-010-0453-x.

Enderle, G. and Tavis, L. A. 1998, 'A Balanced Concept of the Firm and the Measurement of Its Long-term Planning and Performance,' *Journal of Business Ethics* **17** (f11), 1121–1144.

Friedman, B. M. 2005, *The Moral Consequences of Economic Growth* (Vintage Books, New York).

Heilbroner, R. L. 1987, 'Wealth', in J. Eatwell, M. Milgate and P. Newman (eds.) *The New Palgrave: A Dictionary of Economics*, Vol. 4 (Macmillan, London), pp. 880–883.

Kaul, I., Grunberg, I. and Stern, M. A. (eds.) 1999, *Global Public Goods. International Cooperation in the 21st* Centure (United Nations Development Programme, Oxford University Press, New York).

Landes, D. S. 1999, *The Wealth and Poverty of Nations: Why Some Are So Rich and Some Are So Poor* (Norton: New York).

Lu Xiaohe, Enderle, G. (eds.) 2006, *Developing Business Ethics in China* (Palgrave Macmillan, New York). (In Chinese published by Shanghai Academy of Social Sciences Press, 2003.)

Myrdal, G. 1968, *Asian Drama: An Inquiry Into the Poverty of Nations* (Pantheon, New York).

Novak, M. 1993, *The Catholic Ethic and the Spirit of Capitalism* (Free Press, New York).

Sen, A. 1999, *Development as Freedom* (Knopf, New York).

Smith, A. 1776, *An Inquiry Into the Nature and Causes of the Wealth of Nations*, edited by Campbell, R. H., Skinner, A. S. and W. B. Todd, 1976 (Clarendon Press, Oxford).

The Economist 2005, *The Good Company*, Special survey, January 22.

Tonge, A., Greer, L., and Lawton, A. 2003, 'The Enron story: you can fool some of the people some of the time . . ., *Business Ethics: A European Review* **12** (1), 4–22.

Van Dieren, W. (ed.) 1995, *Taking Nature Into Account: Toward a Sustainable National Income* (Springer, New York).

Werhane, P. H. and Freeman, R. E. (eds.) 1997, *The Blackwell Encyclopedic Dictionary of Business Ethics* (Blackwell, Malden, MA).

Werhane, P. H. and Freeman, R. E. (eds.) 2005, *The Blackwell Encyclopedia of Management, Volume II: Business Ethics,* Second edition (Blackwell, Malden, MA).

World Bank 1993, *The East Asian Miracle: Economic Growth and Public Policy* (Oxford University Press, New York).

World Bank 2007, *WDI Online* [electronic resource]. *World Development Indicators* (World Bank, Washington D.C.).

World Commission on Environment and Development (WCED) 1987, *Our Common Future* (Oxford University Press, New York).

Yamaguchi, T. 1997, 'The Secret of Matsushita's Success. Five Principles of Rational Humanistic Management', Presentation at the Beijing International Conference on Business Ethics.

Chapter 3
Cultural Values, Economic Growth and Development

Symphorien Ntibagirirwa

3.1 Introductory Background

The intention behind this chapter is to raise awareness of the importance of cultural beliefs and values as an important factor, one of the root-sources of economic development that should be taken seriously, particularly in Africa. So far little or no attention has been paid to the cultural factor in Africa's economic development. Cultural values in Africa have been mostly perceived negatively in economic matters both by African economists, policymakers and planners themselves as well as the consultants of the international institutions and Western donors. As a consequence, there is a tendency to shift away from them, even from those values such as solidarity and cooperation which, nowadays, are important in today's economic business. Much attention is concentrated on the claim that appropriate economic policies (mostly neo-liberal policies) necessarily achieve economic growth and development.

Accordingly, this chapter consists of six major points. In the first point I will outline the issues that are at stake in the whole reflection. The second point considers the sense of neo-liberal's claim and underlines its limits. The third point questions the link between self-interest and economic growth and development by considering the economic experiences of East Asia and Sub-Saharan Africa. The aim of this point is to suggest that one needs to look beyond the mere concept of self-interest as the basis of economic development. In the fourth section I will review the principle of self-interest against its historico-cultural background in order to show that what led to economic development is not the self-interest per se but rather cultural beliefs and values that produced it. My main objective is to show the necessary link between cultural values, economic growth and development (fifth section), by paying more attention on the case of Africa (sixth section). In the conclusion I summarize the macro-argument and give the implications of my reflection.

S. Ntibagirirwa (✉)
Doctoral Researcher, Philosophy Department, University of Pretoria, Pretoria, South Africa;
Director, Revue Ethique et Société, South Africa
e-mail: nsymphorien@yahoo.fr

G. Moore (ed.), *Fairness in International Trade*, The International Society
of Business, Economics, and Ethics Book Series 1, DOI 10.1007/978-90-481-8840-6_3,
© Springer Science+Business Media B.V. 2010

3.2 The Issues at Stake

Four key issues are at stake in this reflection. The first one is the issue of the impact of people's cultural beliefs and values on economic development. I am aware that certain cultural beliefs and values of a people could enhance or hamper their economic development. In this reflection, and as far as African economic development is concerned, I am much more inclined to place weight on those beliefs and values that would likely enhance economic development.

The second issue is a practical follow up of the first: it is the whole issue of how what people believe and value can be validated in terms of policies of economic development. Nowadays, the concept of participation has become the catchword in developing countries. However, it is not enough for people to "participate" if the model of economic development proposed to them is based on a cultural foundation which is not theirs. Participation in a perspective of economic development which is not rooted in one's cultural beliefs and values could only be contingent rather than essential. I believe that participation could only be essential if it applies to those economic development projects that are founded on the beliefs and values of the people concerned.

The third issue is the philosophical foundation of economic development. In effect, what people believe and value are based on their being or ontological status. In other words, the beliefs and values people hold are a reflection of their identity, that is, their sense of self. Thus, ultimately, it is from this ontological status that a given people structure its own economic development that cannot easily be transferred to another people whose ontological status is different. What we are as a people determines the way we structure and shape our economic development (economy being, qualitatively, a cultural phenomenon) (see Throsby, 2001: 7ff).

Yet, and this is the fourth issue at stake, the way people view themselves and live in the world can be enhanced or hampered by others with whom they do not share the ontological status, as has been the case with slavery and colonisation or other forms of domination. The problem here is the refusal of the difference based on the fact that a group of people can feel powerful enough to universalise its way of life, thus undermining the whole issue of particularity. How can what certain people claim to be universal be appropriated in another context that has its own particularities (see Gyekye, 1997)? Cultural values matter (cf. Harrison and Huntington, 2000; Sen, 2006, Ch. 6); and my effort will consist in showing how they matter (see Section 3.6).

3.3 Making Sense of the Neo-liberal's Claim

The proponents of the neo-liberal economics have often tried to make us believe that the freedom to pursue one's self-interest as well as one's rational choice lead to successful economic growth and development. Accordingly, neo-liberal economists, planners and policymakers tended to universalize this claim, and insistently argued that appropriate economic policies effectively implemented produce everywhere the same results independently of cultural values (see Williamson, 1993; Olson, 1982; Hayek, 1949, 1978; Downs, 1957). Some of these economists and policy-makers often support their argument by the view that modern economics is based on mathematical methods that are universal[1] (see Rosenberg, 1992; Yonay, 1998; Hodgson, 2001). Thus, policies and principles of economic development that are derived from it are universally applicable irrespective of the culture in which they are applied. Accordingly, they suggested that developing countries should embrace the neo-liberal economic policies for them to escape from the trap of economic underde-velopment and poverty. This, indeed, has been the case with the ten macroeconomic principles that constitute the core of the Washington Consensus[2] (Williamson, 1990: 1993).

The economic success of South East Asian countries on the one hand and the failure of economic development in Sub-Saharan Africa on the other, are increas-ingly proving that the "economic" argument alone cannot be taken as a dogma: self-interest and rationality do not seem to be the only avenues for economic growth and development to take place in any given society. One other avenue to be explored is the link between cultural values and economic growth and development. My concern is that even though they cannot be taken as the sole fac-tor,[3] cultural values are crucial for economic growth and development. Economic growth and development can occur only if they are a substantiation of a people's beliefs and values. For alien economic policies to be effective in a cultural sys-tem other than that which generated them, they need to be appropriated by such culture.

---

[1] In his recent publication, the winner of the prestigious Myrdal prize 2008, Erik Reinert (2007: 42–46) has complained about the quantification and the mathematics being the only recognized form of doing economics, and thus, requested for room to bring qualitative analysis back into academic economics.

[2] Principle 1: Fiscal discipline;
Principle 2: Concentration of public expenditure on public goods including education, health and infrastructure;
Principle 3: Tax reform toward broadening the tax base with moderate marginal tax rates;
Principle 4: Interest rates to be market determined and positive;
Principle 5: Competitive exchange rates;
Principle 6: Trade liberalization;
Principle 7: Openness to foreign direct investment;
Principle 8: Privatization of state enterprises;
Principle 9: Deregulation – abolishment of regulations that impede entry or restrict competition, except for those justified on safety, environmental, and consumer protection grounds, and pruden-tial oversight of financial institutions;
Principle 10: Legal security for property rights.

[3] For instance, in his *Cultural Factors and Economic Performance in East Asia and Latin America,* Jiang Shixue (2008) argues that "each culture has its own unique positive and negative components, but the positive ones cannot automatically create better economic performance in the absence of other necessary conditions like sound economic policies, effective institutions, favourable world economic situations, the right timing of a nation's entry into industrialisation, and political stability."

3.4 Questioning the Link Between Self-Interest and Economic Growth

The claim that "the freedom to pursue one's self-interest leads to economic growth" comes from Adam Smith's reflection on how the wealth of a nation could be increased (Smith, 1965). Smith believed that human behaviour is guided by self-interest. However, when one looks at the way the economic perspective based on the principle of self-interest is failing in Africa, particularly with the Structural Adjustment Program of the 1980s on the one hand, and the economic success the South East Asia on the other, one cannot but wonder whether self-interest really leads to economic efficiency as neo-liberal economists and policymakers would make us to believe.

The idea of self-interest is apparently, if not obviously, in contradiction with the earlier ideas in his book, *The Theory of Moral Sentiments* (1808) in which Smith developed the concept of sympathy considered to be the concern for the interest of the other. Sympathy requires the benefactor to suspend his own interest for the sake of the beneficiary. Although this altruism does not necessarily give Adam Smith communitarian credentials of the African or Oriental type, one may wonder whether the spirit of sympathy could not increase wealth in the same way as self-interest does, if oriented in economic matters. So that one can say that sympathy could lead to economic success just as self-interest does.

I am aware, as Smith would be, that the motive to satisfy one's self-interest and the interest of others both come from the same human tendency to sympathise with self and with the beneficiary (Khalil, 2001). However, in so far as the economic discourse of neo-liberalism lays much emphasis on self-interest rather than on the interest of the other, the centre of focus in neo-liberal economic ordering is self-interest. There are a number of issues that are raised here. Would people really achieve economic success if they behaved in an exclusively self-interested way (see Sen, 1987: 21)? Even if economic success were to be achieved, to what extent can one really say that it is only the principle of self-interest that led to such a success? Do people really behave in an exclusively self-interested way in economic matters? Are there no other aspects that may serve as catalysts of economic success such that self-interest is but one of them or not even necessary? Amartya Sen has this crucial question: "the real issue is whether there is plurality of motivations, or whether self-interest alone drives human beings" in economic matters (Sen, 1987: 13).

This series of questions led Mark Lutz and Kenneth Lux to explore the possibility of a *Humanistic Economics* as can be seen in their conclusive observation:

> Where it has been acknowledged that human behaviour might have another dimension than self-interest, it has been decided that this part of the person is irrelevant to economics and therefore is outside the scope of science. [...] Such an exclusion is theoretically wanting, empirically questionable, a serious social mistake with unfortunate consequences (Lutz and Lux, 1988: 102).

The idea of self-interest was boldly underlined at the time when the production of goods and services was being developed thanks to the development of natural sciences and their technological dividends, especially in England. Furthermore this increasing production required larger markets which were being conquered in the new English colonies in various parts of the world. This seems to lead one to believe that the principle of self-interest may achieve economic growth and development only for those who can sell or buy and who actually have the means to do so. On the contrary it does not work for those who cannot buy or sell, and hence are excluded. According to Michael Todaro (1989: 84), the principle of self-interest and the so-called invisible hand of the market that results from it often act not to promote the general welfare, but rather to lift up those who are already well-off while leaving others behind.

There is here a whole argument that runs counter to the ethical theory of utilitarianism, but I will not play on this field for the time being. But what Todaro seems to be saying is that for self-interest to work there must be other conditions that must be fulfilled. Thus I would go as far as saying that it is not just having something to sell on the market and/or having the means to buy that matters. But one must also have in oneself self-interest as a value, more precisely, an economic value. The question is to what extent this is the case.

According to Amartya Sen (1987), in the case of the economic success of Japan, there is empirical evidence showing that there were systematic departures from the self-interested behaviour in the direction of cultural values such as duty, loyalty, good will that played an important role in the Japanese economic success (cf. Lutz and Lux, 1988: 84). Sen himself was drawing on the reflection of Michio Morishima (1982), a Japanese scholar who argued that what has played an important role in the Japanese economy is much more the Japanese spirit which is rooted in Shintoist and Confucian values. Nowadays it is being argued that the economic success in other South East Asian countries is also being achieved thanks to the same Confucian values (Granato et al., 1996; Franke et al., 1991; Hofstede and Bond, 1988). Onis (1995) argued that, the East Asian economic miracle has been possible thanks to the developmental state provided by the Confucian heritage which emphasizes hierarchy and group solidarity. The group solidarity provides a ground for cooperation within the same East Asian society, while the hierarchical authority of the government provides incentives, political framework, the infrastructure and other means necessary for the enterprises of its country to compete on the international scene.

Economists and policymakers who defend the philosophy of self-interest in economic growth and development argue that, in the case of Africa, the state has been an obstacle to self-interest and its success, and thus is a hindrance to economic growth and development. This argument is built on the debate between the libertarians defending the priority of the individual over the community, and the communitarians who defend the priority of the community over the individual. Hence those who believe that in Africa the state is an obstacle to the principle of self-interest and its economic achievements are the libertarians who argue that in the African culture, the community is hampering individual freedom and responsibilities, and hence an obstacle to the individual flourishing (Kenyan, 2006; cf. Dalacoura, 2002; Nozick, 1974). It is true that the community can effectively be a limit or an obstacle to individual freedom and responsibility; but it is equally true that the community can be a context in which the individual flourishes more than if one were left alone, particularly when the values which the community cherishes are harmonised with those which the individual cherishes for mutual advantage (see Mbiti, 1970; Tshamalenga, 1985; Shutte, 1993; Gyekye, 1997; Sandel, 1982, 1996, Taylor, 1989, MacIntyre, 1981).

In the case of the Asian economic miracle, it has been observed that the state, far from being a handicap for the market economy that is thought to result from the principle of self-interest, played an important role in the economic development (Biel, 2000: 202; Dasgupta, 1998; Onis, 1995). Furthermore, even in Latin America, the introduction of the neo-liberal principles in the 1980s required an authoritarian state to deal with opposition from the rent-seekers who had benefited from the structuralist import substitution policies.

Of course, my intention is not to advocate for authoritarianism in the present era of political liberalism in so far as I believe that democracy is a historico-political achievement which people embrace as they become aware of their political nature. My point here is that it is possible to achieve economic growth and development with community-centred interest just as it can be achieved with individual self-interest. If this were found to be the case, the traditional values of African communitarian society should be explored to see whether they may not be pregnant with economic potentials. In fact, the point of incompatibility between self-interest as the ground of economic growth and development and African culture has not yet been tackled as an issue. I should say that certain societies, especially the African one, have been misled by the link between capitalism and individualism built in the belief that self-interested individuals and the subsequent invisible hand of the market increase wealth. This has been the case with the introduction of neo-liberalism in Africa in the 1980s and the subsequent trade liberalisation, privatisation of state enterprise, and deregulation of national economies (see note 2). The neo-liberal economists and policymakers have been so dogmatic to the extent that it was easily forgotten that capitalism could be possible even in non-individualistic societies. Yet it is clear that the neo-liberal capitalist (which I consider to be linked with individualism), with its private markets, well defined property right, entrepreneurship, is but one version of capitalism. To be precise, the market-led capitalism of the United States of America and the United Kingdom is not the corporate capitalism of Japan and South Korea; the social-democratic capitalism of Scandinavia and Austria is not the state-led capitalism of France (see Brauer et al., 1999). Is a capitalist version that fits with the structures of African society, for instance, conceivable?

Thus, the problem might not be the belief itself since it might work for some societies. The real problem lies in the tendency to universalize it as if it is the only possibility. The implication is that other avenues are neglected and undermined, especially for those countries which are historically, politically and economically dependent. The consequence is that the victims of this economic dogma find themselves confused about what values really lead to economic growth and development. And under the pressure of achieving this economic growth and development in the short term, they don't strive to make a difference which would be derived from the validation of their cultural beliefs and values.

3.5 Viewing the Principle of "Self-Interest" Against Its Historico-cultural Background

The point I want to substantiate in this section is that what achieves economic success is not the self-interest per se but rather the cultural beliefs and values from which it resulted. If Smith claimed that the freedom to pursue one's self-interest leads to the increase of wealth for a nation, it is apparently because he was reflecting in a new cultural environment where the individual was henceforth sovereign. And indeed, the sovereignty of the individual was a new conception of the human being which came to the fore as a result of the intellectual and historical mutations of 17th/18th century in Europe. This means that the individual who became now the source of wealth of the nation was the product of a new cultural universe in Europe. Here are the salient characteristics of this new culture:

3.5.1 Human Sovereignty

The first characteristic of the new culture is the human sovereignty over the natural world. This aspect is better described by Klaus Nürnberger, in his book, *Beyond Marx and Market* (1998: 31):

> No part of reality is forbidden ground for human investigation and utilisation. There are no uncanny forces, magical powers, divine beings or eternal principles which human beings must fear, respect, or obey. Human beings are masters over the world.

This reality itself was henceforth discovered by means of investigation (empirical philosophy of John Locke and David Hume), penetrated by logical thought (Rationalist philosophy of René Descartes) and manipulated for the desired result (technological advances). The implication of this was a culture which gave human beings a new way of looking at the world and affirming themselves (Nürnberger, 1998: 31).

3.5.2 Individual Sovereignty

This characteristic is, in fact, the implication of the first one and has been emphasized by a great number of western philosophers. The first philosopher who underlined boldly the sovereignty of the individual is René Descartes with his famous principle: "I think therefore I am". The implication of this principle was that from then on, the human being was the creator of his own self, his world, and depended on no one else except his own individual self. John Locke is another defender of individual sovereignty. He argued that people are equal and that every individual has the right to self-preservation. This self-preservation goes with personal property. Every individual has a property in his own person. Locke shares his thought on the sovereignty of the individual with Thomas Hobbes, although this latter viewed the individual from a negative perspective as can be seen in his principle: "Man is a wolf against man". Yet this does not prevent him from sharing with Locke the view of the individual as an atomic unit sufficient unto itself, interacting with others primarily in the pursuit of their self-interest (Ingersoll and Matthews, 1991: 37–38). Another important figure in the defence of individual sovereignty is Kant. The idea that lurks behind Kant's categorical imperatives is that the individual is the starting point of universality.

Finally, that the individual is sovereign means that the society plays a second role. That is what Jeremy Bentham affirms when he views the community as a fiction and a collection of individuals, and that no objective social interest exists except individual interest independently of fictitious society.

One may summarise these different views on the individual as follows: The individual who was now defined by reason (the thinking being) became the source of not only morality (Kant's categorical imperatives), but also of every aspect of life: Political life (democracy as a political system of equal and free individuals), social life (the individual could now act unconstrained by the society and the hierarchical authority), religious life (the individual is no longer defined by any divinity), moral life (against Aristotelian teleological definition of human action), and economic life (one's self-interest and rational choice increase a nation's wealth) (cf. MacIntyre, 1981).

3.5.3 Freedom

The new culture insists on freedom of individuals to organise their own lives, alone or in cooperation with others. According to Klaus Nürnberger (1998: 30), freedom goes with the virtues of taking bold initiatives and using all one's gifts and talents for self-determination, self-realisation and self-responsibility. Freedom is associated with personal choices, self-fulfilment and personal initiatives. Thomas Hobbes, John Locke, and David Hume argued that all people possess the freedom necessary to secure their natural rights, that is, the rights that are not subjected to any other authority other than the human beings themselves. This freedom is the necessary means to pursue one's ends.

3.5.4 Private Property

The fourth salient feature of the culture that fuelled the classical economy is the emphasis on private property which goes with self-interest. Private property is viewed as an expression of human potential and an indication of human creativity (Ingersoll and Matthews, 1991: 39). According to Jean Jacques Rousseau, there is a link between freedom and private property: private property is an instrument without which one's freedom cannot be secured. Linked with private property is the whole notion of self-interest which has been emphasized by Hutchison, Hume, Tucker, Furgeson, Mandeville, and in a particular way Adam Smith (see Haney, 1921).

3.5.5 Materialism

The materialist outlook of the new culture can be seen from two important aspects, namely a new sense of value and labour. According to Jeremy Bentham, the human being is governed solely by the hedonistic principle of seeking pleasure and avoiding pain. And utility maximising is the only standard of evaluation. He further argued that money is the most accurate measure of the quantity of pain or pleasure a human being can be made to receive. Accordingly, the valuation of what is good or bad, profitable or not, pleasure or pain, rests solely on the subjective judgement of the individual with money as the measure of welfare (Bentham, 1970: Ch. 1). Such a notion of value is also connected with the individual and one's self-interest. However, this materialist conception of value is very limited. At most it could cover what people can do (quantification of our pain or pleasure), but it does cover what people can be (qualification of our pain or pleasure). In other words one's pain or pleasure is quantified in terms of money (exchange value) but not qualified.

Materialism can also be seen in the instrumentalisation of labour. The traditional belief in labour as an important social resource and the means by which a society advances was rejected. Accordingly, in his *Political Discourses* David Hume (1987) argued that everything in the world is purchased by labour, and that our passions are the only cause of labour. Jeremy Bentham argued that the love of labour is a contradiction in terms. From the utilitarian point of view labour is not undertaken for the benefit of those performing the labour, but for those hiring labour power to generate exchange value. Workers must be bribed to expend effort through payment of wages. Even Adam Smith tended to limit productivity to tradable commodities to the extent that even people themselves are viewed as other commodities.

3.5.6 Reason

The new culture emphasized reason as the regulator of everything. It is said that when individuals use their reason and industry in the pursuit of personal gain, everyone in the society gains. This means that reason is the criterion for the distribution of profits and burdens in a given society, particularly a utilitarian society. Economically, the role of reason is to instruct people on how to secure these desires most efficiently (Ingersoll and Matthews, 1991: 38). However, from the contractual point of view, the role of reason is to deal with conflicts which arise because self-interest leads people to desire the same object. Thus the traditional understanding of reason as the essential characteristics of human nature is seemingly dropped as reason is considered mostly from an instrumental perspective rather than comprehensively. According to David Hume, reason is and ought only to be the slave of the passions and can never pretend to any office other than to serve and obey them.

The above characteristics underlie the cultural value system which gives the individual a particular ontological status. People in turn orient all the aspects of their life in a way that responds to this ontological status. Thus classical economic liberalism and the liberal revival in the 1980s can be understood against this background. The appeal to a minimal involvement of the state in the economy was the outcome of such a culture and the ontological status it produced. Adam Smith's economic thought has been revived as a ground of universal economic development inherited from this cultural value system. His assumptions of self-interest and *laissez-faire* economic policy developed from and within this cultural environment. That economics is concerned with wealth of the nations, that economic activity is embedded in the pursuit of wealth, and that the mainspring of economic activity is self-interest, can only be understood against this cultural and individual's ontological background.

In today's economic thinking, one major feature of these beliefs that goes with self-interest as a principle of economic growth is rationality. Self-interested producers and consumers mindful of economic growth and development are presupposed to be utility and profit maximizers who respond rationally and efficiently to market signals. Rationality is thus the central characteristic of the self-interested economic people, and consists in the logical application of economic means to attain particular economic ends. The human being becomes that being whose economic behaviour conforms to the dictates of reason. Accordingly, the neo-liberal economists tend to advise the policymakers of the developing countries to simply get "the price right".

Rationality as a major feature that underlies economic behaviour is emphasized by various theorists who treasure the neoclassical economics. Bill Gerrard (1993: 52), for instance, argues that the axiom of rationality is the cornerstone of modern economics. Economic behaviour is interpreted as the outcome of optimizing choices by rational economic agents. Daniel Hausman (1992: 278) posits that "much of the methodological distinctiveness of economics stems from the remarkable fact that a theory of rationality lies at its theoretical core". Ann Cudd (1993: 102) argues that rationality is the capacity inherent primarily in individuals, and these agents act to maximise their subjectively given utility, and thus to give substance to their self-interest.

From what I have developed so far, it is clear that what achieves economic success is not self-interest *per se* but the set of cultural beliefs and values from which it resulted. The claim I am trying to establish so far is that economic growth and development is a product of the validation or substantiation of peoples' cultural beliefs and values. In the next section, I would like to consider this necessary link between cultural values and economic growth and development by paying much more attention to the case of Africa.

3.6 Cultural Values, Economic Growth and Development: The Necessary Link

The cultural outlook I have just reviewed has been so intuitive to its promoters that it tended to be universalised to other societies to the point that their cultural beliefs and values (henceforth viewed as traditional) came to be considered as economically worthless (cf. Mehmet, 1995). Indeed, this has become a background against which the developing nations are viewed and advised for their economic growth and development. In the 1960s and 1970s, for instance, modernisation theorists argued that, for underdeveloped nations to achieve economic growth and development, they have to take the same road that modern societies took (see Rostow, 1960; cf. Weber, 1971).

The consequence of all this is that most of the societies of the south, particularly in Africa south of the Sahara, came to neglect unduly their cultural beliefs and values arguably because they lacked the potentials and the rationality peculiar to the modern economics. But this neglect is more a result of the complex of economic powerlessness felt by some societies that their beliefs and values are economically barren without exploration. For instance, Etounga Manguellé (1990), in his celebrated *L'Afrique a-t-elle besoin d'un programme d'ajustement culturel?*,[4] argues that Africa needs a programme of cultural adjustment that would transform its mentality to one which is consistent with values in the rest of the world. Of course, it is not clear what those universal values are that he is referring to. However, one may presume that Manguellé is referring to western values.

According to Sally Matthews (2004: 380), a project of economic development premised upon a set of values cannot succeed in the absence of those values. A project which has its roots in particular assumptions and values cannot succeed in the absence of the relevant assumptions and values. Thus, Manguellé's suggestion can be interpreted as follows: if Africans want to achieve the economic growth and development of the West, they first have to espouse the type of beliefs and values upon which it is premised. This was the argument developed by the proponents of the modernisation theory. Despite the injunction of this theory in Africa (one may refer to certain colonial approaches such as assimilation practiced by France) as well as Western influences, most Africans still retain most of their values: they still converse in their own languages, still have their African style homes, African food, and Africans' world views and values systems remain noticeably different from those of the West (Matthews, 2004: 379). I shall come to the meaning of this in terms of Africa's economic development later. For the time being, I would like to consider another African who has an argument similar to that of Manguellé.

Axelle Kabou (1991) argues that, although they never appear on the long list of official causes of underdevelopment, African cultures and mentalities are the main

---

[4] Does Africa need a cultural adjustment program (my translation).

obstacles to development. Effectively it may be true that some mentalities and attitudes can effectively be obstacles to economic growth and development. One may refer, for instance, to those mentalities that tend to limit people's production to their immediate consumption with little or no conception of the long term.[5] A communal, paternalistic outlook can hamper the spirit of creativity, initiatives and innovation. Much emphasis on family ties is often the source of nepotistic behaviour linked to incompetence of which Africa is often accused. One may also refer to the fact that some traditional religious faiths do emphasize detachment from material goods and wealth. But those mentalities cannot take priority to the fact that people produce for their subsistence or produce to acquire what they do not produce; this being the starting point of economics. Neither can they take priority on the fact that people produce and exchange as part of their self-realisation or self-actualisation and self-transcendence.

Manguellé and Kabou seem to be biased to the point of considering only the negative aspects of African culture that effectively have a negative impact of economic development. Messay Kebede (2004) might be right to suggest that they need to undergo a mental decolonisation so as to emancipate their views from non-African constructs. The communal outlook thought to be an obstacle to creativity and initiative is also the ground of economic cooperation. In effect, the extended family, for instance, is, indeed, the nucleus for a cooperative spirit, solidarity, care and self-help. The family could be the source of the value which consists in considering and protecting the goods and the services of a company as one's own (see Wong, 1988). Paternalistic behaviour can be the source of authority that managers need to lead their companies (see Reddy, 2009). At the same time, this paternalistic behaviour could be the source of a kind of leadership strong enough to ensure accountability (cf. Asante, 1991: 69).

Thus, there is a link between what one believes and what one lives (*passage du cru au vécu*).[6] In other words, as Asante (1991: 68) puts it, "it is the totality of the values, norms, attitudes, beliefs of a society which shapes its social, political and economic organisation and inculcates a general feeling towards development." This

---

[5] This point could be deepened especially when dealing with the concept of time in the African context. For instance, John Mbiti (1970) argues that in traditional Africa, there are only two aspects of time: the present (*sasa*) and the past (*Zamani*). The consequence of this conception of time would lead one to believe that planning for the future is rather speculative. If this were the case, then it would be difficult to talk of planning of economic development (Nyang, 1994). However Mbiti was obviously mistaken since in all Bantu languages there is the future tense as well. And the akamba culture of which Mbiti is part is not an exception. Yet it may be possible that what Mbiti might have had in mind is that the past, the present and the future merge in the same way as the individual is ontologically part of the community in the African conception of the human being. If this was the case, is it not the prospective nature of economic development that would be endangered along with the meaning that people derive from the future (Diagne, 2004)?

[6] For a more extended reflection on the point, one could refer to my article "Le miracle asiatique": qu'apprendre de l'expérience asiatique du développement (The Asian miracle: what can be learned from the Asian experience of development), in *Ethique et Société*, 2006, 3 (1): 18–34.

is the case irrespective of whether the culture of such a people is individualistic or communal. Thus, Messay Kebede (1999) argues that,

> The depiction of development in terms of mere satisfaction of needs rather than validation of beliefs largely explains the underdevelopment of Africa. By not being a program of corroboration of beliefs, development fails to be animated by a competitive, insatiable, and creative spirit.

Michael McPherson (1987) argues that economics itself is part of a cultural milieu. This point is also echoed by David Throsby when he says: "The fact that economic agents live, breath and make decisions within a cultural environment is readily observable" (Throsby, 2001: 9). The cultural milieu, in large measure, endows economic goods and activities with meaning and presents people with the matrix of constraints and opportunities within which they develop themselves.

3.7 Linking African Cultural Values to Africa's Economic Growth and Development

The crucial question one should ask at this juncture is how African cultural values are structured and what kind of economic development could fit with this cultural value system. I shall attempt a response to this question by considering how the Bantu people conceive of themselves and reality. The Bantu are a group of Africans who occupy almost all the Southern part of the Equator and its surroundings. They cover more than 60% of the African population in Sub-Saharan Africa, and occupy geographically one third of the whole African continent (Kagame, 1976). This may justify why most African and non-African thinkers tend to refer to Bantu philosophical principles to make the point of what unifies Africans (Tempels, 1959; Jahn, 1961; Eboussi-Boulaga, 1981). According to Alexis Kagame,[7] the lowest common denominator of the Bantu people is the fact that their value system is structured according to the way they conceive of the categories of being in their ontology (Kagame, 1976, cf. Kagame, 1956). There are four of these categories (Fig. 3.1), namely:

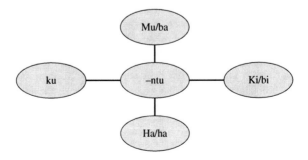

Fig. 3.1 The structure of the Bantu universe

---

[7] Kagame collected data on 180 languages from the Bantu zone, read 300 books on the various Bantu.

- The category of *mu-ntu* (plural: *ba-ntu*): intelligent (or rational) being(s). It is the category of human beings;
- The categories of *ki-ntu* (plural: *bi-ntu*): non-intelligent beings. It is the category of things including animals, plants, and inanimate beings such as stones;
- The category of *ha-ntu*: Spatio-temporal being. It is the category of time and space;
- And finally, the category of *ku-ntu*: Modal being. It refers to the way different beings are shaped, their position, their relation, their colour, etc.

All these four categories (mu, ki, ha, ku) are built on the same root, *ntu* (being)[8] and are arranged in a hierarchical order with the human being standing at the top of the hierarchy. Contrary to what Nhlanhla Mkhize (2008: 41) holds, it is obvious from the above figure that *ntu* is not only reserved to human beings. Mkhize (2008: 38) rightly talks of the cosmic unity but fails to discover that *ntu* underlies it, maybe because the four categories seem to be unknown to him.

There has been a question of why "bu" of *(u)bu-ntu,*[9] for instance, does not constitute a fifth category. According to Kagame (1976), with the concept of *u-bu-ntu,* one is already in the formal logic as a condition for (African) philosophizing. In effect, the Bantu distinguish between the concrete and the abstract. They separate the abstract of accidentality expressing entities which do not exist independently in nature such as *u-bu-gabo* (courage, force, and virility), *u-bu-shingantahe* (integrity, equity); and the abstract of substantiality. Both of them are connoted by *-bu. Ubuntu* (humanity or humanness) enters in the latter category. Of course, *ubuntu* as a metaphysical concept has moral implications. In effect, *ubuntu* is a moral character and even a value of people when they live, act and behave in the way that fosters harmony in the society and the universe around them. The use of *ubuntu* of Southern Africa refers to this moral character or value. In fact, when one says that people are living according to the value of *ubuntu,* one means that these people live in a way that fulfils their nature as intelligent beings.[10]

---

[8] Kagame claimed that these four categories correspond to the ten Aristotelian categories (one substance and nine accidents). However, his biographer, Kagabo (2006: 236), questioned this claim arguing that Aristotelian categories are classes of predicates while Kagame's categories are classes of beings. However, this is not to say that Kagame is wrong since as far as the Bantu languages are concerned, Kagame is right to stress that any conceivable entity comes down to one of those four and there is no entity outside those four categories (Kagame cited by Kagabo, ibid.).

[9] According to Ramose (1999: 41, see also Mkhize, 2008: 41) *ubuntu* has two particles, the prefix *ubu* and the stem *ntu.* But actually there three particles: *u* which is an article, *bu* which denotes the abstract. For instance the Bantu would refer to the dog-ness of a dog as u-*bu*-bwa, the animality of an animal as *u-bu-koko.* When *bu* is combined with the stem *–ntu,* it means the humanness or humanity.

[10] I am also using the word "intelligent" to mean "comprehensive rationality" that allows people to transcend calculations geared to substantiating their personal interests rather than harmony in the universe.

What these Bantu categories of beings underlie is the notion of community. The human being, the *mu-ntu,* is first of all part of the universal community (the community of *ntu*) which includes beings other than the human being. In other words, the different realities of the universe belong together. As Mkhize (2008: 38) rightly puts it, different realities of the universe form the cosmic unity.

Secondly, the human being belongs to the human community (family, clan, village, etc.) from which one is born. One is *mu-ntu* among the *ba-ntu.* The *muntu* is conceived of as part of the social web which incorporates other *Bantu.* These *Bantu* include human beings actually living (the present generation), human beings who are dead (the past generation), and human beings who are not yet born (the future generation). This sense of community which is not limited to the present generation is peculiar to African way of life. For Dickson Kwesi, it is a characteristic mark that defines African-ness (Kwesi, 1977). In Southern Africa, this sense of the (human) community is expressed in the following popular Zulu and Xhosa saying: *"umuntu ngumuntu ngabantu"*[11] (a person depends on other people to be a person; or better, you are a person in that you carry within yourself your humanity and the humanity of others).

Thus, in the African value system, the first value is the value of the community. The ontological primacy of the community in the African value system may lead one to wonder what happens to individual agency. In effect, one may be made to believe that the individual is swallowed up by the community to the extent that one cannot have a freedom and responsibility of one's own. Kwame Gyekye (1997) felt uncomfortable with the seeming radicality of the African sense of community and asked himself whether a moderate perspective of the African community can be envisaged. In fact, his whole book, *Tradition and Modernity* is an effort to substantiate such a moderate perspective. However, the African value system naturally accommodates both the individual as well as the community as ontologically interdependent without reducing the ontological density and the primacy of the community. I have developed this point elsewhere by making a distinction between the human being as a being-with/in-self (*umuntu-w'-ubuntu*) and human being as being-with/in-others (*umuntu-mu-bantu*) (see Ntibagirirwa, 1999, 2003: 75–77). Maybe what I could add here is the fact that the value of *ubuntu* is both an ontological and moral value of people individually as they live according to their nature as well as collectively when their interdependence is geared to achieving social harmony.

There is a host of moral values that go with the value of the community. I will not dwell much on them but will only refer the reader to the reflections of thinkers such Julius Nyerere who tried to build a political and economic system based on the values of the family (*ujaama*), cooperation, sharing, care and compassion (Nyerere, 1968); Kaunda (1968) whose humanism is built on such values as mutual aid, cooperation, responsibility and concern for others; and Senghor (1964) who emphasized communion, participation and sympathy. All these thinkers who also happen to be

---

[11] This saying is also found in other languages such as Sesotho (*Motho ke motho ka batho*), in Kirundi and Kinyarwanda (*Umuntu ni umuntu mu Bantu*).

the fathers of Africa's independence aimed at building a socialist type of economy on the community and the values that flow from it. However, my observation is that their socialist response to the Africa's quest of economic development was rather a question in search of an answer: which economic system is most likely to harmonise with the African value system and its ontological structure?

Today's economic development involves three major actors which tend to compete in the economic order: the state, the markets, and the people. What the Bantu conception of reality leads us to is the fact that the three forces have to interact in synergy for a meaningful development to be achieved. In other words, in the Bantu conception of reality, economic development should be inclusive rather than exclusive. Obviously this goes in the opposite sense of the neoliberal belief that self-interest and rational choice require that the market run the economic show alone, thus excluding the state and the people. The implication is that the market alone becomes the agent of economic growth and development, while the role of the state and the people is reduced to being the patients. On the contrary, the African value system as can be seen from the Bantu conception of reality would not divide the actors of economic development into agents and patients, producers whose responsibility is to produce and accumulate on the one hand, and on the other hand the consumers. The African value system gives us a framework in which all could be agents whose solidarity and cooperation would lead to economic growth and development. In such a framework, one achieves one's humanity as a producer and a consumer, a buyer and a seller, who responds not only to the forces of the market but also to both the material and spiritual needs of the being human. This is the very meaning of *ubuntu;* I mean *ubuntu economy.*

3.8 Conclusion

In this chapter I have tried to challenge the neo-liberal claim that the freedom to pursue one's self-interest and rational choice lead to economic growth and development. I argued that this claim cannot be universalised as neo-liberal economists and policy-makers have led us to believe. I endeavoured to demonstrate that cultural values are an important factor that needs to be taken seriously to achieve economic growth and development. I showed that self-interest and rational choice themselves are part of a cultural value system. This led me to substantiate the claim that there is a necessary link between cultural values and economic growth and development. Against certain arguments that have tried to marginalise the African value system on the ground that it is an obstacle to economic development, I argued a contrary point by considering the Bantu conception of themselves and reality. Such a conception structures a whole system of values that could enhance rather than undermine economic growth and development in Africa. The major advantage of the African value system I underlined is the fact that it guards us against exclusion and the separation of people into categories of agents and patients in the process of economic development. Seen against this background economic growth and development is a product of the synergy of all actors: the state, the market, and the people.

Thus if the argument of the necessary link between cultural values and economic development is convincing enough, it is misleading to try to universalise the values of self-interest and rationality as the only ground of economic growth and development. Accordingly, my reflection has two major implications. The first implication is that my argument should be understood as a reflective invitation to political leaders, economists, policymakers to concentrate much effort on creating a political and socio-economic environment in which cultural values can catalyse economic growth and development. From this point of view I am in the line of the World Bank which, in October 1999, declared that culture is an essential component of economic development that should play an important role in economic processes.

The second implication is rather a warning based on the history of economic development. The experience of the last decades of the 20th century as well as the present financial crisis have shown us that neither the state alone, nor the market alone, can lead societies to a meaningful economic growth and development. The last years have also witnessed to some kind of collective mobilisation of marginalised groups against the disempowerment tendency of the state and the market thanks to the development of civil society movements (Mohan and Stokke, 2000), particularly in developing countries. What one can learn from African values centred on the community is that what would work to achieve economic development is not exclusion but inclusion of all the actors. Accordingly, I am suggesting that, in the African context, what could achieve economic growth and development is the synergy of the state, the market and the people. I called this *ubuntu economy*.

Acknowledgements I thank the Philosophical Society of South Africa (PSSA) and the International Society of Business, Ethics, and Economics (ISBEE) for organising forums from which this chapter benefited valuable comments and suggestions. I express my sincere gratitude to my Ph.D. advisor, Prof. Deon Rossouw from the University of Pretoria, and Prof. Georges Enderle from the University of Notre Dame, USA for their accompaniment on my ongoing research of the link between values and economic development. The chapter has benefited a lot from the comments and suggestions of reviewers. I appreciate very much their enlightenment and help. The friendly insights and kind encouragement of Prof. John Mittelstaedt from Clemson University, USA, on a research visit at the University of Notre Dame, are greatly appreciated. Certain sections have been added to the original text while I was on Robert S. McNamara- World Bank fellowship, at the University of Notre Dame. I am grateful to World Bank for this opportunity.

References

Asante, K. B. 1991, *African Development: Adebayo Adedeji's Alternative Strategies* (Spectrum Books, Ibadan).

Bentham, J. 1970, *An Introduction to the Principles of Morals and Legislation,* in Ed. J.H, Burns and H.L.A. Hart, (The Anthlone Press, London).

Biel, R. 2000, *The New Imperialism: The Crisis and Contradictions in North/South Relations*, (Zed Books, London).

Brauer, J., Van Tuyll, H., and Harriss, P. 1999. The EU and the US: The competing types of capitalism in the 21st Century. Online http://www.aug.edu/~sbajmb/showit/slide1.html (accessed on 20 April 2009).

Cudd, A. E. 1993, 'Game Theory and the History of Ideas about Rationality'. *Economy and Philosophy* 9, 101–133.

Dalacoura, K. 2002, 'A critique of communitarianism with reference to post-revolutionary Iran', *Review of International Studies* 28, 75–92.

Dasgupta, B. 1998, *Structural Adjustment, Global Trade and the New Political Economy of Development* (Zed books, New York/London).

Diagne, S. B. 2004, 'One Prospective: Development and a political culture of time', *Africa Development* 29(1), 55–69.

Downs, A. 1957, *An Economic Theory of Democracy* (Harper and Row, New York).

Eboussi-Boulaga, F. 1981, *La crise du Muntu: Authenticité africaine et Philosophie* (Présence Africaine, Paris).

Franke, R. H., Hofstede, G. and Bond, M.H. 1991, 'Cultural roots of economic performance: A research note', *Strategic Management Journal* 12, 165–173.

Gerrard, B (ed.). 1993, *The Economics of Rationality* (Routledge, London).

Granato, J., Inglehart, R. and Leblang, D. 1996. 'The Effect of Cultural Values on Economic Development: Theory, Hypotheses and Some Empirical Tests', *American Journal of Political Science* 40(3), 607–631.

Gyekye, K. 1997, *Tradition and Modernity* (Cambridge University Press, Cambridge).

Haney, L. H. 1921. *History of Economic Thought* (Macmillan, New York).

Harrison, L. E. and Huntington, S. P. (eds) 2000, *Culture Matters: How Values Shape Human Progress* (Basic Books, New York).

Hausman, D. M. 1992, *Essays on Philosophy and Economic Methodology* (Cambridge University Press, Cambridge).

Hayek, F. A. 1949. 'The Meaning of Competition', in F.A. Hayek (ed.), *Individualism and Economic Order* (Routledge and Kegan Paul, London), pp. 92–106.

Hayek, F. A. 1978, *New Studies in Philosophy, Politics, Economics and the History of Ideas* (Chicago, University of Chicago Press).

Hodgson, G. 2001, *How Economics Forgot History: The Problem of Historical Specificity in Social Science* (Routledge, London).

Hofstede, G. and Bond, M. H. 1988, 'The Confucius connection: From cultural roots to economic growth', *Organizational Dynamics* 16, 4–21.

Hume, D. 1987, *Political Discourses* (Verl. Wirtschaft u. Finanzen, Frankfurt/Main).

Ingersoll, D. E. and Matthews, R. K. 1991, *The Philosophic Roots of Modern Ideology: Liberalism, Communism, Fascism* (Prentice Hall, New Jersey).

Jahn, J. 1961, *Muntu: An outline of the New African Culture* (Grove Press, New York).

Kabou, A. 1991, *Et l'Afrique refusait le développement* (L'Harmattan, Paris).

Kagabo, L. 2006, 'Alexis Kagame (1912–1981): Life and Thought', in K. Wiredu (ed.), *A Companion to African Philosophy* (Blackwell, Oxford), pp. 231–242.

Kagame, A. 1956, *La Philosophie Bantu-Rwandaise de l'Etre* (Académie Royales des Sciences Coloniales, Brussels).

Kagame, A. 1976. *La Philosophie Bantu Comparée* (Présence Africaine, Paris).

Kaunda, K. 1968, *A Humanism in Africa* (Longman, London).

Kebede, M. 1999, 'Development and the African Philosophical Debate', http://www.rrojasdatabank.org/afro.htm (4 April, 2007).

Kebede, M. 2004, 'African Development and Primacy of Mental Decolonization', *Africa Development*, 29(1), 107–129.

Kenyan 2006, 'On a Communitarian Ethos, Equality and Human Rights in Africa', http://iheu.org (accessed on 11 April 2009).

Khalil, E. L. 2001, 'Adam Smith and Three Theories of Altruism', *Louvain Economic Review* 67(4), 421–435.

Kwesi, A. D. 1977, *Aspects of Religious Life in Africa* (Ghana Academy of Arts and Sciences, Accra).

Lutz, M. A. and Lux, K. 1988. *Humanistic Economics: The New Challenge* (The Bootstrap Press, New York).

MacIntyre, A. 1981, *After Virtue* (University of Notre Dame Press, Notre Dame, Indiana).

Manguellé, E. D. 1990, *L'Afrique a-t-elle besoin d'un programme d'adjustement culturel?* (Editions Nouvelles du Sud, Paris).

Matthews, S. 2004, Post-development theory and the question of alternatives: a view from Africa'. *Third World Quarterly* 25(2), 373–386.

Mbiti, J. 1970, *African Religions and Philosophy* (Doubleday, New York).

McPherson, M. S. 1987, 'Changes in tastes', in Eatwell, J., Milgate, Murray, and Newman, P. (eds.), *The New Palgrave: A Dictionary of Economics*, Macmillan, London, pp. 401–403.

Mehmet, O. 1995, *Westernizing the Third World: The Eurocentricity of Economic Development Theories* (Routledge, London/New York).

Mkhize, N. 2008, 'Ubuntu and Harmony: An African approach to Morality', in Ronald Nicolson (ed.), *Persons in Community: African Ethics and Culture* (University of Kwa-Zulu Natal Press, Pietermaritzburg), pp. 31–45.

Mohan, G. and Stokke, K. 2000, 'Participatory development and empowerment: the dangers of Localism', *Third World Quarterly* 21(2), 247–268.

Morishima, M. 1982, *Why has Japan 'succeeded'? Western Technology and Japanese Ethos* (Cambridge University Press, Cambridge).

Nozick, R. 1974, *Anarchy, State and Utopia* (Blackwell/Basic books, Oxford).

Ntibagirirwa, S. 1999, 'A Retrieval of Aristotelian Virtue Ethics in African Social and Political Humanism. A Communitarian Perspective' University of Natal. Unpublished Masters Dissertation, University of Natal, South Africa.

Ntibagirirwa, S, 2003, A wrong Way: From Being to Having in the African Value System http://www.crvp.org/book/Series02/II-7/chapter_v.htm (accessed 22 April 2009).

Ntibagirirwa, S. 2006, 'Le Miracle Asiatique: Qu'apprendre de l'expérience Asiatique du Développement), *Ethique et Société* 3(1), 18–34.

Nürnberger, K. 1998, *Beyond Marx and Market* (Cluster Publication, Pietermaritzburg).

Nyang, S. S. 1994, 'The Cultural Consequences of Development in Africa', in I. Serageldin and J. Taboroff (eds.), *Culture and Development in Africa* (World Bank, Washington, DC), pp. 429–446.

Nyerere, K. J. 1968, *Ujaama: Essays on Socialism* (Oxford University Press, Dar-es-Salaam).

Olson, N. 1982, *The Rise and Decline of Nations: Economic Growth, Stagflation and Social Rigidities* (Yale University Press, New Haven/London).

Onis, Z. 1995, 'The Limits of Neoliberalism: Towards a Reformation of Development Theory' *Journal of Economic Issues* 29(1), 97–119.

Ramose, M. B. 1999, *African Philosophy through Ubuntu* (Mond Books, Harare).

Reddy, Y. R. K. 2009, 'The Ethics of Corporate Governance: An Asian Perspective'. *International Journal of Law and Management* 5(1), 17–26.

Reinert, E. S. 2007, *How Rich Countries Got Rich... and Why Poor Countries Stay Poor* (Constable and Robinson, London).

Rosenberg, A. 1992, *Economics: Mathematical Politics or Science of Diminishing Returns* (University of Chicago Press, Chicago, IL).

Rostow, W. W. 1960, The *Stages of Economic Growth: A Non-Communist Manifesto* (Cambridge University Press, Cambridge).

Sandel, M. 1982, *Liberalism and the Limits of Justice* (Cambridge University Press, Cambridge).

Sandel, M. 1996, *Democracy's discontent: America in search of Public philosophy* (The Belknap Press of Harvard University Press, Cambridge).

Sen, A. K. 1987, *On Ethics and Economics* (Blackwell, New York).

Sen, A. K. 2006, *Identity and Violence* (Norton, New York).

Senghor, L. S. 1964, *Liberté I: Négritude et Humanism* (Seuil, Paris).

Shixue, J. 2008, 'Cultural factors and Economic performance in East Asia and Latin America', Online http://orpheus.ucsd.edu/las/studies/pdfs/jiang.pdf (accessed 10 June 2008).

Shutte, A. 1993, *Philosophy for Africa* (University of Cape Town Press, Cape Town).

Smith, A. 1808, *The Theory of Moral Sentiments,* 2 vols (Bell & Bradfute, Edinburg).

Smith, A. 1965, *An Inquiry into the Nature and Causes of the Wealth of Nations*, Edited by Edwin Cannan, introduced by Max Lerner (Modern Library, New York).

Taylor, C. 1989, *Sources of the Self. The Making of Moral Identity* (Cambridge University Press, Cambridge).

Tempels, P. 1959, *Bantu Philosophy* (Présence Africaine, Paris).

Throsby, D. 2001, *Economics and Culture* (Cambridge University Press, Cambridge).

Todaro, M. 1989, *Economic Development in the Third World,* 4th edition (Longman, New York).

Tshamalenga, N. 1985, 'Language et socialité. Primat de la Bisoité sur l'Intersubjectivité', in Facultés Catholiques de Kinshasa (ed.), Actes de la 9eme Semaine Philosophique de Kinshasa, du 1er au 7 décembre, 1985 (Facultés Catholiques de Kinshasa, Kinshasa), pp. 59–81.

Weber, M. 1971, *The Protestant Ethic and the Spirit of Capitalism* (Unwin, London).

Williamson, J. 1990, 'What Washington Means by Policy Reform' in J. Williamson (ed.), *Latin American Adjustment: How Much Has Happened?* (Institute for International Economics, Washington, DC).

Williamson, J. 1993, 'Democracy and the "Washington Consensus", *World Development,* 21, 1329–1336.

Wong, S.-L. 1988, *Emigrant Entrepreneurs: Shanghai Industrialists in Hong Kong* (Oxford University Press, Hong Kong).

World Bank 1999, *Culture and Sustainable Development: A Framework for Action* (World Bank, Washington, DC).

Yonay, Y. 1998, *The Struggle over the Soul of Economics* (Princeton University Press, Princeton).

Chapter 4
Black Economic Empowerment and the Post-Apartheid South African Quest for the Domestication of Western Capitalism

Munyaradzi Felix Murove

4.1 Lay People's Discussion on South African Black Economic Empowerment (BEE)

We were watching television in a tavern in Sobantu township in South Africa whilst treating ourselves to some nice cold beers and snacks. After some few minutes of adverts, a popular South African black business man appeared on television narrating a story on how he managed to get rich and be where he is today. He looked smart indeed. A three piece charcoal grey suit, elephant leather black shoes, his left hand adorned with a gold watch and a gold marriage ring. His appearance in itself was a story to the effect that he had it all in life. We previously knew him from our memory of the struggle as a tall, slender and cheerful man who had always expressed insurmountable zeal and unsurpassable passion for social, political and economic justice. But now those clothes which he wore during the struggle can no longer fit his body.

His appearance on the national television told a story of someone who had it all in life. Rumours from oral tradition circulating among newspapers has it that since he joined the business fraternity 5 years ago, his fortunes have arisen to tens of billions of dollars, and that he stays in a mansion or palace which many third world presidents might envy. Whilst most of his business associates are from Europe and America, all his businesses are in African names. Like all African indigenous names, the names of his companies are pregnant with symbolism. One could read from the symbolism behind these names messages such as, "A new era has dawned in South Africa", "The sun has risen", "Nothing comes easy without going through turmoil of the struggle", "Follow the ancestors" – and the list is inexhaustible. In pursuit of more and more fortunes, he made himself a friend to all companies and

M.F. Murove (✉)
Senior Lecturer, School of Philosophy and Ethics, University of KwaZulu-Natal,
Durban, South Africa
e-mail: murovem@ukzn.ac.za

G. Moore (ed.), *Fairness in International Trade*, The International Society
of Business, Economics, and Ethics Book Series 1, DOI 10.1007/978-90-481-8840-6_4,
© Springer Science+Business Media B.V. 2010

corporations. His message to them was always clear and the most seductive as it was articulated as follows: (a) Previously white owned companies and corporations have no business future in the new South Africa and a new world order. They needed to tune themselves into the new legislation that stipulates that companies should have those who were previously disadvantaged in management positions as well as transforming those who were previously disadvantaged into shareholders. (b) That his participation in their companies or corporations would be to their own self-interest as he is more knowledgeable in the contemporary political and economic policy landscape. (c) His appearance in overseas business meetings on behalf of these companies and corporations would be a wise business decision as such appearance will inevitably be viewed as "overseas companies doing business with Africans who were previously disadvantaged", hence "overseas companies bringing business transformation to post-colonial Africa".

The appearance of this African business person on national television business programme was aimed at mentoring young aspiring black Africans on how to become successful business people. His speech went as follows:

- It's all about believing in yourself.
- You must tell yourself that you can do it.
- You must be focused on what you want to achieve and set goals on how to achieve your dreams.
- Work hard in whatever you do.
- Don't be discouraged when you don't achieve that which you had set yourself to achieve.
- Tell yourself that next time your dreams will come true.
- Don't wait for others to employ you.
- Tell yourself that you are your own employer.
- You are the master of your own dreams and it's up to you to see to it that they come true.
- Your destiny is within your hands.
- Apply your very best to take advantage of the opportunities before you.

This talk was very touching and inspiring indeed. However the owner of the tavern interrupted and managed to draw all our attention. With a frowned face, and a voice of disbelief in what was being said by our newly empowered businessman, he asked, "Gentlemen how can it be possible for someone who was not even a businessman five years ago to become a multimillionaire within such a short space period of time"? Someone in the group answered this question by saying that Black Economic Empowerment programmes are more lucrative than any other business venture you could ever think of. The owner of the tavern went on to pose a question to the effect that, "Why are these Black Economic Empowerment programmes not accessible to the majority of us who have been involved in businesses for decades? Would it not make empowerment sense if businesses and corporations are to empower the majority of poor people who live under subsistence level than empowering individuals who are already well-off?".[1]

4.2 Introduction

The most controversial issue that is currently sweeping across the post-apartheid South African political and economic landscape is mainly about the ethical justifiability of post-apartheid South African economic policy of Black Economic Empowerment (BEE)/Africanisation/Indigenisation. Such an economic policy has been implemented in many post-colonial African societies without success. Whilst all these post-colonial African economic programmes were prompted by the need to transform capitalism from being a foreign owned economic system to a domestically owned economic system, such transformation did not necessarily result in the domestication of capitalism but rather in a creation of economic inequalities among those who have been previously disadvantaged by colonialism and apartheid. The creation of insurmountable inequalities among those who have been previously disadvantaged has given rise to a situation where the majority of the South African citizens have come to question the morality of such an economic programme, especially in the face of inadequate government provision of basic needs such as education, health and transport.

Arguments that are usually proffered in support of BEE/Indigenisation/Africanisation are as follows:

(1) The African economy under colonialism and apartheid was based on giving business opportunities to whites as opposed to black people, hence to redress this colonial economic legacy, it is imperative that the post-colonial African government should give preference to black people in all sectors of the economy.

(2) Since capitalism has been the handmaid of colonialism and apartheid, the continuous existence of this economic system under the hands of those who were the beneficiaries of colonialism and apartheid can only perpetuate neo-colonialism in post-colonial or post-apartheid South Africa.

(3) Real political power is in the hands of those who own and control the economy. It follows that political power will remain inadequate without economic power by those who were previously disadvantaged to own and

---

[1] I am very much indebted to my friend Muthandeni Duma for introducing me to Zenzele tavern, a place where I managed to interact with ordinary people whom we in academia have often marginalized in our academic discourses. The experience of coming face to face with poor and uneducated people engaging in a conversation that has a strong bearing on economic ethics within South African contemporary political and economic changes has motivated me to embark on African Business Ethics as an appropriate focus for the study of business ethics in post-apartheid South Africa.

control all the sectors of the economy. For that to happen, it is indispensable that governmental legislative authorities should enact laws that promote BEE/Indigenisation/Africanisation in the modus operandi of companies and in the issuing of tenders. In so doing, economic power is being transferred to those who were previously disadvantaged.

(4) Capitalism in Africa has helped to promote the westernization of Africans and operated in ways that only helped to serve western economic needs. To reverse such a scenario, post-colonial Africa needed to domesticate capitalism, and the most effective way towards the domestication of capitalism was for black Africans to wrest control of this economic system such that African values, modes of production and consumption should become prominent in this economic system. Hence the post-apartheid economic policy of BEE/Indigenisation/Africanisation is regarded as the most effective economic policy towards the domestication of capitalism.

On the other hand, those who argue against BEE/Indigenisation/Africanisation have the following arguments in this debate:

(1) BEE/Indigenisation/Africanisation amounts to some form of legalized looting by those who have political power and their closest friends.

(2) BEE/Indigenisation/Africanisation creates a class of African capitalists who will rely heavily on political relatives and friends, thus making it difficult to distinguish between ethical business practices and corrupt business practices.

(3) In an economic context such as that of South Africa with enormous challenges for economic development, government policy and funding priorities should be focused on urgent issues such as education, health and infrastructure. Ignoring these areas amounts to perpetuating the injustices of the past.

(4) Beneficiaries of BEE/Indigenisation/Africanisation will not necessarily lead to the domestication of capitalism in Africa. These beneficiaries will end up identifying themselves with yester-year colonial capitalists instead of uplifting the black communities.

(5) There is no empirical evidence all over post-colonial Africa that can help us to support the view that BEE/Indigenisation/Africanisation will lead to the domestication of western capitalism.

Within the limited scope of this chapter, I will not go into a detailed discussion of all these arguments, rather, my focus will be on ethical challenges that arise from BEE. The first part of this chapter will look into the colonial heritage of BEE in which it is argued that the failure to transmit capitalist values led to the failure of the ascendency of capitalism. In the second part it will be shown that while the idea of BEE/Indigenisation/Africanisation as a post-colonial African economic transformation policy was aimed at domesticating capitalism or giving it an African flavor, there is no evidence where the policy has succeeded in many parts of post-colonial Africa. This claim will be supported in the third part of the chapter where it is argued that BEE/Indigenization/Africanisation does not necessarily lead to the domestication of capitalism, but to a creation of a class of capitalists whose economic behavior is based on the emulation of other capitalists in all parts of the world. In this vein, this chapter will argue that BEE/Indigenisation/Africanisation policies are mistaken policies when seen from an economic developmental perspective. Lastly, it is argued that such policies do lead only to weak participation in global capitalism by African countries.

4.3 BEE/Ingidenisation/Africanisation and the Colonial Heritage

The world renowned African scholar, Ali Mazrui advanced the argument that capitalism failed in post-colonial Africa because of the inherent historical problem that originated in the transmission of capitalist values during the colonial epoch. As he put it,

> The colonial master did not normally dig his own land physically, or clean his own cattle, or sweep his own barn, or wash his own clothes, or change his own tyres. There was always a Black man around to do the physical chores. ...The aristocratic legacy of masters and servants had its adverse consequences for the work ethic in post-colonial Africa, just as it had on industrial relations in Britain. White masters in Africa drinking their gin and tonic leisurely while their servants pulled off their boots – this was the colonial caste which transformed physical labour into a burden of servitude (Mazrui 1986: 233).

The implication of the above quotation is that it was part and parcel of the colonial economic practice that one could accumulate wealth without necessarily sweating for it. The idea of capitalism through accumulation was severed from accumulation through hard work and frugality as advocated by Max Weber. Thus one finds one of the owners of Lever Brothers say that, "...the organizing ability is the particular trait and characteristic of the white man...I say this with my little experience, that the African native will be the best, and live under the larger conditions of prosperity when his labour is directed and organized by his white brother who has all these million years' start ahead of him" (see Davis 1973: 385).

Whilst Weber depicted rational organization as one of the elements inherent in the spirit of modern capitalism, this element of organized labour was violated in colonial Africa because colonial capitalistic production often involved manipulation when the African work force did not appear voluntarily. In this vein, Karl Polanyi alleged that the colonists used to "impose a hut tax on the native [in order] to force him to barter away his labour" (Polanyi 1968: 164; see Murove 2005: 394–395). Karl Polanyi's argument can be supported by taking recourse to the observation that was made by Felix Gross about Cecil John Rhodes. Gross said that in order to make Africans work for him, Rhodes had to devise a plan: "It called for special enticement to lure them to the farms, and a good psychological understanding of their primitive though complicated mentality to keep them there. Cecil found out that many Natives needed money to pay their hut-tax. He lent them the money on their promise to work for him. And they never let him down. 'Karrirs', he wrote home, are really safer than the Bank of England" (Gross 1956: 11).

It is from such historical evidence where it is argued that BEE/Indigenisation/ Africanisation policies are intended to redress the injustices of the past whereby black Africans had their labour used and at the same time found themselves excluded from reaping the fruits of their labour. This is evident where one finds the then Minister of Bantu Affairs, Verwoerd stating that, "There is no place for [the Bantu] in the European Community above the level of certain forms of labour...it is of no avail for him to receive a training which drew him away from his own community and misled him by showing him the green pastures of the Europeans but still did not allow him to graze there" (see Lipton 1986: 24). It is in such utterances that it is argued that the demise of these political systems also called for the restructuring of the capitalist economic system in post-colonial or post-Apartheid South Africa as a way of redressing the economic injustices of the past.

In this regard, advocates of BEE/Indigenisation/Africanisation argue that one could not redress the injustices of the past solely through political control, rather political control is supposed to be complemented by economic control. It was the greatest conviction of African nationalists that economic control could only be effected through the domestication of capitalism because during colonialism, capitalism had turned Africans into victims of expropriation. Kwame Nkrumah referred to this expropriation as follows, "While missionaries implored the colonial subject to lay up his 'treasures in Heaven, where neither moth nor rust doth corrupt', the traders and administrators acquired his minerals and land. There was no intention of processing locally the discovered raw materials. These were intended to feed the metropolitan mills and plants, to be exported back to the colonies later in the form of finished commodities" (Nkrumah 1970: 22). Here the main argument is that African economic relations under colonialism were not about developing or transferring capitalistic values to the colonized. It is also for this reason that Nkrumah argued against those who gave moral support to colonialism on the grounds that it was indispensable to Africa's appropriation of capitalism and modernity.

According to Nkrumah, colonialism represented the expropriation of African resources. He writes, "In her African colonies, Britain controlled the export of raw materials by preventing their direct shipment to foreign markets. After satisfying the demands of her home industries, she sold the surplus to other nations and netted the profits herself. The colonial farmer and worker had no share in those profits. Nor was any part of them used in providing public works and social services in the colonies" (Nkrumah 1970: 22–23). The economic modus operandi of colonial economic practices could not be severed from the idea of legalized robbery on the grounds that African resources were controlled by their respective colonial powers – be they French, British or Portuguese. The coming of political independence was also followed with what Julius Nyerere called economic nationalism. For Nyerere, economic nationalism was about the control of the economy. In support of economic nationalism Nyerere had this to say,

Such an economic expression of nationalism is nothing new in the world; although the manner of the action may have been peculiarly Tanzanian, its motivation is common enough. Every country – whether it be capitalist, communist, socialist or fascist – wants to control its own economy. . . .At independence we achieved political control, but all important industries remained in foreign hands. . . .Whatever economic system the peoples of different African countries eventually adopt, it is quite certain that sooner or later they will demand that the key positions of their economy are in the hands of their own citizens (Nyerere 1968: 262).

It is evidently clear that the post-colonial concept of economic nationalism was about the control of capitalism which African nationalists for so long had suspected to have been controlled externally. For this reason, an externally controlled capitalism as it was under colonialism was deemed exploitative. In pursuit of economic nationalism, Nyerere became hostile to the whole concept of economic growth and development through direct foreign investment. He writes, ". . .I do not think there is any free state in Africa where there is sufficient local capital, or a sufficient number of local entrepreneurs, for locally based capitalism to dominate the economy. Private investment in Africa means overwhelming foreign private investment. A capitalistic economy means a foreign dominated economy. These are the facts of Africa's situation. The only way in which national control of the economy can be achieved is through the economic institutions of socialism" (Nyerere 1968: 264).

Those who argue against the idea that colonialism was about the expropriation of African resources maintain that since African traditional values were prohibitive to the appropriation of capitalism, there was no way in which Africa would have developed its own capitalism without the colonial intervention. In other words, the providential aspect of colonialism to Africa lay in the fact that Africa would have remained poor and backward if intercourse with western economies did not occur. One of the most notorious defender of the providence of colonialism, A. J. Hanna did not mince his words when he said,

. . .[I]t is virtually certain that conditions in Africa would still be roughly what they were a century ago, had it not been for the introduction of European administration, European instruction, and contact with the European economy. . . .It has often been asserted that investment in Africa involved injustice to the Africans, since it was a device for draining the wealth of their continent into the pockets of investors in Europe. This is an elementary misconception. The mineral and other resources of Africa were useless to the native inhabitants until they were developed, and they could not be developed without transport, machinery and skill. By making these things available the European investor, however self-interested he may have been, was serving Africa; and if his enterprise came to an end through bankruptcy, Africa gaining nothing through his misfortune (Hanna 1961: 11–17).

As it can be deduced from the above quotation, Hanna's main argument was that colonialism was morally justifiable on the grounds that if it were not for colonialism, then the African economy would not have accrued economic benefits from its contact with the western world. In other words, it was to the benefit of the African economy that there was colonialism. It is also part of Hanna's argument that the expropriation of African resources is morally justifiable because those resources were not being used at all. Since those African natural resources were not being used at all, it becomes a reckless mistake for one to interpret the whole colonial economic enterprise as stealing and expropriation of African resources. But Hanna's reading of the colonial history was not shared by everybody who officially participated in colonial administration. Thus one finds the French Colonial Secretary of State, Albert Sarraut arguing passionately that colonialism was mainly about the expropriation of African resources. As he puts it,

> What is the use of painting the truth? At the start colonization was not an act of civilization, nor was it a desire to civilize. It was an act of force motivated by interests. An episode in the vital competition which, from man to man, from group to group, has gone on ever increasing; the people who set out to seize colonies in distant lands were thinking primarily of themselves, and were working for their own profits, and conquering for their own power. ...The origin of colonization is nothing else than enterprise of individual interests, a one-sided and egotistical imposition of the strong upon the weak (see Nkrumah 1970: 21).

Surely Sarraut was a pragmatist who did not hesitate to call a spade a spade. In this type of pragmatism, colonialism was solely about economic expropriation of the colonized Africans. Accordingly, there wasn't any room for moral justification of colonialism at all. Since colonialism could not promote the ascendency of capitalism in colonial Africa, it is also the argument of post-colonial African scholars that colonialism should be seen solely as a moment of expropriation within African history. This is the argument that was advanced by Ali Mazrui when he said that,

> The greatest mockery about Western imperialism does not lie in its promotion of capitalism in Africa; it lies in its failure to do so. ...the West destroyed traditional African economies without really creating capitalist foundations to replace them. In this sense, the problem of dependency in African is about who controls capitalism within Africa, rather than about the merits of capitalism as such. ...Western imperialism transmitted capitalist greed to Africa – but without capitalist discipline. It transmitted the profit motive – but not the entrepreneurial persistence and risk-taking (Mazrui 1986: 215).

In the light of Mazrui's argument as stated above, colonialism failed to promote capitalism nor did it create any alternative economic system, hence the problem of dependency became the main pre-occupation of post-colonial scholars and policy makers on ownership and control of capitalism in Africa. In this vein, one finds that most post-colonial African scholars have persistently maintained that the west were the real owners of capitalism in Africa, hence the second phase of Africa's struggle for independence was to be focused on economic decolonization. In this regard, the post-colonial African economy came to be understood as a remnant of colonialism. Thus one finds Chinweizu saying that, "Political decolonization and formal independence in Africa have not meant the end of imperialism. They have only meant a change in the *guise* of imperialism. Political decolonization has not been accompanied by economic decolonization" (Chinweizu 1999: 769).

The idea of economic decolonization fueled the post-colonial African economic policy of BEE/Indigenisation/Africanisation. Whilst western capitalism tends to agree on the importance of such a policy in the domestication and appropriation of capitalism, Chinweizu argued that these western countries are only in favour of such a policy in so far as it provides fertile ground for the perpetuation of western economic interests. It is on these grounds that Chinweizu said that the decolonization of the economy through indigenization of capitalism remained a contentious

issue between the west and post-colonial Africa. He writes, "On economic decolonization, the African states and the West were in sharp conflict. The African states
wanted to wrest control of their economies from a West which has determined
to retain that control. For the West, losing control would mean giving up what
a century of conquest and colonization had achieved for them, and what political
decolonization had aimed to preserve. For the African states, however, not to wrest
away that control would be to defeat the economic aim of their struggle for political
independence" (Chinweizu 1999: 771).

As indicated previously, in post-colonial Africa, the most effective instrument
for economic decolonization was indigenization or Africanisation. In this regard,
"Decolonisation was generally seen as no more than Africanisation, in the sense of
putting more Africans into the economic structures inherited from colonial times."
(Chinweizu 1999: 777). To those western countries who were owners of capitalism
in colonial Africa, Africanisation was preferred on the grounds that those educated
Africans who were also westernized through education would not endanger their
economic interests, but rather they will simply give an African face to western
capitalism. But Chinweizu (1999: 790) argued that the Africanisation of capitalism
could not succeed because those Africans who were supposed to be the agents of
this policy "had enormous appetites for material consumption". Since they had this
insatiable appetite for consumption, "They craved the best that the industrial world
could offer, and were therefore preoccupied with the distribution for consumption of
whatever income was available from an economy which remained colonial in character". Contrary to the economic behavior of African capitalists, "the bourgeoisie of
the Western core were habitual accumulators of capital, highly experienced at it, and
with highly developed productive organization as well as vast sums of already accumulated capital which they could deploy for further accumulation" (*ibid*, 790). Here
Chinweiuzu's argument is that the idea of creating a group of African capitalists
who will be responsible for the domestication of capitalism will not prevail because
the consumption habits of African capitalists are contrary to the spirit of accumulation and saving as is the case among western capitalists. The same observation was
also made by Nkrumah when he said that,

> Thrift has not been a characteristic of our people, largely because they have not enjoyed
> enough income to make the question anything but academic. How to instill a need to spend
> and save wisely among them has become a major preoccupation now that they are beginning
> to enjoy higher incomes and the taste for amenities. Our family system actually discourages
> family heads from saving, for the system, in effect, penalizes the man with initiative in
> favour of the lazy and the weak. The indigent members of the family live upon the more
> fortunate ones. A praiseworthy and useful practice in our past, more or less stagnant soci-
> ety based on subsistence farming, it acts today as a break upon ambition and drive. At
> the present time, the man who makes a reasonable living finds his money eaten up by his
> relatives...so that he simply cannot meet his personal obligations, let alone save anything
> (Nkrumah 1970: 100).

Nkrumah's pessimism on the domestication of capitalism through indigenization
was based on Max Weber's theory that said that there was some early connection
between the Protestant ethic of thrift, frugality and hard work and the ascendance

of modern capitalism in western societies. According to Nkrumah, the stumbling-block to the domestication of capitalism through indigenization was in the African traditional communalism which puts emphasis on the need for the individual to demonstrate a sense of concern for the well-being of others through sharing of material possessions. This African traditional prestige motive is thus seen as an inherent hindrance to saving and accumulation of wealth.

Unlike Nyerere, Nkrumah was convinced that the domestication of capitalism was supposed to be attained through indigenous capitalists. For this reason he was distrustful towards foreign capitalists as much as he was towards indigenous capitalists. Since foreign capitalists and indigenous capitalists could not be trusted Nkrumah suggested that the government was the most appropriate agent to bring about the domestication of capitalism. He writes, "We have had enough of European monopoly domination of our economy. We have emancipated ourselves politically, and we have now to take off the economy monopoly that was the objective of foreign political control. This is the crux of our economic policy, and the essential heart of our endeavours. For unless we attain economic freedom, our struggle for independence will have been in vain, and our plans for social and cultural advancement frustrated" (Nkrumah 1970: 102). Many scholars have come to argue that the idea of domesticating capitalism through policies of indigenization/Africanisation/BEE does not have any empirical evidence that shows that such economic policies have yielded the intended results. Many economic developmental theorists have argued that such policies tend to perpetuate the previous colonial economic situation where wealth ends up cornered by a few at the expense of the majority of the populace. Some argue that the indigenized African capitalists are most likely to emulate the accumulation and consumption habits of other capitalists all over the world.

4.4 BEE/Indigenisation/Africanisation and the Problem of Emulation

It has been argued repeatedly by some post-colonial African critics of indigenization that for government to embark on policies aimed at creating a class of African capitalists was an exercise in futility. African scholars such as Claude Ake argued that those who end up benefiting from governmental economic interventions in favour of black economic empowerment are mostly in solidarity with international capitalism rather than with their fellow African poor (Ake 1981: 32). The idea of solidarity between those Africans who are economically empowered and international capitalism has its explanatory logic in Thorstein Veblen's Institutional Evolutionary Economics. In his *The Theory of the Leisure Class*, Veblen argued that the capitalistic practice of economic predation is a shared characteristic among all capitalists despite their backgrounds because, "In order to stand well in the eyes of the community, it is necessary to come up to a certain, somewhat indefinite, conventional standard of wealth..." (Veblen 1931: 30). According to Veblen, this predatory habit has no proper explanation besides the seeking of power and honour through endless accumulation and acquisition of wealth. The appetite for acquisition and accumulation of wealth among the leisure class (capitalists) manifests itself as insatiable. The need to acquire more becomes too addictive to such an extent that it leads to compulsive acquisitiveness. He writes,

> But as fast as a person makes new acquisitions, and becomes accustomed to the resulting new standard of wealth, the new standard forthwith ceases to afford appreciably greater satisfaction than the earlier standard did. The tendency in any case is constantly to make the present pecuniary standard the point of departure for a fresh increase of wealth; and this in turn gives rise to a new standard of sufficiency and a new pecuniary classification of one's self as compared with one's neighbours. So far as concerns the present question, the end sought by accumulation is to rank high in comparison with the rest of the community in point of pecuniary strength (Veblen 1931: 31).

In the light of Veblen's theory of the evolution of institutional economics, solidarity between the rich and the poor becomes untenable because those who are capitalists are driven by an insatiable need for wealth whereby that which has been acquired is always inadequate because, as Veblen put it, "the normal average individual [among the leisure class] will live in chronic dissatisfaction with his present lot" in the sense that, "when he has reached what may be called the normal pecuniary standard of the community, this chronic dissatisfaction will give place to a restless straining to place a wider and ever-widening pecuniary interval between himself and this average standard" (Veblen 1931: 31). The main psychological reason behind this insatiability comes from the fact that in the leisure class, individuals are always driven by the urge to emulate those who belong to their class – thus setting a path to an endless economic state of competitive accumulation without stipulating standards for sufficiency. Within this psychological state of a compulsive urge for endless accumulation, the individual thus severs himself from communal belongingness. According to Veblen, the leisure class is endowed with conspicuous consumption patterns that can only be appeased by extraordinary lifestyles. He writes, "The quasi-peaceable gentleman of leisure, then, not only consumes of the stuff of life beyond the minimum required for subsistence and physical efficiency, but his consumption also undergoes a specialization as regards the quality of the goods consumed. He consumes freely and of the best, in food, drink, narcotics, shelter, services, ornaments..." (Veblen 1931: 73).

Veblen maintained that such consumption habits are vicarious because they are done as a way of expressing one's economic status within the leisure class. But such conspicuous consumption habits are something which the individual is expected to maintain if s/he is to remain honourable within the circles of the leisure class. In characterization of the leisure class which was rendered by Veblen was that "the wealthy class is by nature conservative" in the sense that this class "opposes innovation". Its opposition to innovation is not only caused by the factor of vested interest, but this conservatism has "a certain honorific or decorative value". As he puts it, "Conservatism, being an upper-class characteristic, is decorous; and conversely, innovation, being a lower-class phenomenon is vulgar" (Veblen 1931: 198–200). In other words this conservatism

> makes it incumbent upon all reputable people to follow their lead [i.e., the wealth class]. So
> that, by virtue of its high position as the avatar of good form, the wealthier class comes to
> exert a retarding influence upon social development far in excess of that which the simple
> numerical strength of the class would assign it. Its prescriptive example acts to greatly
> stiffen the resistance of all other classes against any innovation, and to fix men's affections
> upon the good institutions handed down from an earlier generation (Veblen 1931: 200).

In other words, the conservatism of the leisure class is inevitable because it is parasitic or predatory on the poor. This conservatism of the leisure class becomes a mechanism that safeguards its own class-interests. Consequently, the leisure class adopts an understanding of evolution based on the belief that, "Whatever is, is right'; whereas the law of natural selection, as applied to human institutions, gives the axiom: Whatever is, is wrong'". Veblen went on to say that such a type of class-interested conservatism perpetuates the existence of unjust or inhumane institutional practices (Veblen 1931: 207). The conservatism of the leisure class is not so much concerned with perpetuating the received moral values, rather, moral values can only be conserved when they help to support the long entrenched economic interests of the leisure class. Thus he characterized the industrial processes and the economic institutions of this leisure class as follows, "Their office is of a parasitic character, and their interest is to divert what substance they may to their own use, and to retain whatever is under their hand. The conventions of the business world have grown up under the selective surveillance of this principle of predation or parasitism. They are conventions of ownership; derivatives, more or less remote, of the ancient predatory culture" (Veblen 1931: 203)

For Veblen, the business world of the leisure class is simply predatory and parasitic in as far as it feeds on the labour of others whom it denies access to the tastes of its class. Such a business practice was archaic; hence it could not be applied in the present context. The continual survival of such business practices owes its indebtedness to the past economic outlooks that cannot be applied to today's socio-economic conditions.

The implications of Veblen's theory of Institutional Evolutionary Economics to BEE/Indigenisation/Africanisation economic policy has already been observed by many African developmentalist scholars. Among some of their observations was the idea that BEE economic programmes would inevitably create a class of African capitalists whose economic standing will make it impossible for them to be in solidarity with the majority of the African poor. Claude Ake advanced the argument that BEE/Indigenisation or Nationalisation economic programmes do not necessarily lead to the decolonization of the African economy as it is generally assumed. Such programmes "[e]essentially. . .amount to a new partnership between the African ruling class and international capitalism to their mutual benefit and often reduce areas of conflict between them. By operating under the umbrella of the state, foreign capital reduces the visibility of its exploitation while enjoying new immunities" (1981: 39). Ake went on to say that,

> Imperialist exploitation of Africa occurs precisely because of the existence of capitalism in
> Africa. For the most part, the African ruling class is the creation of Western imperialism and
> remains largely a tool of Western imperialism. . . .their interests coincide on the fundamental

issue of maintaining capitalist relations of production. The African ruling class survives in so far as capitalist relations of production are maintained. And international capitalism maximises its exploitation of Africa by keeping African economies capitalist and dependent (Ake 1981: 35–36).

Within such an analysis, there is obviously an echo of Veblen's theory that the leisure class (which Ake has identified as the ruling class) tends to form bonds of solidarity based on their own conventional methods of acquiring and consuming of wealth. Such a solidarity drives the poor to the peripheries of the economy, thus further perpetuating the legacy of economic imperialism which the BEE/Indigenisation/Africanisation policy had purported to terminate. It is partly for this reason that other African scholars have sarcastically argued that indigenisation or BEE is about the indigenisation of privatization. These scholars argue against the old argument that has often been proffered by advocates of indigenisation which says that indigenisation of capitalism does avoid the externalization of profits that are made on African soil. Related to this is also the claim that international capitalism thrives on the mobility of capital, that is, foreign capitalists can easily relocate their business operations to other countries or regions depending on profitability of such a venture.

Against all those arguments, Chanda Chisala argued that we should accept capitalist practices as they are practiced all over the world and concentrate on improving our African economic environment. Thus Chisala writes,

The only way is to change our environment and this will start by changing our attitude to the whole idea of capitalism. Capitalism simply means allowing the environment to be as free as possible. We destroy the environment when we start intervening in it in order to force our ideas of who should own what; how much should what he bought for [sic]; how should this one pay that one; who should pay less taxes than who; etc. ...The answer to our economy simply lies in a true understanding of the capitalist philosophy, period. And the logic is really simple: the most capitalist nations in the world are the richest countries in the world – can it get simpler than that? It really has nothing to do with constitutions (even though we do need a good constitution); with foreigners; with agriculture; or even with national airlines (Chisala C. "Indigenisation of Privatisation (Part 2): Some General Comments on Privatisation and Capitalism", file://E:\Indigenisation%200f%20Privatisation –Botswana.htm, Accessed 22 April 2007).

Chisala's argument as stated above is that African states should just embrace capitalism as it has been practiced in the western world. Programmes that tend to go against the logic of the capitalist system can only be counter productive. The capitalist logic is based on the idea that in economic matters, the free market should decide on who gets what and who deserves what. A whole hearted embrace of capitalism would also imply that government should not come up with legislation with the aim of aiding a particular segment of the population against the other. Obviously the moment government tries to assist the individual's efforts to accumulation of wealth through legislation and incentives, such actions become ethically problematic. Here the problem arises with reference to who should be indigenised among those who have been previously disadvantaged by colonialism or apartheid. If indigenisation is aimed at correcting the economic oppressions of the past, the question that also arises is that are the beneficiaries of indigenisation the only ones who were disadvantaged? Thus Ray Matikinye critiqued indigenisation in Zimbabwe on the grounds that,

> A first attempt at indigenisation succeeded in creating a legion of briefcase business-men and petty traders. It also created a small clique of *nouveaux riches*, largely thriving on crony capitalism and feeding on an intricate patronage system. ...Many complaints revolve round the repeated appearance of the same beneficiaries in different deals and guises. ...Black empowerment can only succeed in an environment of economic growth buttressed by a vibrant private sector with full accountability all the way down the line (www.theindependent.co.zw/news/2).

Matikinye's argument is that the economic policy of BEE/Indigenisation/ Africanisation does not solve the problem of economic decay and the resultant poverty among the poor; rather it creates a small African elite class whose economic privileges are the direct result of governmental efforts. A popular critique of BEE among South Africans has been that those who are politically well connected end up remaining the only beneficiaries of BEE.

Recently Finance minister Trevor Manuel was interviewed by the London based *Financial Times* in which he suggested that the South African government's economic policy of BEE has to be reviewed. As a followup to Manuel's suggestion, the chief director of BEE, Polo Radebe conceded that, "The problem he highlighted is in the implementation, it's not a problem in the content of the policy. It's the practice of BEE that we need to rectify" (*Mail & Guardian*, April 20–25, 2007). Asked whether it was crucial for there to be a sunset clause, Polo retorted that, "You cannot put a sunset clause on transformation, [because as things are, BEE was] self-propelling" so that the economy will reach a point in the future when 'legislation was no longer necessary'. "That's when the market starts taking care of itself, when equity becomes part of our psyche. ..At that point I would like to remove that 'B' from BEE so that people stop talking about black people and see empowerment as an integral economic driver"

> Whilst criticisms of BEE have raged on the grounds that it was mainly enriching a few indi-viduals that were properly connected to the ruling party, Polo Radebe refuted this criticism on the grounds that, "But if we assume that the 67% votes that went to the ANC are a reflec-tion of their support throughout the economy, then it suggests that 67% of the population are in one way or another connected to the ANC. So when you make the argument that politicians, or those with political connections are the ones benefiting, then you are almost suggesting that BEE should be confined to 30% of the population. So for me the discussion always baffles me" (*Mail & Guardian* April 20–25, 2007).

Polo however admitted that it was difficult in the light of the present codes to reg-ulate those who are using BEE for their own personal enrichment: "But how do you determine how rich is rich enough. ..Even if we were ready to go the route of regu-lation, would these guys give us access to their balance sheets? Much of their wealth is still on paper too. We would start entering murky territory" (*Mail & Guardian*, April 20–25 2007). Whilst Polo is admitting that BEE is being abused by a few individuals, she does not spell out explicitly what has to be done in order to rectify the situation. It is abundantly clear that she admits that the BEE economic policy is beset with enormous moral problems in the sense that such a policy empowers those who are already privileged whilst ignoring the majority of the previously disadvantaged. It is mainly for this concern that such an economic policy creates strong bonds of solidarity between the newly economically empowered black people and capitalists from the previous colonial or apartheid era. The main presumption of the advocates of BEE/Indigenisation/Africanisation policies is usually based on the idea that domestic capitalists are indispensable to the domestication of capitalism, "and that factors characteristic of traditional society, especially 'traditional values', inhibited the emergence of such elites" (Leys 1994: 16). In this regard, domestic capitalists are presumed to be in the position to do so. However, since capitalism is about accumulation, it also follows that those who have accumulated more and more as a result of BEE/Indigenisation/Africanisation policies will always retain the advantage of opportunities that present themselves for further accumulation of wealth. The argument that such policies will inevitably lead to continuous accumulation of wealth by the same individual cannot be easily explained away. For example, Vuyo Jack said that after making lots of accumulation of wealth through BEE deals, Mzi Khumalo "notified the public that he was no longer available for BEE deals". Jack went on to commend that,

> Herein lies a good lesson. Once BEE beneficiaries operate in the mainstream economy without the need for assistance envisaged by BEE, they should no longer monopolise the opportunities presented by BEE but allow other people to use the policy to gain access to the mainstream economy. The principle of graduation is simple – if no one graduates, the school will soon become too full and all students will suffer. . . .The graduation from BEE will most commonly be based on wealth levels, which government cannot set. Individuals must determine their own graduation level (Jack & Harris & Harris 2007: 59–60).

Here I would like to argue against Jack by saying that graduation by essence is marked by a completion of a certain set of requirements that are known and accepted by everyone. As stated above, Jack's view is that graduation is by self-determination informed by self-satisfaction of accumulation of limitless wealth. In a desperate attempt to support this confused rendering of self-graduations he cannot help but to cite one graduand as adequate representation of the whole BEE empire of accumulation. What a representative sample! But Jack also raised an issue of ethical concern to the effect that BEE was actually empowering the same individuals who are in most cases politically well connected to national centres of political power. Thus within BEE, Jack avers,

> The more influential the politician, the greater the attraction the suitors have for him or her. Furthermore, the more deals the former politician can conclude, the more bankable he or she becomes as a deal-maker and the stakes get higher. The trend is evident when tracking the deals entered into, for example, by Tokyo Sexwale, Cyril Ramaphosa and Saki Macozoma. Their early transactions were smaller in value but increased substantially as they landed more deals. . . .BEE does not intentionally advocate empowering the same individuals. Companies seeking Black ownership credentials frequently choose the same individuals and do not cast their nets wider in search of other Black people to partner with (Jack & Harris 2007: 60).

Obviously if what is stated by Jack is a true expression of how BEE operates, then the previous claim that has been made by people that this economic policy was designed to help a few is valid. If such a policy can only benefit a few of those who are well connected politically then in no way can BEE policy ever lead to the domestication of capitalism. My argument here is that if capitalist accumulation requires hard work, thrift and frugality as it is generally agreed by economists, an economic policy that is mainly oriented towards accumulation and political connectivity as the ultimate value without hard work degenerates into some form of legalised looting. For this reason, other critics of BEE have raised their moral agitation towards this policy on the grounds that such a policy betrays the spirit of *Ubuntu* which is at the heart of African ethics. This moral agitation was expressed by Mike Boon when he said that African capitalists "are self-serving and care nothing for the community other than what it can deliver to them personally. . ."(Boon 1996: 48). Other developmental economists have maintained that an economic policy that elevates individual accumulation without limit does militate against broad economic development of the country. It is for this reason these critics have argued that BEE/Indigenisation/Africanisation is just a mistaken policy prompted mainly by political opportunism and the desire for a luxurious life without any sense of concern for the well-being of others or the greater good.

4.5 BEE/Indigenisation/Africanisation as Mistaken Policies

Adebayo Adedeji argued that the idea of indigenisation as a development policy objective has evolved through various stages of evolution. As he puts it,

> As a policy, however, one gets the impression that the approach to its development and application has been rather *ad hoc*, piece-meal and lacking in internal consistency. It has been a product of circumstances, and at times mainly of politicians reacting to unfavourable economic situations and the demands of small groups of indigenous businessmen who felt that the prevailing economic conditions put them in an unfair position *vis-à-vis* their foreign competitors. It was hardly the original work of development planners, although their involvement became inevitable after political decisions have been made. Just as the articulation of a policy of indigenisation came about in a piece-meal fashion, so the measure for its realization was equally *ad hoc* and unplanned (Adedeji 1981: 45).

The implication of the above quotation is that the economic evolution of indigenisation does not reflect a well reflected and planned economic policy. Its implementation carried with it some form of reaction on the part of African businessmen to foreign economic relations. Ali Mazrui is more radical on this issue when he said that the whole thrust towards indigenization policy was aimed at making multinational companies more relevant to the African context. He writes,

> The economic interests of the newly westernized Africans become interlinked with those of the multinationals at some levels. More and more jobs within the multinationals become accessible to the locals. More and more decision-making roles are Africanised. Increasingly the faces behind the managerial desks are local. Increasingly the boards of directors co-opt westernized locals to lend further legitimacy to their operations (Mazrui 1978: 294).

In the light of Mazrui's observation we can deduce that the aims of indigenization in post-colonial Africa was partly to give a local semblance to multinational capitalism by co-opting local personnel. Once co-opted into multinational capitalism, Africans become representatives of multinational capitalism par excellence. In this way, Mazrui maintained that, "The growth of [the market] for western consumer goods partly depended on the spread of western tastes and life-styles. . . .Some aspects of African culture have reinforced the temptation to emulate and imitate the West. Most of western political and economic culture has been conditioned by the respect given to both political individualism and the profit motive" (Mazrui 1978: 295). Within this state of emulation of western patterns of consumption, "western consumer goods started to widen their culturally relevant market" (Mazrui 1978: 296). According to Mazrui, "The pace-setters in all this world of status and prestige were the more educated and more westernized Africans. Some of these later owned mines and not just jewellery, rode in a Mercedes-Benz and no longer on a bicycle, and drank imported liquor and mineral water from Europe and not merely imported foodstuffs. . . .Those few leaders that are struggling to control the revolution in consumption patterns risk their own survival in so doing unless they combine these efforts with a revolution in education" (Mazrui 1978: 296).

In other words, in historical origins of BEE/Indigenisation/Africanisation policy the orientation of such a policy created a class of Africans who became indispensable instruments for the ascendency of western capitalism in post-colonial Africa. Whilst proponents of BEE/Indigenisation/Africanisation have always maintained that such a policy is aimed at transferring colonial capitalist institutions into African hands so that Africans would have effective control of these institutions, African dependency developmental theorists do argue that such a policy can only lead to strong solidarity between African capitalists and global capitalism. These critics maintain that the economic power of foreign owned companies has managed to successfully contain the momentum of expropriation of their wealth through BEE/Indigenisation/Africanisation policy. It is partly on these grounds that Africa dependency theorists insist that African capitalists were contributors of post-colonial African underdevelopment. To illustrate the validity of this argument, Chinweizu said that,

Nigeria's inability to accumulate and properly invest its enormous oil income was largely due to the origins, ideology and aspirations of its governing class. The dominant section of the elite were mandarins, largely originating from the non-producer sections of the colonial *petite-bourgeoisie*. Even those who originated from the producer sections had been turned into mandarins by their long, academic preparation for bureaucratic careers. As a result, they were, on the whole, inexperienced in production, averse to its rigours and risks, and even superciliously hostile to material production. On the other hand, they had enormous appetites for material consumption. Forgetting that hunting is not the carcass on the plate, they conceived development planning as the making of shopping lists of modern artifacts to be imported and consumed. They craved the best that the industrial world could offer, and were therefore preoccupied with the distribution for consumption of whatever income was available from an economy which remained colonial in character (Chinweizu 1999: 789–790).

According to Chinweizu, African capitalists will always be outsmarted by western capitalists especially when it comes to what to do with the wealth which has been overaccumulated. African capitalists are prone to lavish spending whilst western capitalists put all their energies mainly on accumulating insatiably on that they could lay their hands on. For this reason, African capitalists "were ill disposed to capital accumulation for productive investment". On the other hand, "In contrast, the bourgeoisie of the Western core were habitual accumulators of capital, highly experienced at it, and with highly developed productive organisations as well as vast sums of already accumulated capital which they could deploy for further accumulation" (Chinweizu 1999: 790). In this comparative study of western capitalists and African capitalists Chinweizu is arguing that African capitalists cannot be seen as agents of development because of their consumption habits. The same argument was also made by Mazrui when he said that, "When Westerners call upon African countries to privatize, they are expecting the profit motive to be given free play. But in fact, the problem in most of Africa is not simply how to liberate and activate the *profit motive*, but also how to control and restrain the *prestige motive*. Arguably the latter crusade is even more urgent than the former. Indeed, the ultimate crusade may well turn out to be how to tap the prestige motive in such a way that it serves the goals of production and not merely the appetites of consumption" (Mazrui 1999: 493). The behaviour of African capitalists in relationship to profit and prestige motives that go hand in glove with capitalism is always seen as something that is predetermined by African culture and values. In African culture, someone who eats alone or who accumulates wealth without sharing that wealth with others in community is mainly regarded as anti-social and such wealth is usually seen as some products of wicked machinations on the part of the business person concerned. Whatever is to be eaten by the individual should be made accessible to everybody. In this regard, to what extent can African capitalists through BEE/Indigenisation/Africanisation policy find their way in global capitalism? To what extent can African capitalists lead to the evolution of a globally competitive African capitalism?

4.6 BEE/Indigenisation/Africanisation and Global Capitalism

However, with the globalisation of neo-liberal capitalism there is no way where one can expect a unique capitalism that is distinctively African without some influence of the processes of global capitalism. Chinweizu argued that from the word go, policies and programmes of indigenisation or Africanisation were met with economic resistance from the western world. The western world suspected that such policies were only another way whereby Africans try to expropriate the western wealth. According to Chinweizu,

> Expropriation, whether by nationalisation or indigenisation, did not go without responses from the West. Western governments in the 1960s threatened crippling reprisals against those who nationalised their assets. ...There was also a shift from parent-company direct control of African subsidiaries to management participation, technical assistance and

training arrangements, production sharing and supply contracts. French investors began to rely on investment guarantee and insurance schemes provided by their home governments to cover non-commercial risks like war, revolution and expropriation. Other European powers followed suit. Such schemes were applicable for investments in countries with whom their home governments had Investment Protection Agreements (IPAs) which provided for fair and prompt compensation in cases of expropriation. . . .By such devices, the West often under both French and American leadership contained the momentum of expropriation, and made it safe for Western companies to keep investing in Africa (Chinweizu 1999: 779).

As stated above, Chinweizu's argument was that the economic power of western owned companies successfully contained the momentum of Indigenisation or Africanisation through protective schemes such as Investment Protection Agreements (IPAs). Another way in which western governments managed to avert the momentum of expropriation of their companies in post-colonial Africa was through international trade. Within international trade, Chinweizu writes, "Neither partial nor total African ownership of companies operating in Africa improved the prices Africans got for their exports, the quantities they could sell, or the prices they had to pay for imports. They discovered that the power over these lay with the handful of Western companies which dominated world trade in each commodity" (Chinweizu 1999: 779). Chinweizu's argument is also that it is the reality of unfair trade conditions within the international market that rendered indigenization or Africanisation a mere exercise in economic futility. Within South Africa, the government has been very cautious in its application of BEE requirement for multinational companies. In the BEE Codes, a multinational is defined as "a measured entity with a business in the Republic of South Africa and elsewhere, which maintains its international headquarters outside the Republic" (see Jack & Harris & Harris 2007: 221). Within such a definition a multinational with its headquarters outside South Africa can hardly be expected to comply with BEE. The problem here is that a multinational is mainly concerned with a standardized form of business operation and is mostly interested in its profits and the protection of its investments. In cases where economic policies of particular countries become unbearable the multinational company can easily relocate somewhere.

4.7 Conclusion

In this chapter I started by giving an ordinary people's conversation about BEE. I have shown through this story that BEE does create some ethical questions with regards to whom this economic programme is benefiting. Through this story, the main ethical problem is that such an economic policy is only benefiting those who are well connected politically. I have also shown that BEE was not an invention of post-apartheid South Africa, rather, such an economic policy has been experimented with in many parts of post-colonial Africa with the aim of domesticating capitalism.

An analysis of BEE/Ingidenisation/Africanisation policy has also revealed that such a policy only leads to the creation of African capitalists who will end up being in solidarity with other capitalists. By applying Thorstein Veblen's theory of Institutionary Evolutionary Economics, it was argued that African capitalists cannot be seen as different from other capitalists because by belonging to the capitalist class, they are bound to emulate fellow capitalists in terms of accumulation and consumption. Many post-colonial economic dependency theorists have argued that BEE/Indigenisation/Africanisation does not have any developmental contribution to make towards the socio-economic upliftment of the majority of the citizens in post-colonial African society. The gist of their argument here was that there was no empirical evidence that BEE/Indigenisation/Africanisation will lead to the domestication of capitalism or to the development of African economies.

The questions I would like to pose for future research are as follows:

1) Why does BEE/Indigenisation/Africanisation enrich a few when the majority of the citizens are living in desperately poor conditions?
2) Would it not make sense to have some Economic Empowerment that is directed towards education, infrastructure and health?
3) Does not BEE/Indigenisation/Africanisation policy pose a conflict of interest when politicians or former politicians collude with businesses in pursuit of best deals?

References

Adedeji, A. (ed.) 1981, *Indigenisation of African Economies* (Hutchinson University Library for Africa, London).

Ake, C. 1981, 'Historical and Theoretical Background: The Political Context of Indigenisation', Adedeji, A. (Ed.) *Indigenisation of African Economies* (Hutchinson University Library for Africa, London), pp. 32–41.

Boon, M. 1996, *The African Way: The Power of Interactive Leadership* (Zebra Press, Johannesburg).

Chinweizu, 1999, 'Africa and the Capitalist Countries', Mazrui, A. A. and Wondji, C. (eds.) *General History of Africa: VIII Africa Since 1935* (Unbridged Edition) (James Currey, UNESCO), pp. 769–797.

Davis, R. H. 1973, 'Interpreting the Colonial Period in African History', *African Affairs* 72 (289), 385.

Gross, F. 1956, *Rhodes of Africa* (Cassell, London).

Hanna, A. J. 1961, *European Rule in Africa* (Routledge and Kegan Paul, G., London) p. 46.

Jack & Harris, V. and Harris, K. 2007, *Broad-Based BEE: The Complete Guide* (Frontrunner Publishing (Pty) Ltd, Northcliff).

Leys, C. 1994, 'African Capitalists and Development: Theoretical Questions.' in Berman, B. J. and Leys, C. (eds.), *African Capitalists in African Development* (Lynne Rienner Publishers, Boulder & London), pp. 11–38.

Lipton, M. 1986, *Capitalism and Apartheid: South Africa, 1910–1986* (David Philip, Publisher, Cape Town).

Matikinye, R. at www.theindependent.co.zw/news/2

Mazrui, A. A. 1978, *Political Values and the Educated Class in Africa* (Heinemann, London).

Mazrui, A. A. 1986, *The Africans: A Triple Heritage* (BBC Publications, London).

Mazrui, A. A. 1999, *Cultural Forces in World Politics* (James Currey, London).

Murove, M. F. 2005, "The Incarnation of Max Weber's *Protestant Ethic and the Spirit of Capitalism* in post-Colonial subSaharan African Economic Discourse: The Quest for an African Economic Ethic", *Mankind Quarterly* XLV(4) Summer, 389–394.

Nkrumah, K. 1970, *Africa Must Unite* (Heinemann, London).

Nyerere, J. K. 1968, *Freedom and Socialism: Uhuru na Ujamaa* (Oxford University Press, Oxford).

Polanyi, K. 1968, *The Great Transformation: The Political and Economic Origins of our Time* (Renehart and Company, New York).

Veblen, T. 1931, *The Theory of the Leisure Class: An Economic Study of Institutions* (The Modern Library, New York).

Chapter 5
Ethical Sourcing and Moral Responsibility in Global Business: Is 'the Common Good' the Missing Factor? The Case of the Cut Flower Industry in Kenya

Christine Wanjiru Gichure

5.1 Introduction

International business today is estimated to constitute a singularly big employment capacity in developing countries (Chang 2003). For the rich countries, global marketing has stimulated the search for areas in which to outsource production at low cost, with a view to reducing the prices of a wide variety of goods, while increasing purchasing power and accelerating the availability of consumer goods. This trend prompts competition between countries, as they seek to set up production centres around the globe. In Africa, some studies say that global business has facilitated much economic growth in terms of resources and certain skills (Roozendaal, 1994; Hennock, 2002; Lehmann, 2004). However, that growth is increasingly being questioned when compared to the huge benefits that the North, the developed world, reaps from the labour and environment of the South, the developing world (Ngotho, 2005; Esipisu, 2007).

This scepticism is justified on various accounts. In the first place, global investors want a 'favourable fiscal' regime and regulation of the labour market. This, in many instances, means downsizing of social security systems as the price to be paid for seeking greater competitive advantage in the global market with consequent grave danger for the rights of workers and for fundamental human rights (Kenya Human Rights Commission [KHRC], 2004: 11, Benedict, 2009: 25). On their part, the developing countries, in order to attract investment, strive not only to compete with each other, but also to provide a favourable, conducive or enabling environment for the investors (Mwakungu, 2003; KHRC, 2004: 16–17).

'Favourable conditions', 'favourable environment' or 'deregulation' generally mean labour processes characterised by casual or informal work, flexible working days or hours in order to meet the needs of employers or the business cycle, and wages that are often pegged on profit margins achieved by the business (Majtenyi, 2002; KHRC, 2004: 17–22; Benedict, 2009: 21). In addition, the management in

C.W. Gichure (✉)
Associate Professor of Applied Ethics, Department of Philosophy and Religious Studies,
Kenyatta University, Nairobi, Kenya
e-mail: gichure.christine@ku.ac.ke

G. Moore (ed.), *Fairness in International Trade*, The International Society
of Business, Economics, and Ethics Book Series 1, DOI 10.1007/978-90-481-8840-6_5,
© Springer Science+Business Media B.V. 2010

many types of global businesses in the developing world tends to opt for a workforce that is expendable. As a result, the opportunity cost of offering these incentives results in a shift of the social cost to the workers in sweatshops or farms and environmental degradation of the natural resources (Gibbon, 1992; Food and Water Watch Canadians [FWW] 2008; Benedict, 2009: 25). This practice is typically exemplified in the Export Processing Zones (EPZ) and in the cut flower industry in Kenya, which is the focus of this chapter.

Within this context, an example of the problematic can be explained as follows. A developing country, A, that wants to attract a cut-flower growing company will offer strong tax incentives. In the meantime, two neighbouring countries, B & C, which are also interested in attracting the same growers, will each try to offer investment deals that undercut the tax incentives offered by the others. From there a race and row arises between the two or three developing countries to see who can offer the most 'favourable condition'. Finally, the government with what the global investor happens to consider 'favourable fiscal' and deregulation conditions hosts the flower growers and is happy with the short-term benefits. These benefits are usually employment opportunities for some of its people and prospects of some gain on taxes and work permits. In the meantime, it may realise that it has sacrificed the ability to provide its own citizens with some basic legal, human and infrastructural support (FWW, 2008). Due in part to these factors, the success of floriculture has been tempered by an extremely politicized backlash centred on allegations that flower farms generate profits at the expense of Kenyan environments and workers.

5.2 Kenya Floriculture in Global Business

Floriculture first arose in Kenya in the 1970s, fuelled by development aid aimed at integrating African producers into the global economy (Kenya Flower Council [KFC], 2008; Hennock, 2002). In the last two decades, Kenya has turned into a successful cut flower exporter, thereby becoming a strong competitor on the European cut flower market. However, the country seems to be heavily dependent on ownership, knowledge and technology from the North (Roozendaal & Commander, 1994).

The major destinations for the Kenyan flowers are the Netherlands, United Kingdom, Germany, France, and other European Union (EU) countries. The EU is believed to consume over 50% of the world's flowers and, of these, 25% is exported from Kenya (Roozendaal, 1994). In the UK alone, an ETI media briefing indicated that, on a day like Valentine's Day, one in every four flowers sold in the UK comes from Kenya. That makes Kenya the third-largest exporter of cut flowers, after Colombia and the Netherlands (Roozendaal, 1994; Ethical Trading Initiative [ETI] Briefing, 6th February 2008).[1]

---

[1] The Ethical Trading Initiative [ETI] is an alliance of companies, trade union organisations and non-government organisations (NGOs) committed to working together to achieve that aim. "Our

The value of the export of cut flowers from Kenya to the European market is estimated at approximately 43 billion Kenya Shillings (approximately USD 12.9 billion) ranking them among the most important agro-export products of the country (Roozendaal, 1994). But the development of the cut flower sector often involves large governmental investments in infrastructure, such as roads and cold storage facilities, to enable the rapid export of the perishable product. That means that, in reality, only a small portion of the investment is recovered through tax income. This makes it an expensive sector to invest in, especially for a government that suffers from declining budgets. Recently, some municipal leaders, such as those from Naivasha, the city bordering the lake which is the hub of the flower farms, are pushing for a law to enable it to tax the farms 1% of their annual output. But with this proposal a high percentage of growers have threatened to move their operations to neighbouring Ethiopia (Interview, Human Flower Project [HFP][2] with Naivasha Town Clerk, July 2009).

The accredited body to monitor floriculture activities in Kenya is KFC. It is, therefore, the legal body that oversees the audits, gives certification for good practice to the flower growers, and collects standard levy fees on behalf of the Kenya Bureau of Standards (KEBS). Working closely with KFC is the ETI, which regularly reports on what is going on in the horticulture industry. In its briefing report of February 2008, the ETI estimated that over 55,000 Kenyan workers and their dependents rely on jobs within the industry (ETI, 2008). These figures vary from report to report, however, with the KFC putting it at 100,000 direct workers, but claiming that all in all approximately 1.2 million people rely on it, if one adds other people indirectly employed in transport and packaging roles (KFC, 2008).

These large numbers of employees in the cut flower industry, coupled with the apparently huge earnings for Kenya, show the industry to be capable of improving the economy and the lives of Kenyan people. However, this perception has been disputed by other reports. The Town Clerk of Naivasha laments that, while "these farms earn billions of shillings every year, a municipal council like the one of Naivasha only benefits from the industry through the meagre levies it charges for business permits and the land it owns – not sales. That means Naivasha takes in only about $32,835 annually (2.2 million Kenyan shillings) from the flower industry. Furthermore, wages at the flower farms amount to only between $37 and $104 per month" (Interview with Ardery, HFP, 2009).

These complaints are corroborated by a Kenya Human Rights Commission (KHRC) survey of 2002–2004, which was carried out in various flower farms and the EPZ sector in the Kenya. Its findings showed that, despite the huge profits, the Kenyan people, including local Kenyan flower growers, gain little foreign exchange from the cut flower business (ETI Survey, 2005). Other researches give similar observations (Smith et al., 2005; Dolan & Opondo, 2005; Black, 2004).

---

ultimate goal is to ensure that the working conditions of workers in companies that supply goods to consumers in the UK meet or exceed international standards." See www.ethicaltrade.org.

[2] The Human Flower Project is an international newsgroup, photo album and discussion of how people live through flowers.

A special report carried in Kenya's *Sunday Standard* of April 17, 2005 (which has not been refuted) highlighted various discrepancies between the apparent huge earnings from the flower industry for Kenya and the reality on the ground in terms of gains for the Kenyan people. Firstly, just like the coffee, tea and tourism industries, the floriculture sector remains largely a foreigners' affair. Specifically, of the approximately 500 flower farms in the country, a total of 76% is concentrated in foreign-owned flowers farms around Lake Naivasha in the Rift Valley. The largest are the Homegrown, Sulmac, Sher, Oserian and Finlay flower companies. Oserian alone employs more than 5,000 workers and has been the subject of many workers' strikes (Smith et al., 2005).

Other complaints come from local indigenous flower growers, who lose in the manner that flowers are assessed and sold in Amsterdam. While their flowers are sold as Kenyan flowers and taxed as such, the Dutch companies growing their flowers in Kenya tend to sell theirs as Dutch flowers, because in that way they receive preferential treatment at the auction. This includes exempting those flowers from the EU-imposed export rules (Harper, 2009; Ngotho, 2005). Ultimately, this means that the indigenous Kenyan grower earns less than his expatriate or foreign counterpart who has a flower farm or company in Kenya. In addition, most of the earnings gained at the auctions are banked in the investor's home country.

A third and more alarming observation has to do with the working conditions of the employees in the flower farms. Generally, the people who seek work in this industry are poor, which makes them vulnerable to exploitation. Their plight eventually leaks out to the media and the human rights groups. For many years, the cut flower industry in Kenya has been covered by the media, revealing the poor labour practices and treatment of the workers and the adverse effects of some of the growers' practices on the environment, especially on Lake Naivasha. Among the most recent, one can mention Ngotho (2005), Esipisu (2007), FWW (2008), Riungu (2009), Ardrey (2009) and the scientist Harper (2009). All of these reports confirm the ETI Report findings of 2002–2004. That research revealed widespread discrimination against women workers, workers kept on rolling temporary contracts, poor health and safety, low wages, long working hours and low levels of union representation. That report gave some recommendations for the improvement of human rights, but going by later media reports, the improvement cannot be significant.

The fourth and most pernicious problem is the ongoing destruction of Lake Naivasha, the centre of most of Kenya's flower business. Nestled in the Rift Valley, the lake is a source of abundant wildlife and a rich variety of bird species. Tens of thousands of people rely on the fragile ecosystem to preserve their livelihoods in an environment that has increasingly come under threat. These threats are of various kinds. In the first place, the fishing communities around the lake complain of the increasing spread of water hyacinth, a weed that thrives due to the continuous supply of phosphates and nitrates used in the water farms, which are later drained into the lake. With the growth and spread of this weed, the sunlight, much needed by species living below for breeding and sustenance of life, is blocked, thereby reducing fishing stocks. In addition, fishermen who depend on the lake for their livelihood claim not only that the pesticides and fertilizers also drained into the lake pollute the water, but also that, in the process of pumping it into the flower farms, many fish eggs and small fish are sucked in and killed.

After 25 years of conducting research in the Lake Naivasha area, a leading scientist, Dr. David Harper is reported to have told ScienceNews:

> Roses that come cheap are grown by companies that have no concern for the environment, who cut corners and avoid legislation, who sell their flowers into the auction in Amsterdam so that all the buyer knows is the flowers 'come from Holland (Harper ScienceDaily, Feb. 14, 2009).

The shrinking water levels of Lake Naivasha are an evident environmental problem, much publicised, and still largely ignored by the farmers. About a half of the good cut flower companies breed their flowers around this lake. On paper, the country has strong legislation on the use of water for the flowers, which should come from boreholes, but its enforcement is weak. So, companies whose only interest is profit take advantage of that (Harper, 2009; CEO KFC, 2009; Riungu, 2009; Ardery, 2009; Food and Water Watch Canadians [FWW], 2008). The lake has immense potential for sustainable, small-scale agriculture and ecotourism that could protect both the lake and the livelihoods of the communities around it. The former would promote food security for Kenyans; the latter would attract even more local and foreign visitors, who would help the local economy, while causing little or no damage to the environment.

The flower companies, on their part, and with them the KFC, either deny that these things are happening, or consider them solely from an economic point of view. They, too, have complaints: the costs of production are higher in Kenya than in the developed countries, owing to various factors. They cite poor infrastructure, inadequate air cargo capacity and high airfreight rates, high prices of inputs such as fertilizer and chemicals, inability to sustain high quality of the fresh flowers due to transportation problems and lack of sufficient technical knowledge (Roozendaal & Commander, 1994; Author's personal interview with CEO Lankas Ltd, 2008).[3]

Thus far, we have looked at four major types of problems involving the Kenya cut flower industry, problems which are evidently complex and certainly beyond the scope of one chapter. The focus of this chapter is ethics and, therefore, it will limit itself to the theoretical question of what appears to be a paradox, whereby Kenya's cut flower industry is one of the most heavily audited sectors for 'ethical sourcing' using multi-stakeholder designed ethical codes but, on the other hand, the same industry continues to be in the spotlight frequently for the ethical malpractices that I have highlighted.

Having given this background and stated the problem and objectives of this chapter, I now turn to the notion of 'ethical sourcing' as a concept in global business, in order to examine how it is understood within the two major business management models, namely, the shareholder organizational theory and the stakeholder model. That analysis will be followed by an examination of the facts on the ground, guided by the results of the three related researches that explored the trajectory of 'ethical

---

[3] Not real name of the Farm in question.

sourcing' in Kenya, namely the report by Dolan and Opondo (2005), Smith et al. (2005) and the ETI Report 2002–2004 (2005). Since these reports already question the factors underlying the design and implementation of the Horticultural Ethical Business Initiative (HEBI) codes, purportedly designed through a multi-stakeholder processes (MSP) to audit the farms for 'ethical sourcing', the objective of this chapter is to identify what might be missing from the management philosophy governing the concept of 'ethical sourcing' and social responsibility, and to make some recommendations. Unfortunately it has not been possible to obtain permission to work with what the researches term 'base code' for purposes of this chapter.[4]

5.3 The Concept of 'Ethical Sourcing' and Social Responsibility in Global Business: The Problematic of Its Application in the Kenya Cut Flower Industry

Ethical sourcing is described as a process whereby a company at one stage of the supply chain takes responsibility for the ethical, social and environmental performance at other stages of the chain, especially for that of primary producers (Blowfield, 2000: 1). However, the way it is understood by the different players within the global business chain, from the production, packaging and distribution stage, depends largely on the kind of perception of ethics a company may have, and the management theory to which it subscribes. That perception is what guides their particular codes of ethics. The implementation of the codes is, in turn, expected to give ethical assurance, especially if there are annual audits, as in the case of Kenya's flower farms. Given the fact that there are divergent theories and models of business management and its moral responsibilities, no one should be surprised that each company or business sector can easily have its [their] own understanding of the kind of issues that constitute 'ethical sourcing', a process that has grown in popularity from the early 1990s, when national and international trade unions and non-governmental organisations (NGOs) started to campaign about social and environmental conditions in the cut flower industry worldwide. These campaigns were geared towards raising awareness among consumers in market countries, about the conditions in the industry in both Latin America and Africa (ETI Report, 2005).

Within the present decade, following various workers strikes, particularly at Oserian Farm, one of the largest flower holdings with 50,000 acres on Lake Naivasha, and media exposés, there have been efforts to alert the consumers of the fact that the goods they buy could possibly have been acquired at the cost of human basic rights (Smith et al., 2005; ScienceDaily, 2009; FWW, 2008; HFP, 2009). But, as we have seen, excessive exploitation of resources, both human and the natural environment, continues to be highlighted with the aim of pressurizing companies to become more ethically responsible. The result has been a proliferation of good

---

[4] A special permission is required by the KFC in order to see and use the code. This permission was not given to the author.

practice mechanisms, such as codes of ethics, good practice statements, vision and mission statements and agendas for 'social responsibility' initiatives, with varying degrees of success, which can be found in nearly every company and organization today.

5.3.1 Flower Labelling Program (FLP)

To ensure the implementation of those initiatives, many markets in the North now require 'labelling' as a sign of ethical sourcing (Holtshaussen, 2007). In the cut flower industry, this is done through the Flower Label Program (FLPs). However, while those efforts may have addressed certain aspects of ethical practice, it appears that in Kenya they have not managed to provide significant ethical or social responsibility, corporate or otherwise. The indication from studies carried out in those parts of the world (Hughes, 2000, 2001) is that the consumers of goods bearing such labels as the FLP, more often than not, have little clue of what it means for a product to have been 'ethically sourced'. They are happy to see that the product they purchase bears the label, because that gives them some kind of comfort. They feel that at least they are acting responsibly towards the promotion of ethical business. An empirical study carried out by graduate students in the UK among 34 respondents within the food and agricultural industry showed that no strict definition of 'ethical sourcing' was discernible, even among people who are not only active defenders of 'ethical sourcing', but would not knowingly use a product sourced otherwise (Holtshaussen, 2007). According to this research, however, when asked what they meant by 'ethical', for example, most of them spoke of fair trade. But, as to what makes such trade fair or unfair, they had absolutely no notion. This, they believed, depends on the interpretation of each person. Hence, to different respondents it meant different things. In some instances, according to the report, companies were found to adopt a holistic interpretation of the concept of 'ethically sourced' product, where it could mean anything from the manner of producing and packaging a product to the treatment of the workers, fair remuneration for work, and their rights to certain social benefits which everyone seemed to admit must all be part of 'ethical sourcing'. Very few individuals focussed on social benefits for their workers, the protection of children, equal opportunity and occupational health and safety (Holtshaussen, 2007: 2).

One other factor, as noted by the Canadian human rights body, Food and Water Watch, that the consumer at the other end of the market may not be aware of, is that one can easily be fooled by the market chain: for example, through false labelling. This is what Harper is cautioning the flower buyer about in relation to Lake Naivasha. The flowers may continue to bear the labels, despite the fact that the lake is literally being drained dry by flower growers. But, since these flower growers know about the bad publicity that Kenyan-grown flowers have been receiving for lack of environmental responsibility and other malpractices, they sell their flowers at the flower auctions in Amsterdam as being Dutch- or German-grown, so that when people buy their flowers, they think they are buying them from the

Netherlands instead of Lake Naivasha (2008). The surprising thing is that nobody talks about corruption in these cases.

5.3.2 The Ethical Sourcing Audits

The usual instrument used to measure 'ethical sourcing' is the code of ethics. A code of ethics is commonly defined as "a written, distinct, and formal document which consists of moral standards used to guide employee or corporate behaviour, but it is recognized that such documents can take a variety of forms" (Moore, 2006: 411). Codes take a variety of forms, depending on the kind of ethical issues they want to address. Moore identifies three clusters of codes, namely "those dealing with issues impacting primarily on employees, on companies or on wider society" (ibid.).

Most companies like codes of ethics, because, once drafted and launched, that fact alone gives the impression that the company is taking ethics seriously. However, since companies are presumed to be voluntary entities, the content of the codes and their implementation is largely dependent on the management model governing the business (Samet, 2003; Gichure, 2008: 202–206). This can explain, in part, why so far it has not been proved anywhere that codes of ethics significantly influence the practice of ethics in business and, secondly, there remains the delicate side to their use. "This may be the core to the problem in 'ethical sourcing'. For a code to be comprehensively effective depends largely on various factors, such as how it was designed, who designed it, what interests it was primarily designed to serve, how it was supposed to be implemented, how often, and who would audit the company for good practice" (Gichure, 2008).

The motivation for producing and implementing a code of ethics is an important factor in ethical sourcing, for it determines the effectiveness of the audit document. This motivation, according to Moore (2006), focuses more often than not on internal issues and on issues relating to the company itself, rather than on issues relating to external stakeholders, such as consumers and the wider public. "This suggests that the motivation for introducing a code relates more to firm protection and compliance issues (preventing harm, particularly to the company) than to a more positive and outward-looking motivation" (Moore, 2006: 411). Applied to ethical sourcing, this means that there are varying degrees of its implementation, with equal possibility for some important stakeholders to be omitted, even legally, from the improvement process (Moore, 2006).

This assumption is affirmed by the findings of Dolan and Opondo (2005) in the case of the cut flower industry in Kenya. Their findings showed that, despite being one of the most codified industries, ethical violations of basic rights of the workers and the natural environment continue to be rife. A further investigation revealed that the codes used to audit the farms had originally been imported from the Dutch flower industry, where the workers' conditions and the environment are very different from those of Kenya. Wood (1995) points to another reason why such codes may not serve to provide ethical sourcing in a situation like that of Kenya. Generally, corporations in the North assume that, because developing countries 'appear' to operate at lower ethical standards (often due to lack of education and means), it is not ethically wrong to operate with values and norms that would otherwise be questionable in their own countries. As a result, with only superficial changes in supplier practices, products sourced under questionable ethical standards reach the developed countries where the markets are bearing FLP tags as guarantee of having been sourced ethically.

5.3.3 Business Management Models, Ethical Sourcing and Social Responsibility

It would not be justified to attribute blame to any party along the production, supply and distribution chain without having first examined ethical sourcing as a concept within the business organizational models in vogue in global business. The two most commonly used models of business organization are the agency/shareholder/stockholder model and the stakeholder model, to which we shall now turn.

According to the proponents of the shareholder model, the purpose of the firm is to maximize shareholder value, since all corporate profits belong by right to the stockholders as the owners of the firm. Hence company managers are simply agents of the stockholders and, in that capacity they have a moral obligation to manage the firm solely in the interest in the owners. That interest is to maximize shareholder wealth (Friedman, 1970; Boatright, 2001). This is the rationale behind Friedman's famous statement: "The social responsibility of business is to increase its profits".

Freeman (1984) speaks of a narrow and a broad way of understanding the stakeholder model of the purpose of business, and how it should be managed. In the narrow sense, the stakeholders of a business are those groups who are vital to the survival and success of the corporate firm, such as owners, employees, customers, suppliers, and local community (Freeman, 1984: 31). In the broad or wider sense, the concept of stakeholder includes any group or individual who can affect or be affected by the corporation. Furthering this notion, other scholars have affirmed that the stakeholders not only have interests in the affairs of the corporation, but that the interests of all stakeholders have intrinsic value (Donaldson & Preston, 1995: 81).

Schaefer (2008), Phillips (2003) and Melé (2008) have attempted to show the complexities underlying the relationship between these two theories from a moral point of view. In the following section of this chapter, I attempt to characterize those complexities within the paradigm of 'ethical sourcing' in the cut flower industry in Kenya. The points of departure are the testimonies of workers within this industry, unearthed by the two researches already cited: the exploiting of the unfortunate plight of workers, pollution of the lake, unfair competition with local flowers at the market end of the chain, downsizing without warning. All of these practices should have been detected by the ethics audits, but never were. They should have been within the demands of the code of good practice, but for some reason they do not appear to have been violated at the time of the audits. Faced with such accusations, what do the traditional management models say with regard to, say, moral responsibility?

5.3.4 'Ethical Sourcing' Under the Agency Model of Business Management

This model assumes that the purpose of the firm is to maximize shareholder wealth. Therefore, the managers are agents of the shareholders, who are the business owners or its principals. As such, the managers have fiduciary duties to do their best to serve their principals' interests. From an ethical perspective, fiduciary duties of managers are moral duties and, in most countries, legal duties as well (Melé, 2008), because managers are fiduciaries or trustees of the shareholders. Hence, the fulfilment of the duties corresponding to that relationship entails an ethical obligation, because a fiduciary relationship is based on good faith, loyalty and trust.

The question then arises: is it ethical to serve the principal's interests at the cost of unethical behaviour toward others? In other words, can fiduciary duties be ever overridden by moral duties towards other constituencies affected by the business activity? This, according to an analysis of this model by Schaefer (2008), does not appear to be the case, because "from a shareholder management perspective, the purpose of the corporation is to realize the specified ends of the share holders, with the caveat that those ends are legal and basically non-deceptive" (Schaefer, 2008: 297). Those ends are nearly always to maximize the corporation's profits – so much so that to characterize shareholder theory by reference to maximization of corporate profits has been accurate for all practical purposes. Friedman, the best known proponent of this theory explains that,

> In an ideal free market resting on private property, no individuals can coerce any other, all cooperation is voluntary, all parties to such cooperation benefit or they need not participate. There are no values, no 'social' responsibilities in any sense other than the shared values and responsibilities of individuals (Friedman, 1970, in Boatright, 2001).

The next question is: what is the content of the morality that holds in an ideal free-market capital society? Schaefer's analysis of the above statement suggests that it is one in which individual freedom and private property take on the highest priority, that is to say, "property, where the freedom of the capitalist [read principal] takes priority over all other considerations" (Schaefer, 2008: 298 footnote 56). He further observes that, whereas this model frequently emphasises non-interference, or 'negative duties', towards one another as strong moral duties of the manager, there is a loud silence on the presumably 'positive duties' that one would expect to be also highlighted. By 'negative duties' is meant "to respect one another's individual freedom and private property, while 'positive duties' are said to be, by their very nature, coercive in a way that disrespects the values associated with those [former] goods" (Schaefer, 2008: 300).

There is a discrepancy here between the emphasis of 'negative duties', on one hand, and on the other hand, the understatement of what are the 'positive duties'. This discrepancy, in my view, renders this approach to criticism on various grounds. Firstly, by getting overly concerned to protect the rightful interests of the shareholders, the model ends up out-rightly rejecting moral responsibilities for all other constituencies outright. Secondly, its proponents equate legality with morality.

When drafting and implementing a code of ethics, the management cannot help but address only those issues which the law recognizes, with the argument that legality means that the behaviour of a corporation is right when its activities seek to maximize profits and wrong when they do not.

Secondly, the model appears to overlook the fact that the law, especially in the developing countries, may not be able – for any number of reasons, some of which were highlighted in the introduction to this chapter – to guarantee adequately that the rights and interests of all current and future generations of local stakeholders will be represented satisfactorily by the law. In such cases, under this model, those concerns, or 'positive duties', fall beyond its immediate concerns, for it is not the business of companies to take responsibilities that should be catered for by government.[5] To this objection should be added Melé's observation that "laws are not themselves a moral justification and, unfortunately, they do not always respond to ethical principles, but to ideology; and the law in favor of maximizing shareholder value as the purpose of business is not an exception. In addition, laws do change over time, and no country has identical laws" to another (Melé, 2008: 14).

Thirdly, this model suggests, though implicitly, that people are mere human resources; hence, their relationship to the firm is simply a matter of ownership, in which certain services are bought and sold, in some cases forgoing the fact that the corporation is basically formed of persons. Some scholars have tackled this problem, which they considered to be "an affront to natural justice, in that it gives inadequate recognition to the people who work in the corporation and who are, increasingly, its principal assets" (Handy, 2002, in Melé, 2008: 14).

Finally, in our democratic era, in which the tendency is to be more tolerant in considering the interests and rights of other people or stakeholders, the principles of maximization of shareholder value are rather anachronistic. Yet, this business management model continues to be predominant in many companies and democratic countries, even those which presumably have taken on stakeholder interests, as we shall now see. In doing so, they make the model increasingly controversial (Melé, 2008).

The crucial question and the basis from which we can judge this model, from an ethical point of view, is the market logic, from both the shareholder and stakeholder points of rationality, especially in those cases when a situation arises where the law does not provide the proper regulation to protect possible violation of basic human rights. Without such considerations, it becomes difficult for the model to make any honest claim of 'sourcing ethically'.

This is the problem highlighted by Benedict XVI:

> One of the greatest risks for businesses is that they are almost exclusively answerable to their investors, thereby limiting their social value. Owing to their growth in scale and the need for more and more capital, it is becoming increasingly rare for business enterprises to be in the hands of a stable director who feels responsible in the long term, not just the short term, for the life and the results of his company, and it is becoming increasingly

---

[5] An interview of the author with the CEO of an important cut flower farm in Naivasha and member of the KFC, confirmed that this is indeed the stance taken by the shareholders in this sector.

rare for businesses to depend on a single territory. Moreover, the so-called outsourcing of production can weaken the company's sense of responsibility towards the stakeholders — namely the workers, the suppliers, the consumers, the natural environment and broader society — in favour of the shareholders, who are not tied to a specific geographical area and who therefore enjoy extraordinary mobility (Benedict, 2009: no. 40).

Today, the growing conviction is that business management cannot concern itself only with the interests of the proprietors, but must also assume responsibility for all the other stakeholders who contribute to the life of the business (Melé, 2008) and take proactive responsibility to avoid any negative effects that their business may have on all stakeholders including the environment. This portrays the logic of the shareholder model as being less consistent with 'ethical sourcing' and moral responsibility in global business.

5.3.5 'Ethical Sourcing' Under the Stakeholder Model of Business Management

This model borrows from the rights theory, and particularly the Universal Declaration of Human Rights (1948), which provides that all men and women every-where in the world have the right to life, liberty and security of person, freedom from slavery and servitude and to proper legal process. Thus, any employee, shareholder, creditor, consumer or member of a similarly interested group is regarded as a rights bearer, whose diverse claims must be respected by the organization's management. Because the Universal Declaration of Human Rights casts its net so wide, it is not easy to pin down firms on violations of their duties using the model.

In essence, however, the stakeholder model contends that firms have obligations to parties beyond shareholders. In recent years, it has gained strength in international development circles in forging coalitions between business, government and the civil society, a fact noted by Dolan & Opondo (2005) in their survey report of the cut flower industry and confirmed by, among others, the works of Freeman (1984), Phillips (2003) and Schaefer (2008).

A stakeholder theory of the firm holds "that the corporation should be run for the benefit of all stakeholders regardless of whether doing so maximizes the corpora-tion's profits" (Schaefer, 2008: 297). Although it is generally agreed in this model that the relation of each stakeholder to the firm may be different, there is within that common understanding a disagreement amongst scholars regarding the degree of stakeholder status. Donaldson and Preston (1995) tried to solve this difficulty by introducing the notion of legitimacy and illegitimacy of stakeholders, but, as Phillips notes (2003: 27), this concept remains imprecise within the stakeholder literature.

In Phillips' view, stakeholder obligations and, therefore, stakeholder status are created when the organization voluntarily accepts the contributions of some group or individual. This voluntary acceptance is likened to consent, contract, or promise in its capacity for generating obligations. Such obligations are not imposed or stip-ulated from outside the relationship, such as those duties and rights that are one's simply on account of being a human being (Phillips, 2003: 27). From this reasoning, the employment of a person does *ipso facto* create moral duty for the employing body on at least two counts: the duty to respect the unwritten basic human rights arising from the fact of being a human, or human dignity, and the moral obligation of stakeholder fairness. Phillips puts it this way:

> Obligations of stakeholder fairness are additional moral obligations that are created based on the actions (in this case the voluntary receipt of benefits) of the parties. They are the obligations that are created among persons and organizations within the sphere of 'private associations' rather than at the level of the 'basic structure of society' and are therefore better adapted for use as an ethics of organizations (Phillips, 2003: 27–28).

To sort out the distinction between various kinds of stakeholder rights and duties, some scholars take recourse to the notions of normative and derivative stakeholder legitimacy, with the aim of creating a middle ground in the broad and narrow notions of stakeholder given by Donaldson and Preston (1995). Phillips describes normative stakeholders as "those stakeholders to whom the organization has a moral obligation, an obligation of stakeholder fairness, over and above that due other social actors simply by virtue of their being human beings. These", he continues "are those who would fit in the stakeholder question: 'for whose benefit. . .should the firm be managed?'" (Phillips, 2003: 30). But he still cares for the apparently non-normative stakeholders who, he reckons, should "still be morally considered and their human rights respected and protected. However, *no additional moral consideration is due to them in managerial decision making, and the organization has no special obligation to attend to their well-being*" (Phillips, 2003: 30).[6]

By limiting the radius of its moral responsibility to only those groups to whom a moral obligation is owed, this model, in a manner analogous to that used by the shareholder model, leaves out a large group of sensitive constituencies, who are considered to fall under the 'broad stakeholder' category. This point has important significance in the 'ethical sourcing' concept and the kind of draft code used to do the audits. It is possible for some constituents such as casual workers, to be locked out from the status of legitimate stakeholders for which the organization has moral obligation (Phillips, 2003: 29). Other constituents likely to suffer the same fate are the environment and communities that are directly or indirectly affected by a company's presence and activities. Even from a strategic theory of management view, this renders the model significantly incomplete and ethically questionable. The notion of legitimate and illegitimate appears to run "contrary to much of stakeholder scholarship and literature on stakeholder legitimacy in other fields, such as law, politics, moral theory and in organizational studies" (Phillips, 2003: 29). It was from within this complexity of the many nuances of stakeholder and moral obligation that a multi-stakeholder process (MSP) came into existence (Dolan & Opondo, 2005).

The proponents of the MSP base code envisaged the formation of an alliance of normative and derivative stakeholders through dialogue, from which solutions to problems such as those concerning 'ethical sourcing' in developing countries

---

[6] Emphasis in the original.

could be adequately addressed. It was hoped that the alliance would also prepare codes of ethics to foster greater accountability in the business practices of global corporations. Once a multi-stakeholder framework for each sector of business was in place, a code and its implementation were presumed to become the panacea for ethical malpractices in local and international business (*ibid.*).

5.3.6 The Betrayal of MSP-Generated Base Codes in Kenya Cut Flower 'Ethical Sourcing' Audits

When the Kenyan cut flower producers started to embrace codes,[7] they borrowed codes already generated in similar establishments overseas, with the idea that with time they would design their own. It was with this spirit that the Horticultural Ethical Business Initiative (HEBI), a Kenya flower stakeholder group, was formed to guide and monitor social accountability in the cut flower industry by identifying the points of consensus and conflict as articulated by all member flower growers. The HEBI framework was based on that of the ETI, the international organization based in the UK that monitors ethical trading worldwide. HEBI's base code was launched in 2002, and thereafter became the basic ethical code in Kenya's floriculture. The issues involved in it are, however, determined by the KFC. On its part, the KFC's membership comprises the major flower growers (principals), with representations of some non-governmental organizations, a few members of the departments of foreign governments such as DfID and the Royal Netherlands Embassy (RNE), plus three representatives from the Ministries of Agriculture, Trade and Labour. At the end of the day, it is not clear that the workers from the grassroots are in truth represented.

The ETI code, the model through which the Horticulture industry created the HEBI base codes is a MSP-generated base code that had been in use for some years in Britain. A number of factors, however, seem to limit the extent to which this kind of code could address the needs of workers or assure social responsibility for the communities surrounding the places where the flowers are grown. The first factor is the nature of the codes itself. As noted above the motivation for introducing a code is important and, more often than not, this relates more to firm protection and compliance issues (preventing harm, particularly to the company) than to the more positive and outward-looking motivation, such as the welfare of the workers. For this reason, the question, "who writes the code is itself an important issue, with wide involvement generally recommended if employee acceptance is to be high" (Gichure, 2008).

Both Moore (2006: 411) and Dolan and Opondo (2005) seem to agree that MSP base codes can be effective when and where there is flexible application, and local

---

[7] Multi-stakeholder codes: ETI Base Code developed by company, trade union and NGO members of the UK's Ethical Trading Initiative; International Code of Conduct for Cut Flowers, developed by NGOs and trade unions in Europe, and used by the German-based 'Flower Label Programme' (FLP).

ownership in the process of code implementation and verification. This is not the case in the Kenyan cut flower industry, because, as we have seen, the ownership of the cut flower industry in the South is mostly foreign. Consequently, while it is possible that some MSP codes may have emerged in the South, those currently in use are mostly replicates of codes from the North, where the process of implementation, the agenda of implementation, and the standards of implementation are different. This is largely the case with HEBI and EUREPGAP[8] base codes, which give the standard criteria for 'ethical sourcing' in the horticultural sector. One could safely say that the effectiveness of the MSP, at least in Kenya's cut flower sector, has not been encouraging.

The experience of the Kenyan cut flower industry seems to indicate that, despite their noble aim, the multi-stakeholder base codes may have served to fulfil some 'negative duties' but, in the process, they have neglected those of other very crucial stakeholders and the environment. Hughes' (2001) explanation of this discrepancy is that the presence of codes does not, by itself, guarantee greater social or environmental justice. This view is corroborated Moore (2006: 412) in regard to the influence of codes in general and attested to by Dolan and Opondo (2005) in their evaluation of the Kenya cut flower industry, using the MSP HEBI base code. What they considered to be the major setback for effective application of the code was the fact that, instead of addressing important local considerations, as replicas from another country, these codes represented the interests of the UK and Dutch companies (Holtshaussen, 2007: 5).

There are two other reasons why the MSP-generated base codes may not have provided genuine 'ethical sourcing' results. The first one has to do with the nature of regulation. As we saw earlier, part of the package in global business is relaxation of laws to attract investors and to ensure that they do not relocate. The second and most basic reason is the fact that these, just like most other codes, generally address the minimum requirements, remaining mute on issues that could make a significant impact on the societies of the countries in which the businesses operate. Consequently, the North ends up having an economic advantage over the South which can be termed 'exploitative'. This advantage is what we earlier saw enshrined in the notion of 'favourable conditions'. That is to say, the North can lay certain conditions on the host country, such that, if a country through its representatives in a body like the KFC demands the flower growers to meet certain regulations, if those regulations are not favourable to them, they threaten to relocate. This is something which governments in the South do not like very much, among other reasons, because that creates massive unemployment. And so the 'arm twisting' continues.

So long as companies operating in the cut flower and other similar businesses continue to limit their concerns to the 'deregulated' system and follow the law as stipulated in their base codes, certain basic human goods will necessarily be violated. And, so long as those human goods are overlooked, the sourcing of products cannot be considered genuinely ethical. Unfortunately, the flower auctions in the

---

[8] Euro-retailer Produce Working Group on Good Agricultural Practice.

European markets either do not know about these background problems or prefer not to know about them so long as the flowers bear the hallmark that they have been sourced ethically. At best, businesses, both foreign and local, may claim that the workers offer their services 'freely' or that they are better off working for low wages than not working at all, but not that ethics has been observed in the sourcing of the product at the different levels of the chain.

5.3.7 Exploitation: A 'Grassroots' Experience in the Cut Flower Industry in Kenya

Exploitation as a concept is tied to that of unfairness, and unfairness to that of injustice. Morally, fairness is an important property of institutions, organizations, schemes, games and activities at all levels of human interaction. It is usually associated with ideas like justice, equality, proportionality, reciprocity, and impartiality.

To exploit something means to take an unfair advantage of it or to make the most of it irresponsibly. We can speak of exploiting people or a natural resource. In both cases, the implication is that an unfair use is made of, or taken advantage of, by one party over another, which is presumed to be unable to protect itself or its citizens. Exploitation as a concept does not usually apply to actions that can be described using other terms, such as corruption, robbing, stealing, murdering, etc. Rather, it specifically signifies taking advantage of someone else's unfortunate situation, for example, taking advantage of someone's indigence, ignorance, physical weakness, or utter need, where there are no alternatives. From the exploiter's point of view, the aim is to secure an advantage or profit for oneself.

The *Encyclopaedia of Ethics* (1992) makes four distinctions of exploitation. One form is where an exploiter may or may not coerce or defraud the person whom he is exploiting. In this case, the person being exploited may or may not voluntarily consent to the transaction. A second form, typical in all cases of exploitation, is where, in the act of exploitation, the exploited person is made worse off than he was before the exploitation. A third form is where the exploited person neither benefits nor becomes worse off than he was before. The fourth is where the exploited person may profit from the transaction but disproportionately less than the benefits that the exploiter gains. It is worthy of note that, in all the four of the forms of exploitation, the exploited party is treated unfairly because an agent (the exploiter) systematically uses another person to his or her own advantage, and in so doing acts unfairly. Looking at the workers in the cut flower industry, and the country itself, it is clear that both suffer from one or another of these four forms of exploitation.

Developing countries are aware of this fact. For some time now, they have been pointing fingers at the industrialized North on grounds of exploitation. Their argument is invariably that the North is creating wealth at the material expense of the South in terms of natural resources and labour, but the South, and especially the labourer, is left out of stakeholder benefits. Specifically, it is pointed out that it must be morally wrong for global investors to create so much wealth from the resources and hard labour of poor countries, only to repatriate it in one way or another, leaving the land and the people who made those profits possible bereft of their resources, energies, and even their self-esteem. If, by way of example, a company repatriated 99 to 100%[9] of its gross earnings, could it still claim to have upheld moral responsibility towards its stakeholders, when some of them earn and live and work under substandard conditions? One typical excuse is to claim that the investor has complied with the law. Often, however, that is not the whole truth, as we shall soon see. Even where this may be the case, the question of 'ethical sourcing' remains dubious. The problem here consists in the excision of the notion of *moral responsibility* from that of *ethical sourcing*.

The problem of exploitation and abuse of human rights in the cut flower industry was first highlighted in the early 1990s through the activities of some national and international trade unions and NGOs. The major aim of those activities was to raise awareness among consumers in market countries regarding the workers' conditions in the industry in Southern countries. The outcome was a variety of networks of interested organizations, created to work together in order to address those problems. Subsequently, several conferences were held, including two in Nairobi in 2002, on 'Corporate Responsibility and Workers Rights' and 'Human Rights and Development of International Obligations for Corporations', respectively. These conferences were held under the auspices of the Workers Rights Alert (WRA), a coalition of non-governmental organizations that monitors workers rights in various industries in Kenya. It was in the course of these two conferences that the possibility of gross ethics violations in Kenya's flower industry first emerged. Following on that cue, some researchers soon got involved in the field, whose findings we shall now explore briefly.

One of their findings was that workers on flower farms tend to be predominantly women. This was what triggered the interest of the representatives of Women Working Worldwide (WWW) a UK-based NGO, which participated in the two Nairobi conferences and heard what was unfolding in some of the local presentations. Thereafter, WWW urged and sponsored a Kenyan NGO, Kenya Women Workers Organization (KEWWO), to conduct a survey of labour rights violations on flower farms in Kenya. That survey conducted 120 random interviews with workers, and compiled its findings as part of the ETI Report (2005). The issues raised by workers representing their experience in face-to-face meetings were:

- Low pay, as low as Ksh 64 a day, which is less than US$ 1
- Lack of adequate housing
- Excessive overtime
- Unfair dismissal
- Health and safety issues, in particular with regard to pesticide spraying

---

[9] The CEO of Lankas Ltd., farm known for its Best Practice in Ethics Audits, disclosed in an exclusive interview with the author that the company leaves behind around 5% of the gross earnings which includes wages, purchases and other services. This is much more than what many of the other flower companies leave behind.

- Deductions from pay
- Denial of severance pay
- Sexual harassment, in particular by supervisors
- Lack of contracts
- Short-term contracts
- Social security payments not met
- Lack of freedom of association
- Denial of maternity leave and day care

The ETI survey (2005) highlights two basic concerns;

1. The evidence was gross abuse of a variety of labour rights in the management of the industry.
2. That the Ethics Audits somehow could not detect those abuses.

Smith et al. in their survey report the following as being a typical example of the interview with the workers:

> When asked if their wage covered their basic needs, a woman in Kenya replied, 'It is not enough at all. For housing I pay Kenya Shilling (Ksh) 400,[10] school fees are about Ksh 500 per month, food about Ksh 1,500,[11] water about Ksh 200, clothing about Ksh 600, and sickness which varies… since the salary is about Ksh 3,000 per month, then I strain (to make ends meet) (Smith et al., 2005).[12]

What the researchers found most puzzling was that these problems had not come out into the light earlier. Even more surprising was the fact that many farms named by the workers, either because they worked or had worked there sometime, included large holdings with direct supply relationships with the UK and Amsterdam, with smaller farms selling to those larger farms at peak season. Some of these had excellent or 'Best Practice' reputations. From the foregoing, only two possible explanations can be found: either that the ethical/social auditing methods being employed by retailers abroad, the flower farms owners, and other industry players in Kenya were all defective, or that the concept of 'ethical sourcing' in vogue was a camouflage one (Smith et al., 2005), or both.

This takes us back to the concept of stakeholder and its different nuances. Into what category does the ordinary worker, permanent or casual fall in, in global business, and what are his or her rights? From the delineation of stakeholder categories and the moral obligation appertaining to each category (Freeman, 1984; Phillips,

---

[10] Housing in a slum area is the only one which can cost this amount of money (author's interpretation).

[11] *Ugali* with or without *Sukuma Wiki* and *Githeri* are the only foodstuffs which can cost this amount of money. Ugali is a stiff porridge made solely of maize flour and water; Sukuma Wiki is kale while Githeri is meal of boiled maize with beans.

[12] Between 1 May 2002 and 31 April 2003, the statutory minimum wage for unskilled employees in Kenya agriculture was Ksh 1,642 per month, or Ksh 68.90 a day, i.e. equivalent to 1 US$. Today this is slightly higher.

2003) it appears that such workers are normative stakeholders. If that be the case, then, in this industry, these stakeholders are being exploited on at least two different accounts:

a) "As social actors and simply by virtue of their being human" (Phillips, 2003: 30), the workers do not get their rightful due from the organizations. In addition, as members of communities living in the lake areas, these people are exploited in various indirect ways, such the egregious pollution of the water deprives them of much needed fishing and a good ecosystem. Phillips contends that: "Simply because a person or group does not merit the additional moral consideration conferred upon normative stakeholders does not mean that they may be morally disregarded. One still may not break promises without sufficient cause, kill competitors for market share, and violate the rights of or otherwise act immorally towards these groups" (*ibid.*).

b) As normative stakeholder of the organization, the latter can be said to exploit the workers from the point of view of *stake*holder fairness, over and above that due to them by virtue of their being human. Under this proviso, Phillips includes the violation of human rights by an organization, the use of forced labour, racial/ethnic/sexual discrimination, lying and breaking contracts, are some of the "likely examples of activities that would be wrong irrespective of the stakeholder status of the victims. These violations may occur against a group or individual who is also a normative stakeholder, but it is not due only, or even primarily, to this stakeholder status that these actions are morally prohibited. They are wrong for reasons prior to any stakeholder obligation that may obtain" (Phillips, 2003: 30).

It should be evident from the foregoing that the use of MSP 'base codes' alone cannot suffice to adequately address the real needs of this class of stakeholders. There is a default in the ethical or moral and the non-ethical, similar to that which governs, and also limits the shareholder model with regard to moral responsibility. That is to say, despite the efforts to delineate, categorize and demarcate stakeholder categories and the kind of moral responsibility a firm should have towards each of these categories, there is still a missing factor for moral responsibility to effectively cut through all the categories. This is the topic to which we shall now turn.

5.4 Common Good: The Missing Factor in 'Ethical Sourcing' and Social Responsibility in Global Business

5.4.1 Globalization and Ethics

Sometimes *globalization* is viewed in fatalistic terms, as if the dynamics involved were the product of anonymous impersonal forces or structures independent of the human will. In this regard it is useful to remember that while globalization should certainly be understood as a socio-economic process, this is not its only dimension. Underneath the more visible process, humanity itself is becoming increasingly interconnected; it is made up of individuals and

peoples to whom this process should offer benefits and development as they assume their
respective responsibilities, singly and collectively (Benedict, 2009: 42).

Thus, if globalization is viewed from a deterministic standpoint, the criteria with
which to evaluate and direct it can dissipate. But, if we sincerely want to speak of
or observe a global ethic, there has to be a common understanding of the tenets of
that ethics in global business. The truth of globalization as a process, and its fundamental ethical criterion, should necessarily emerge from what all human beings
share as humans. That is to say, from the unity of the human family and its development towards what is good. For that project to be sustainable there is need for a
commitment on the part of the principal stakeholders and governments "to promote
a person-based and community-oriented cultural process of world-wide integration"
(Benedict, 2009: 42).

This concept has its origins in the classical philosophy of Plato, Aristotle, and
the Stoics. Later, it was adopted in Judeo-Christian ethics, but its vestiges are clear
in all virtue ethics. For contemporary ethicists, one could say that it is based on
the Kantian maxim to always see every human person as an end in himself who
should not be used as a means. There have been many nuances to the notion of the
common good, but basically it refers to the right social order that permits and, as far
as possible, facilitates upright living based on the right of every human being to a
minimum of material well-being in order to lead a virtuous life.

As a guide to ethical business management the concept of common good can
be defined as a broad composite reality embracing the private and public spheres,
which does not exclude profit, but instead considers it a means for achieving human
and social ends. It grants that the manner in which the individual company dis-
tributes its dividends and its juridical structure can vary, but what is constant is
the willingness to view profit as a means of achieving the goal of a more humane
market and society. Hence, its economic activity pursues not only the commercial logic, but it also endeavours to cater for the overall human good of all its
stakeholders, especially the most vulnerable, based on the simple fact of their dignity as human beings. The common good model seeks to create a convergence
between economic science and moral evaluation, based on the financial ability of
each organization. In the long run this model should also benefit the company
because of the well known economic fact that "structural insecurity generates anti-
productive attitudes wasteful of human resources, inasmuch as workers tend to adapt
passively to automatic mechanisms, rather than to release creativity" (Benedict,
2009: 46).

There are increasingly more contemporary business ethicists who see the viabil-
ity of this concept as a management guide if we are to have a more comprehensive
understanding of the moral management of business beyond the two traditional
ones. One can mention, among others, Argandona (1998), Velasquez et al. (1992)
Alford & Naughton (2001), and Melé (2008). All of these scholars argue that the
classical understanding of the 'common good', based on the intrinsic worth of every
human being, is a defensible "model of market economy capable of including within
its range all peoples and not just the better off" (Benedict, 2009: 39).

Appeals for the consideration of the common good concept as a management model are surfacing in different discussions of ethical and social responsibilities, from environmental pollution to problems related to crime and poverty. Different authors may give it different names, but irrespective of the name used, the bottom line is always that of a 'Balanced Concept of the Firm' (Enderle, 2006; Franceschi, 2004) and the underlying concern is always the same. This is not to say that everybody agrees on the significance of this concept, because, as Koslowski (2008) notes, history is replete with examples in which the notion of common good was distorted for the manipulation of the masses, or to serve non-ethical practices, even within the agency and stakeholder management models.

The term 'common good' has been criticized on another score: its ethical basis in morally pluralistic societies, as we find in contemporary ethics. Already in 1987 MacIntyre showed how difficult it is for the followers or heirs of the different moral theories such as, say, Hume, Kant or Mill, to engage in moral decision making. According to him, the different factions get into "a battle in which no one is finally defeated, only because no one is ever a victor". And, adds, "One interesting response to the recognition of the situation is the recent redefinition of the task of moral philosophy (ethics) as that of rendering coherent and systematic 'our' intuitions about what is right, just, and good where 'we' are the inhabitants of a particular social, moral-political tradition of liberal individualism" (MacIntyre, 1987: 176). This could not be truer in global business. Viewed from this perspective, the common good could easily be misunderstood to mean a widespread pursuit of individual interests; interests that are defendable through a notion of moral pluralism in which nearly every stance, including ethical egoism, can find a theoretical grounding. This is contrary to the notion of the common good that this chapter proposes.

The concept of the common good that is envisaged here is one that rests on truth regarding the dignity of man and woman and that asks three basic questions: one, why should we never treat humanity, whether in oneself or in another, never as a means but always as an end (Kant)? The second one derives from the first, based on Socratic wisdom, and asks: 'how should we live', and how should we treat one another if all human beings have intrinsic worth? And, finally, what is the basis of that intrinsic worth? In the tradition that upholds the concept of the common good, the intrinsic worth of every human being is human dignity based on the fact of having a rational nature. In other words, a spiritual nature; this factor sets humans apart from the rest of Nature and gives their actions moral value. Hence, "when business ethics overlooks this reality of man, it inevitably falls prey to forms of exploitation. More specifically, it risks becoming subservient to theorisations which, rather than correcting the dysfunctional aspects of management, try to justify their unethical actions as being ethical. The word 'ethical' then becomes the instrument to justify ideological distinctions in such a way as if to suggest that initiatives not formally so designated would not be ethical" (Benedict, 2009: 45).

Under this light, it appears that the glaring scandals of exploitation and the violation of basic human rights are consequences of the consideration of ethical action in dealing with other human beings only from a purely legal and obligatory point of view. And this is what justifies looking for an overarching attitude and model for business management that always seeks human good. The common good model calls for virtue on the part of the acting agent, rather than on the legal obligation which may or may not apply in a given situation.

5.4.2 Ethical Sourcing and Social Responsibility from a Common Good Perspective

The difficulty arises when we come to the effective participation in the common good management of the firm. This is not something automatic. It requires the internalization of certain attitudes and convictions, among them a sense of justice and goodwill, especially at the management level. Hence, the grounding factor for the exercise of the model is a notion of justice, rooted in virtue ethics tradition, with an emphasis on its distributive and legal forms.

The market is subject to the principles of so-called *commutative justice*, which regulates the relations of giving and receiving between parties to a transaction. "Distributive justice refers to the duties and obligations of the whole – in this case, the firm – to its parts, while legal justice spells out the duties and obligations of the parts – primarily, workers and other stakeholders – to the whole" (Sison & Fontrodona, 2008: 24). In business practice, it demands of the firm to pay a just wage, just in proportion to the profits generally obtained and the needs of its normative stakeholders in the first place. The legal form of justice requires that workers dedicate their best efforts to the firm and take care of its resources (Sison & Fontrodona, 2008).

A fundamental consequence of the exercise of distributive and legal justice in regard to any 'ethical sourcing' should be responsibility for the integral welfare of the employees. The term 'responsibility', according to Enderle (2006), derives from the idea of *re-sponding* or giving valid answers to questions asked by others. In this sense, the notion of responsibility is similar to that of accountability. It would be reductive, therefore, to limit the scope of one's ethical responsibility to merely fulfilling roles and rules. Under the common good notion of responsibility, one must distinguish between moral responsibility understood from the minimal requirement, such as those defined by regulation and which must be met under all circumstances, to moral responsibility based on the aspirations of an ethical ideal that goes beyond strict regulation. This latter considers that even when one may claim to have acted legally, if those actions violate any aspect of the human standards that regulate distributive justice and gratuitousness, even if these are not legally spelt out, one cannot be said to observe moral responsibility.

This is the missing factor in the plethora of codes of ethics in global business. Here, too, we find why the flower farms in Kenya have failed to deliver the promise of better lives for the poor. 'Ethical sourcing' on a common good understanding demands practising moral responsibility in a manner that respects, provides and protects both the material and the non-material needs of integral human development and association. Even in economics, this has important and beneficial repercussions. The economy needs ethics in order to function correctly; not any ethics, but an ethics which is people, and environment centred. This is the common good content of management.

'Ethical sourcing' of products starts with the observance of the basic human rights among ones' own immediate stakeholders, such as the employees and the environment that supports neighbouring communities. People may have wants that fall outside what a company can provide, but at the outset, the scale of their remuneration ought to be commensurate to their cost of living. From a distributive justice point of view, this means that for a company that can afford to pay a living wage proportionate to the qualifications and skills of the employees, failing to do so does not look ethical. Similarly, failing to grant permanent employment in order to avoid responsibility for workers and instead hiring them as intermittent casual labourers must be understood as exploitation of their indigent condition.

5.5 Conclusion and Recommendations

The aim of this chapter is to give an overview of the ethical challenges of global business in poor countries. To this purpose, I have used the cut flower industry as the model. We have seen how, at times, the political, social and economic conditions can make a country vulnerable to the interests and, often, inconsideration of richer countries. We have seen how an entire sector of the Kenyan population is succumbing to poverty, even as they pour their whole energies into serving an industry that drains them but has nothing to give back in return. It would not be false, then, to argue that a new form of poverty is emerging, occasioned by the notion of global business.

Benedict XVI observes: "Among those who sometimes fail to respect the human rights of workers are large multinational companies as well as local producers. For the 'super-developed' countries the craving to provide their consumers creates an unacceptable contrast with the ongoing situations of dehumanizing deprivation" (Benedict, 2009: 32). To turn this trend round, the proposed common good notion of the purpose of the firm needs to be taken serious by the different acts in global business: the business owners, governments and the international organizations.

5.5.1 The Role of Global Business

In all business, global or local, it is clear that the "simple application of *commercial logic* cannot solve all social problems" (Benedict, 2009). As alternative, it is necessary to consider the company as a multi-purpose organization that encompasses economic, social and environmental purposes, all of which have their intrinsic value and are related to each other in a circular rather than hierarchical manner. To act in an adequate social and morally responsible manner, there are other values beyond profits that need attention. These values form the fabric on which the moral responsibilities are built and which we have termed the common good concept of the firm.

The practice of this model can benefit from the guidance of the three basic principles of moral responsibility, namely, *the principle of human dignity,* the principles of *non-maleficence and beneficence,* and the principle of *justice* (fairness). We shall now summarise the significance of each of these in the common good approach of ethical management.

5.5.1.1 The Principle of Human Dignity

Dignity is something people are born with. It denotes an intangible value or worth. The good of dignity, therefore, sets a limit to what can be done to a person. As a guiding principle of management wisdom, it enjoins the principals and management to see that economic choices do not cause excessive disparities in wealth in a morally unacceptable manner. Under the common good model, 'ethical sourcing' the fulfilment of such responsibilities is not simply 'helping' people, rather, it is carrying out one's *moral obligations* to one's stakeholders in a balanced manner. For that reason, codes of ethics, even comprehensively generated ones, may serve as a guide for ethical sourcing, but can never sufficiently cover moral responsibility for all one's stakeholders.

That demands the good-will of all actors. Specifically, it enjoins the management to look beyond rhetoric, beyond the mandatory vision and mission statements, which are also needed, and to address the real needs of society. Such corporate community engagement (CCE) should not be limited to merely what the law demands, which is always a minimum, but rather should be a morality guided by respect for the basic human goods, respect for human rights, societal values and the environmental context within which an organisation works. This is an essential part of the understanding of 'ethical practice' and moral management. It is hoped that this will be the interpretation that ISO 26000 makes of its ethics provision.[13]

5.5.1.2 The Principles of Beneficence and Non-maleficence

These are two related principles that derive from the classical First Principle of Morality that 'Good must be done and evil must be avoided' (Gómez-Lobo, 2002). In contemporary ethics, this translates to the 'Golden Rule'. Hence, the principle of *beneficence* entails concern for people's safety, protection from harmful products

---

[13] ISO, the International Organization for Standardization, has decided to launch the development of an International Standard providing guidelines for social responsibility (SR). The guidance standard will be published in 2010 as ISO 26000 and be voluntary to use. It will not include requirements and will thus not be a certification standard.

or work environments, provision of means for medical attention when they suffer illness, hunger or exhaustion, and care for the environment. This focus is often broken further into other logically related norms such as: *Not to do harm* or the duty of *non-maleficence*. All rational beings know this within themselves. In a proactive sense, it means *to do good* by providing benefit wherever possible.

5.5.1.3 The Principle of Justice

We have already considered justice. Under this principle of justice we are urged to observe the requirements of fair dealing. Newton (2005) and Sison & Fontrodona (2008) focus on certain general tenets of justice that are basic for the existence of even the minimum of respect and consideration of human dignity in the treatment of other people:

- The obligation to acknowledge our membership and dependence on human community in which we live and operate;
- The need to contribute to its life, obey its laws and policies;
- The need to be honest in all our dealings with them and, above all, the need to hold ourselves accountable to them for our actions.

Benedict XVI explains this principle as follows: "Economic life undoubtedly requires contracts, in order to regulate relations of exchange between goods of equivalent value. But it also needs just laws and forms of redistribution governed by politics, and what is more, it needs works redolent of the spirit of gift" (Benedict, 2009: 37).

5.5.2 *The Role of International Bodies*

International business ethics would be next to impossible without the good-will of other players to whom the international community has entrusted certain tasks, such as International Labour Organization (ILO), the World Trade Organization (WTO) and environmental programmes such as the United Nations Environmental Program (UNEP). Through their firm intervention, presence, and supervision, these organizations can require global business to entrench more responsible ethical practice in the manner products are sourced and in the treatment of the environment. "Human beings legitimately exercise a responsible stewardship over nature, in order to protect it, to enjoy its fruits and to cultivate it in new ways, with the assistance of advanced technologies, so that it can worthily accommodate and feed the world's population" (Benedict, 2009: 48).

To date, the actual effectiveness of some of the international organizations, such as the UNEP, whose headquarters in Nairobi are less than seventy kilometres from Naivasha, the hub of much of the floriculture in Kenya, is inconspicuous.

5.5.3 The Role of Political Authorities

The temptation to solve immediate economic problems through global business is understandable. However, through inter-continental of states and the collaboration of international organizations of such bodies as the United Nations, it is possible to protect the long-term interest of the developing countries rather than make deals that have no long-term sustainability because they do not cater for the overall development of the citizens. The relaxation of regulation to create a favourable atmosphere for global business has proved to be open ground for the exploitation of humans and nature, without making any significant contribution to the welfare of the local society. In this sense, the criterion to guide the political authorities with regard to global or local business is the fact that "the primary capital to be safeguarded and valued in any nation is the human person in his or her integrity" (Benedict, 2009: 32).

References

Alford, H. and Naughton, M. 2001, *Managing as if Faith Mattered* (University of Notre Dame Press, Notre Dame).

Ardery, J. 2009, Desperate Compromise in Kenya's Rose City. *Human Flower Project* http://www.humanflowerproject.com/index.php/weblog/comments/riots_in_naivasha/Julie). Accessed 29 July 2009.

Argandona, A. 1998, The Stakeholder Theory and the Common Good, *Journal of Business Ethics* 17, 1093–1102.

Benedict XVI. 2009, Encyclical Letter, *On Integral Human Development (Caritas in Veritate)* (Libreria Vaticana, Rome).

Black, R. 2004, Cultivating an Ethical Flower Trade. *BBC News World Edition*, 10 March.

Blowfield, M. 2000, Ethical sourcing: A contribution to sustainability or a diversion? *Sustainable Development* 8, 141–200.

Boatright, John. R. 2001, *Ethics and the Conduct of Business* (Prentice Hall, New Jersey).

Chang, Ha-Joon. 2003, Regulation of Foreign Investment in Historical Perspective – Lessons for the proposed WTO Agreement (Institute for New Technologies, United Nations University).

Dolan, C. and Opondo, M. 2005, Seeking Common Ground Multi-stakeholder Processes in Kenya's Cut Flower Industry. Archive http://www.nri.org/projects/NRET/idswp223.pdf. Accessed 4th April 2008.

Donaldson, T. and Preston, L. 1995, The Stakeholder Theory of the Corporation: Concepts, Evidence, and Implications. *The Academy of Management Review* 20 (1), 65–91.

Encyclopaedia of Ethics. 1992, Edited by Lawrence Becker and Charlotte B. Becker (Garland Publishing, New York).

Enderle, G. 2006, Corporate Responsibility in the CSR Debate. In Wieland, J. et al. (eds), *Unternehmensethik im Spannungsfeld der Kulturen und Religion* (Kohlhammer, Stuttgart) pp. 108–124.

Esipisu, I. 2007, Flower farms' workers still not safe. *Daily Nation*, Nairobi, November.

Ethical Trading Initiative (ETI). 2005, Addressing Labour practices on Kenyan flower Farms, ETI Report 2002–2004. www.ethicaltrade.org/Z/lib/2001/11/codeviolguid/index.shtml. Accessed 20 February 2008.

ETI Media briefing for Valentine's Day. 2008, Workers conditions in the cut flower industry, 6th February 2008 http//:www.ethicaltrade.org. Accessed 20th February 2008.

Food and Water Watch Canadians 2008, http://www.canadians.org/water/documents/ NaivashaReport08. Accessed 29th July 2009.

Franceschi, Luis. 2004, The Misapplication of the Concept of Agency to Financial Management. In Paul Mimbi and David Lutz (eds), *Shareholder Value and the Common. Good* (Strathmore University Press, Nairobi), pp. 292–317.

Freeman, R. E. 1984, Strategic Management: A Stakeholder Approach (Pitman, Boston).

Friedman, M. 1970, The Social Responsibility of Business Is to Increase Its Profits, in *New York Times Magazine*, September 13, 1970.

Gibbon, P. 1992, A Failed Agenda? African Agriculture under Structural Adjustment with Special Reference to Kenya and Ghana. *Journal of Peasant Studies* 20 (1), 50–96.

Gichure, C. 2008, *Ethics for Africa Today. An Introduction to Business Ethics* (Paulines, Nairobi).

Gómez-Lobo, A. 2002, *Morality and the Human Goods* (Georgetown University Press, Washington D.C.).

Handy, C. 2002, 'What's a Business For?' *Harvard Business Review* 80, 49–55.

Harper, D. 2009, Cheap Roses Cost The Earth, *ScienceDaily*, Feb. 14. http://www.sciencedaily. com/releases/2009/02/090213070917.htm. Accessed July 30, 2009.

Hennock, M. 2002, Kenya's Flower Farms Flourish. *BBC News, World Edition,* 14 February.

Holtshaussen, L. 2007, What is Ethical Sourcing? Royal Holloway University of London www.ethicaltrade.org/Z/lib/2001/11/codeviolguid/index.shtml. Accessed February 14, 2008.

Hughes, A. 2000, Retailers, Knowledges, and Changing Commodity Networks: The Case of the Cut Flower Trade. *Geoforum* 31 (2), 175–190.

Hughes, A. 2001, global Commodity Networks, Ethical Trade and Governmentality: Kenya Flower Company, membership and activities. www.kenyaflowers.co.ke/market%20data.htm. Accessed 20th March 2008.

ISO 26000, http://www.iso.org/iso/socialresponsibility.pdf. Accessed 14th April 2008.

Kenya Human Rights Commission (KHRC) Report, 2004, *Manufacture of Poverty: The Untold Story of EPZs in Kenya*, Nairobi, www.khrc.or.ke.

Kenya Flower Council. 2008, Kenya Flower Council (KFC) Activities and Floriculture Industry in Kenya. http://www.kenyaflowers.co.ke/market%20data.htm. Accessed 20th April 2008.

Koslowski, P. 2008, The Purpose of Business and the Future of Society. Paper presented at the Conference and workshop on 'Humanizing Management'. IESE Business School, University of Navarra, June.

Lehmann, J. Pierre. 2004, Kenya: Globalizing with Flowers. *Yale Global*, 9 April.

MacIntyre, A. 1987, *Whose Justice? Which Rationality?* (University of Notre Dame Press, Notre Dame, Indiana).

Majtenyi, C. 2002, Cut Flower Industry Accused of Human Rights Abuse. *East African Standard,* 1 June.

Melé, D. 2008, 'Three current views of the firm and its purpose. Toward a more complete model', Unpublished Workshop paper On Humanizing Management. IESE Business School, University of Navarra.

Moore, G. 2006, 'Managing codes in Higher Education: implementing a code or embedding virtue? *Business Ethics: A European Review* 15 (4), 407–418.

Mwakungu, N. 2003, Anxiety as Kenyan Lake Dries Up. *BBC News, World Edition*, 10 November.

Newton, L. 2005, *Business Ethics and the Natural Environment,* Oxford, Blackwell Publishing.

Ngotho, K. 2005, Kenya's wealth in foreign hands. Sunday April 17.

Phillips, R. 2003, Stakeholder Legitimacy, *Business Ethics Quarterly,* 13 (1), 25–41.

Riungu, C. 2009, Can Lake Naivasha be saved? *The EastAfrican* 20 July.

Roozendaal, Gerda van. 1994, Kenyan Cut Flower Export Blooming, *Biotechnology and Development Monitor,* No. 21, December.

Roozendaal, G. and Commander, P. 1994, The Case of Cut Flowers: Biotechnology in a non-traditional export sector. *Biotechnology and Development Monitor* No. 20, September.

Samet, A. J. 2003, 'Voluntary guidelines may be mandatory,' Commentary In *Journal of Commerce,* NY, Oct 20, p. 1.

Schaefer, B. 2008, Shareholders and Social Responsibility, *Journal of Business Ethics* 81 (2), 297–312.

Sison, A. J. and Fontrodona, J. 2008, The Common Good of the Firm in the Aristotelian Tradition. Paper presented at the IESE Business School, University of Navarra, June.

Smith, Sally, Diana Auret, Stephanie Barrientos, Catherine Dolan, Karin Kleimbooi, Chosani Njobvu, Maggie Opondo and Anne Tallontire. 2005, Report on Ethical trade in African horticulture: gender, rights and participation. IDS working paper 223.

Velasquez, Manuel, Claire Andre, Thomas Shanks & Michael J. Meyers. 1992, The Common Good. In *Issues in Ethics* 5 (2), 45–60.

Wood, G. 1995, Ethics at the purchasing/sales interface: an international perspective. In *International Marketing Review,* 12 (4), 55–61

Part II
Fairness in International Trade–A Global Perspective

Chapter 6
Fair Global Trade: A Perspective from Africa

Piet J. Naudé

6.1 Introduction

I consider it a great honour to be part of the global panel on fair trade, and thank
my colleagues for their constructive comments and co-operation. I am proud to be
an African and wish to present the view of my continent in an open and objective
manner.

6.1.1 Personal and Hermeneutical Limitation

My academic background has been shaped by philosophy and Christian theology and I have only recently ventured into the relationship between ethics on
the one hand and economics and business on the other. My knowledge of economics and the financial world is therefore extremely limited and it restricts my
ability to make informed judgments on technical data, or intra-disciplinary arguments and counter-arguments. However, issues related to fair global trade, require
an open inter-disciplinary approach like the one attempted in this chapter. A possible
weakness in this chapter is a lack of depth and specific detail in certain instances.
However, the strengths are – hopefully – the breadth of scope and the presentation
of new questions that extend beyond the boundaries of the traditional disciplines
that usually engage in global economics.

Debates concerning fair global trade and analyses of globalization are notori-
ously emotive.[1] There are ideological positions over a wide spectrum and data
(both historical and current) are interpreted differently according to the economic

P.J. Naudé (✉)
Professor of Ethics and Director, Nelson Mandela University Business School,
Port Elizabeth, South Africa
e-mail: piet.naude@nmmu.ac.za

[1] No wonder books by Joseph Stiglitz (2002, 2006) and Jagdish Bhagwati (2004) on globalization have become international bestsellers! There is a growing mountain of literature on the
subject from all different perspectives. See the excellent overview of contrasting views by Held
and colleagues (1999).

G. Moore (ed.), *Fairness in International Trade*, The International Society
of Business, Economics, and Ethics Book Series 1, DOI 10.1007/978-90-481-8840-6_6,
© Springer Science+Business Media B.V. 2010

or social development assumptions of the proponent of a particular view, for example, the neo-liberal, structuralist, "left", "right" or Marxist viewpoints. Perhaps a debate about assumptions and presuppositions would aid the hermeneutics of dialogue. Unfortunately, this chapter does not have room for an extensive debate on historiography, the benefits or not of the free market and the contradictory impact of globalization. At certain points in the chapter, convictions will merely be stated without the requisite ground-argumentation.

6.1.2 The Complex Notion of "Africa" and Its Dire Socio-economic Development Needs

If one wishes to bring historical and contemporary perspectives into the debate on fair global trade, one is struck by the complexities of what we call "Africa". There is no single history for Africa, only a multitude of regional histories. "Sub-Saharan Africa" is mostly used as a geographical demarcation[2] of the "southern" half of the continent, but even in this region slavery, colonialism, post-colonial politics, and current socio-economic developments are widely divergent, defying in most cases any unifying terms. Therefore, for the purposes of an overview such as this, we have to accept generalizations beyond what would make serious historians, economists or political scientists feel comfortable. There are always exceptions to whatever is claimed in the name of "Africa".

This chapter is not an attempt to speak "on behalf of" Africa. This I cannot do, as I neither have the necessary knowledge nor the mandate to do so. What is presented here, though, is a perspective on fair trade and related issues from Africa, based on the work of the African Union, developed through my own views and auxiliary literature.

The African Union (AU) was established as an inter-governmental organization in July 2001, as an amalgamation of the former African Economic Community (AEC) and the Organization of African Unity (OAU). Its headquarters are in Addis Ababa, Ethiopia, where the African Union Commission (AUC) co-ordinates the work on behalf of the 53 member states. The AU has ambitious goals to achieve greater unity among African countries via the creation of a free trade area, a central African bank, a common currency and the creation of a single customs union. The AU aims "to promote and defend common African positions on issues of interest to the continent and its peoples" (www.african-union.org). The main sources for this chapter are the *Strategic Plan of the African Union Commission* (3 volumes, 2004 quoted as AUC 1, 2 and 3) and the *Economic Report on Africa 2007: Accelerating Africa's Development through Diversification (ERA)* drafted by Economic Commission for Africa.

Africa is in serious need of socio-economic development, but is currently under threat due to marginalization, in an increasingly globalized economy. Unlike Asia

---

[2]The African Union insists that one of Africa's greatest challenges is exactly to overcome divisions based on so many differences, for example, culture, language, religion, economic status and political systems (AUC 3, pp. 4–22).

and Latin America that have succeeded in taking advantage of the global economy, Africa has failed to become an important member of the international economic community. The results are a deep cause for concern and the source for a general Afro-pessimism inside and outside of Africa itself. Here is some basic information[3]:

- Africa's population of 832 million represents 13% of the world population, but Africa accounts for only 1% of Foreign Direct Investment, 1% of gross domestic product and about 2% of world trade[4]
- Of the 48 least developed countries in the world, 35 are in Africa and African countries are mainly in the lowest 20% of the UN Human Development Index
- Over 40% of the sub-Saharan population live below the international threshold of $1 a day
- Nearly 80% of the continent's labour force "remains mired in manual and archaic agricultural practices" (AUC 1, p. 6) compounded by hostile climatic conditions and persistent animal diseases that threaten food security. Per capita food production fell in 31 of the 53 African countries in the period 2000–2005
- Diseases like malaria and AIDS (a deadly combination in many cases) are taking its daily toll on life-expectancies (2 million AIDS deaths in 2005) and the economy: 60% of HIV-positive people world-wide live in Africa and on average adult HIV prevalence is 6.1% of the population (UNAIDS, 2006 *Report on the global AIDS epidemic*)
- Africa's isolation, marginalization and even exclusion (Hoogvelt 2002) is increasing due to the continued widening of the digital divide (AUC 1, p. 13) with huge backlogs regarding intra-African communication and the inability to "log-in" into the digital global economy

This list can be extended, but is adequate to highlight the dire socio-economic development needs of Africa and the danger of remaining a marginalized continent. From an African perspective, a fair global trade regime must contribute to the continent's development and enhance Africa's ability to participate in the processes of global decision-making, overcoming its marginalized position and weak negotiating power, and ensuring that benefits accruing from global economic interaction are sustainable.

6.2 Historical Background to the Current Debates About Fair Global Trade

As Africans we argue that our current marginal position must be viewed from an historical perspective. According to paleo-anthropological studies, Africa is the

---

[3]This information is mostly available in AUC 1, p. 9 ff.

[4]If one accepts that a very high percentage of international trade is "virtual" (shares, futures), Africa's share of real commodity trading – minerals, and increasingly oil – would be considerably higher. The lack of participation in all forms of trade is a sign of Africa's marginalization as it points to weak financial institutions and a lack of connectivity in a widening digital divide.

motherland of *Homo sapiens*. It was a major force in world affairs over the centuries with its various empires and kingdoms from long before the Christian era up to the fifteenth century (AUC 1, pp. 4–5). An understanding of the marginalization and exploitation of Africa and Africans, between the fifteenth century and the present time, illustrates the reason for the asymmetrical trade situation in which Africa finds itself today. This disproportionate economic and technological situation arose over many centuries and is the cumulative result of at least three factors: (1) the Atlantic slave trade (1440–1870); (2) the colonization of Africa (1884–1961) and post-colonial misrule in Africa (1950–present day); and (3) the creation of a global monetary system (1878–1990).

Hundreds of books have been written on each of these topics. For the purpose of this chapter, I will spend more time on the emerging monetary system (as this is the current context in which the fair trade debates occur), and make only very brief comments on the other two factors.

An important pre-observation is required: This chapter does not attempt to apportion "blame" for Africa's current weak position in international trade. The aim of the historical material is to provide a context in which the current situation may be interpreted. Such context can then provide credence to the moral and material claims made by Africa and other developing regions, in order to support such concepts as "special and differential treatment" (see below) with a view to establishing a new trade order for the global economy. History, in this case, is not to be used as a cheap moral propaganda tool. However, there is mounting empirical evidence to support the argument that there is an implicit causal link between history and the current economic performance of Africa, and indeed this should be credibly demonstrated.[5]

6.2.1 The Slave Trade[6]

The Atlantic slave trade developed over a period of just over 400 years (1440–1870). There is no scholarly consensus as to the origin, extent and effects of the slave trade on Africa and slave importing nations. A middle position would probably agree on the following encapsulation of the African slave trade.

Slave trading was an integral part of African societies, long before the actual Atlantic slave trade started. In the absence of clear rights to property, slaves (cheap labour) were an important means of production and slaves were taken from African tribes themselves, in the normal course of inter-tribal conflicts.[7] However, it must be

---

[5]For an empirical argument, see Nathan Nunn (2007) and his many references to literature from development economists defending the link between Africa's current underdevelopment and historical legacies.

[6]For this section I rely on: Hugh Thomas (1997). *The slave trade. The history of the Atlantic slave trade 1440–1870* and John Thornton (1998) *Africa and Africans in the making of the Atlantic world, 1400–1800.*

[7]See Thornton's persuasive argument of the link between slavery and African social structure (1998, pp. 72–97).

stated, that the rising demand for slave labour in the Americas led to an enormous expansion of intra-African trade in human capital, with competitive co-operation amongst European slave merchants and the African elite. Only in rare cases were slave raids undertaken by Europeans, normally occurring through the course of war on the African continent.[8] However, this does not imply a passive role by Europeans, who entered into agreements with their African counterparts to ravage the lives and social structures of ordinary Africans.

The outcomes for Africa were mixed: On the one hand the barter trade in goods like iron, textiles and liquor, and the opportunity to access more advanced arms brought about many positive economic effects, including a diversification of the local economies. On the other hand, there were devastating demographic[9] and social effects on African societies that were built primarily on kinship and patriarchy. The increasing power of African rulers, as a result of the slave trade, led to them selling even more people into slavery, thus perpetuating the social crisis.

The effect on the Americas and Europe were more uniformly positive. Africa provided a market for produced goods and was a source for labour that made possible the agricultural revolution in what is now known as Latin America and parts of North America (then under European colonial rule). Contrary to Eric Williams' argument,[10] no linear causal relationship between the slave trade and the subsequent emergence of industrialization is feasible. However, there is no doubt that industries like ship-building, marine insurance and rope-making were stimulated by the slave trade and that the capital gained from trading humans and agricultural production by slaves (virtually free labour!) made a variety of industrial projects possible (Thomas 1997, p. 795).

The thesis by Walter Rodney that the Atlantic slave trade was a first step in the under-development of Africa, is no longer supported by main-stream academics. However, one has to state clearly that between 10 and 13 million slaves were exported from Africa[11] and this played an indispensable role in the economic and cultural[12] development of Europe and the Americas. In fact, the rapid progress in agriculture in these regions would have been very difficult – if not impossible – without enslaved African human capital.

---

[8] See Thornton's discussion of early slave raids in Angola by the Portuguese army (1998, p. 115), but also his sober conclusions regarding the link between European war-abilities and enslavement (1998, p. 116ff).

[9] The AUC refers to this as a "demographic haemorrhage occasioned by the paroxysm of the slave trade" (AUC 1, p. 5).

[10] Williams was the prime minister of Trinidad and wrote the controversial book *Capitalism and slavery* in which he argues for a link between slavery and industrialization.

[11] See the estimated statistics of the slave trade as cited by Thomas (1997, pp. 805–806) in terms of carrier countries (Portugal 4.6m and Britain 2.6m); destinations (Brazil 4m); origins (Congo/Angola 3m) and type of labour (sugar plantations 5m).

[12] See Thornton's very interesting chapters (5–9) on the effect of slaves on the cultures of the so-called New World and how reciprocal transformations occurred.

6.2.2 Colonialism[13] and Post-colonial Africa

The abolition of the slave trade eventually led to a markedly different economic and political relationship between Africa and Europe. What slowly emerged was that Europe no longer needed to control human capital, but rather it needed economic and political control over actual African territories. This was necessary to secure trade in goods like gold, ivory, timber and palm oil, and the drive for such control was also influenced by the competitive intra-European rivalries over the period 1870–1945.

Trade in pre-colonial times was essentially co-determined by Africans and their European counterparts, where Africans (although mostly rulers and the trading elite) had a direct influence on events. However, we now enter a phase where asymmetrical power relations play themselves out on the African continent. Commenting on the nineteenth century, Fage observed: "In any clash between European and African interests or beliefs, Europe now possessed both the material means – steam power, firepower, medical power – to impose its will upon Africa, and the moral strength – the certainty that European civilization would prevail, and also that it was in the interest of the African peoples to do so" (Fage 1988, p. 333, see also p. 352).

Starting in West Africa and spreading over into South, East and North Africa, the major European countries increased their administrative, economic and eventually military-political control over Africa. By 1914, Africa – with rare exceptions in cases such as Liberia – were under foreign control[14] (see map in Fage 1988, p. 402), and lost the ability to compete equally in the commercial exploitation of its own natural resources.

Both the process toward and the "reasons" for colonization are too complex when examined over various regions, to summarize in one sentence.[15] Colonization occurred in phases and whereas the initial phases of partial control were motivated by factors as diverse as securing the abolishment of the slave trade and expanding commercial trade in products such as palm oil, the later phases were more directly linked to European political events (the two World Wars and the depression of the 1930s). As Europe's industrialization reached its fulfilment, greater emphasis was

---

[13]For this section I rely heavily on J.D. Fage (1988). *A history of Africa*. He commences his study with early African societies (part 1), the impact of Islam (part 2) and more importantly, for this chapter, he discusses European expansion and colonial power in parts 3 and 4. The well-known book by Thomas Packenham (1991). *The scramble for Africa*, reads like a novel and focuses more closely on the colonial period and actual territorial invasion of Africa between 1870 and 1906. Each region is discussed in detail, and makes clear how complex the process of colonization was. A more journalistic book with a fairly critical view of Africa is Robert Guest's (2004). *The Shackled Continent*. He starts off by arguing that Africa's basic problem is not its past, but its lack of leadership in the post-colonial period (see pp. 12, 23).

[14]Fage remarked that: "Europe and the world had accepted by 1902 that the whole of Africa was the property of one or other of the European colonial powers" (1988, p. 391).

[15]See Packenham's (1991) fairly detailed accounts of the various regions, starting with King Leopold II of Belgium's dealings with the Congo.

placed on the direct economic benefits that the colonies could provide in the form of raw material (rubber, iron ore) and precious goods like oil, gold and diamonds.

Not all the colonies brought immediate profit and wealth to the colonizers and the idea that colonies ought to be invested in only emerged much later in the colonization process. The colonies were considered to be indispensable political building blocks in the intra-European conflicts among countries like Britain, France, Belgium, Italy, Germany and Spain (see Packenham 1991, p. xxii). The proverbial "scramble for Africa"[16] was driven by a powerful combination of economic and political forces, and was based on the emerging assumption that European civilization was superior to Africa's and that the latter needed developing towards a societal model based upon European religion and values.[17] The first comprehensive development plans for the socio-economic upliftment of Africa occurred only after the Second World War (Fage 1988, pp. 422–423).

The rapid de-colonization of Africa started in the late 1940s and occurred *inter alia* due to the rising tide of nationalist liberation movements, political instability, and the acceptance of the Universal Declaration of Human Rights by the newly established United Nations. Post-colonial Africa was ill prepared by its colonial and cultural histories to accept responsibilities for its own affairs. A number of factors contributed to a somewhat sombre picture of Africa after independence. Colonial powers neglected to invest in general education, and training in political-administrative rule. Power transitions were poorly managed and new rulers compiled economic policies that could not be sustained and which lead to indebtedness. Dictatorships emerged due to weak civil societal structures, and corruption and misrule became widespread. Tribal wars escalated, and multi-party democracies were not sustainable due to inadequate levels of preparation for governments of this nature.

There is just no way in which we as Africans can escape the failures of leadership in many parts of post-colonial Africa and which have contributed to a general Afro-pessimism. The AUC mentions slavery and imperialism only in passing. It notes that we should not forget, but "we must learn to put things behind us" and focus on Africa's own responsibilities (AUC 1, p. 7). The self-judgment is fierce and candid: "Distrust for constituted authority, corruption and impunity, coupled with human rights abuses have kept Africa in a situation of conflict, thereby undermining all initiatives towards sustainable development" (AUC 1, p. 14). Coupled to this, is the deep and enduring socio-psychological impact of a colonized self-perception and a mind-set that leads to cultural diffidence and a notion that "foreign" must be "better".

---

[16]*The scramble for Africa* is – as indicated above – the title of the magnificent account of colonization by Thomas Packenham (1991), but the use of this expression probably originated as early as 1884.

[17]The link between Christian mission and colonial power is an ambiguous one. Packenham states unequivocally that the scramble for Africa was led by "the empire-building alliance of God and Mammon" (1991, p. 673), introduced as "Christianity, commerce and civilization" by British explorer, David Livingstone. For us in Africa, a fourth "c" is added: conquest.

Although Africa eventually regained her political independence, an important factor – crucial to the overall argument of this chapter – must be kept in mind. Between 1935 and 1950 there were dramatic increases in foreign trade in areas like the Belgian Congo, French West Africa, Uganda and Northern Rhodesia (see table 5 in Fage 1988, p. 423), and by the mid 1950s "African colonies were participating in the world economy as never before" (Fage 1988, p. 423). The question then arises: How was this world economy in which Africa was participating, structured? The answer to this important question lies in the emerging monetary system from approximately 1870 to the present day.

6.2.3 The Evolution of the Contemporary Monetary and Trade Regime

The growing economic integration of the world[18] implies that decisions taken by one actor in the economic sphere affect other actors much more directly and intensely than ever before in history. It necessitates forms of co-operation to ensure orderly trade, generally accepted rules and regulations regarding the stabilization of the various monetary systems *inter alia* through the "standardizing" of exchange rates.

Economic historians[19] generally agree that three such attempts at "standardized monetarization" (SM) developed between 1870 and our present time: The Gold Standard, the Bretton Woods system and the current emerging system of free capital flow that is subject to negotiated trade rules.

The Gold Standard (GS), formalized in 1878, remained in force until the advent of the First World War.[20] In simple terms, the monetarization at work here was to link the value of major currencies to a fixed price of gold, setting up a system of regulated exchange rates. The initial key-currency areas committed themselves to a free flow of gold and to convert national currencies at a fixed rate into gold, when requested to do so.[21] This created a system of standardized monetarization, facilitating international transactions and protecting participants against currency volatility.[22]

---

[18] Madison (2001) shows how this integration has grown by indicating that for the world as a whole, the ratio of merchandise exports to GDP rose from 5.5% in 1950 to 17.2% in 1995.

[19] I am not an expert in economics or monetary policy and for this section rely heavily on the exposition by Peter Isard (2005), who was for many years a senior adviser at the IMF, and writer of *Exchange rate economics* (1995).

[20] There was fractional support for the GS up until 1933 – see Isard (2005, p. 15), footnote 5.

[21] For a simple explanation of the orthodox account of the Gold Standard, see Held et al. (1999, p. 196).

[22] In theory at least, this is the first example of a system embodying globally integrated financial markets, where domestic or national economies were subject to international financial discipline, to which they were required to adjust. One might refer to the Gold Standard as the origin of what has

However, the collapse of the GS did not remove the need for international monetary cooperation. Already, during the Second World War, negotiations commenced that eventually led to a monetary agreement amongst the forty-four nations at a conference in Bretton Woods, New Hampshire, July 1944. This became known as the Bretton Woods System (BWS) and entailed the declaration of fixed exchange rate parities by a substantial group of countries (Held et al. 1999, pp. 199–201).

In contrast to the GS, the BWS was a managed multilateral system that left individual countries with considerable autonomy to pursue national economic goals, whilst they subjected their exchange rate and international trade practices to international agreements. Two important institutions embodied the BWS: The IMF focused on monetary cooperation and an orderly exchange rate system, whereas the World Bank financed economic reconstruction and development (Isard 2005, pp. 27–29; 69–118).

Gold still played a role, although a considerably different international gold standard was established in this new exchange rate system. The US was the only country that actually pegged its currency to gold (at a par value of $35 per ounce), but other countries in turn pegged their currencies to the dollar. The BWS was thus a monetary system based on the dollar. In this system, private financial flows were restricted, and to diminish market volatility, the US undertook to sell gold only to foreign central banks and governments, and to licensed private users (Isard 2005, p. 29).

According to Held et al. (1999, pp. 201–202), the BWS that formally operated between 1946 and 1971, broke down under exactly the three forces that shaped the current situation of financial globalisation. Firstly, the dramatic increase in highly mobile private capital put the control systems of the BWS under severe stress. Secondly, the emerging Eurocurrency markets (dollar deposits in European banks from multinational companies and the Soviet Union) were also not easily subjected to national capital controls. Thirdly, the OPEC crisis of 1973 resulted in huge flow of funds from oil-exporting to oil-importing countries. This increased the liquidity of international banks with an even greater flow of capital across national boundaries, and higher speculative trading. In short, the intensity and increasing diversity of global financial flows broke the back of the BWS and its intended stable monetary system. In place of the fixed system, where the value of gold, or the dollar acted as a "standardization measure", there emerged a floating exchange rate system where the only remaining "standard" was the value assigned to a particular currency by the day-to-day trading on foreign exchange markets (Held et al. 1999, p. 209). Needless to say, in such a system volatility is higher and the power to determine market perceptions is a crucial factor in who will gain or loose. The "hot money" of private speculators moves with great velocity and intensity. This has a significant impact on financial markets, in some cases leading to currency crises that threatened national

---

become known as economic globalization, i.e. "the increasing flow of goods and services, financial resources, workers, and technologies across national borders" (Isard 2005, p. 4).

and regional economies, due to the contagion effect of emerging market economies (Held et al. 1999, pp. 209, 213).[23]

This third, and still evolving international monetary system, has retained the major institutions of the BWS (the IMF and World Bank), although their roles have been redefined, due to lessons learnt about currency instability and development economics. To ensure some coherence in the increasing volume and extent of trade, the WTO replaced the failed GATT, and has become the only global organization dealing with the rules of trade between nations, acting as tribunal in the case of disputes. General trade agreements reached at the WTO are ratified in the parliaments of participating nations, of which there were 146 in 2003 (Bhagwati 2004, p. 270).

In the first era, the gold standard was fairly tightly controlled with restricted national autonomy. In the BWS, there was more freedom to pursue national economic goals, but the stability was provided by the gold-dollar price and restrictions on private capital flow. In the current era, there is such a high degree of interconnectedness, and such a rapid flow of (speculative) capital that national autonomies are severely restricted – especially in weaker nations.

Consequently, there has been a structural shift in the balance of power between public and private authority in the global financial system. This is a matter of fierce debate and one may cite examples and counter-examples, but without being a "hyperglobalist", one must admit that, "there is much compelling evidence to suggest that contemporary financial globalisation is a market-driven rather than a state-driven phenomenon" (Held et al. 1999, p. 234). The nation-state is, according to Stiglitz, squeezed between political demands at local level, and the economic demands of a global system. The problem is that economic globalisation has outpaced political globalisation, resulting in uncoordinated systems of global governance, which is particularly evident in issues of global health and the environment (Stiglitz 2006, p. 21). The power vacuum has been filled by the most powerful proponents of unlimited trade liberalization, and by staunch believers in only partially successful "trickle-down" economics (Stiglitz 2006, p. 23).

For the purposes of this chapter, I wish to point out a common element in all three monetary systems. *From the beginning they created a fundamental differentiation between "central" and "periphery"*: The gold standard was managed by the Bank of England in London; the BWS was dependent on dollar policies in Washington; the current emerging financial system is determined by the triad of New York, London and Tokyo. Today's poorer countries were for the most part still colonized when these monetary systems took shape and they played only a marginal role in their origin and current direction. The consequence is that a hierarchical, uneven and asymmetrical system has emerged (Held et al. 1999, pp. 213, 224) with clear democratic deficits in decision-making power, and trade agreements that make the poorest countries worse off (Stiglitz 2006, p. 58). This forms the background to

---

[23] For a discussion of the different currency crises between 1994 and 1999 in Mexico, the Asian countries and Russia, read Isard (2005, pp. 119-151).

the establishment of the WTO, the current trade negotiations, and the expectations that Africa has of the latter.

6.3 Africa's Expectations of the WTO and Doha Trade Negotiations

The Doha Development Round of the WTO trade negotiations commenced in 2001 and halted in July 2006, continuing on an informal and bi-lateral level. As the promise of multilateral trade negotiations continues to disappoint, Africa is clearly seeking to develop closer ties with the rising giants of China, India[24] and to a lesser extent Latin America, in the form of South-South-partnerships. The movement toward a truly "Development Round" of trade negotiations raised Africa's expectations and brought the following salient factors to the fore.

6.3.1 Values[25]

Despite experiments in "African socialism" in early post-colonial times, Africa accepts the principles of a market economy to maximize her potential. But contrary to a narrow mercantilist view of trade negotiations, based on the principle of self-interested bargaining, "economic efficacy and solidarity, efficiency and equity, growth and sustainable development, short term gains and long term prospects" must be combined (AUC 1, p. 10) to inform trade negotiations and to judge their outcomes.

6.3.2 Participation

Like many other developing regions, Africa has low negotiation capacities both in terms of human resources[26] and technical knowledge. "Africa could in effect remain in a 'spoke' situation while richer countries with more negotiating capacities are able to place themselves at the centre – the hub – of a network of trade agreements" (ECA 2007, p. 90). Africa is in the process of self-developing its trade negotiation capacities, but would need the assistance of the WTO to participate effectively.

---

[24] At the first major bi-lateral meeting between Africa and India in New-Delhi (8 April 2008), it was announced that India would grant priority trade access to the least developed countries of the world.

[25] See the discussion of *ubuntu* as a value expression under section 5. See also the passionate arguments for embedding fairness and social justice in the WTO by Stiglitz and Charlton (2005).

[26] There are hundreds of meetings and informal negotiations to be conducted, but some developing countries can scarcely afford a permanent trade representative in Geneva, and are outnumbered by other countries and the special interest groups that represent them.

6.3.3 Agenda

An explicitly pro-development agenda holds the potential to overcome the imbalances of earlier trade negotiations (e.g. the Uruguay Round) by actually reforming the multilateral trading system to ensure a more equitable share in the gains of global trade (ECA 2007, p. 76). Africa has a particular interest in negotiations concerning agriculture and services. Although the outcomes have not been finalized, there is at least agreement in principle that the distorted subsidies in the North, and market access for the South should be realized by 2013, though intermediate deadlines have yet to be achieved.

6.3.4 Trade Liberalization and "Aid for Trade"

Africa accepts trade liberalization as the general aim of trade negotiations, but has been at the receiving end of failed development interventions in the form of enforced structural adjustment programmes (AUC 1, p. 9). Therefore, allowance must be made for trade liberalization according to the development needs and adjustment capacities of a particular country or region, because a "one size fits all"-strategy creates huge adaptation costs and actually retards development (ECA 2007, p. 87). In this regard, Africa supports the notion of aid specifically aimed at meeting the adjustment cost of trade liberalization. However, it is important that this aid is not misused as a political weapon in the negotiation process, or as a replacement for current aid commitments (0.7% of Gross National Income) (Stiglitz & Charlton 2006).

6.3.5 African Union Initiatives and the Question of Identity

The underlying question facing the AU is how to regain relative autonomy and initiative for a continent that has lost its sense of self-worth over the past 500 years? This is extremely difficult for a continent that is emerging from colonial rule, and finding itself on the margins of a global system from which it cannot and does not want to escape, but where the power to shape that system towards justice and equity is clearly lacking. This fundamental question of identity underlies initiatives like NEPAD and the African Renaissance. In a courageous paragraph the AUC writes:

> Therefore, as far as Africans are concerned, it is no longer a question of catching up with anything; it is no longer a question of trailing behind any one or being relegated to the sidelines by anyone; rather, it is a question of being at the centre of their own affairs. Africans should devise for themselves watchwords, namely self-development, self-reliance, self-reliance for recognition and development... Having thus clarified the direction of its endeavors for full development, Africa can seek to integrate itself into the globalization process without losing its soul (AUC 1, p. 10).

One could translate the above as follows: Without reconstructing the African identity, socio-economic reconstruction will be extremely difficult. This brings trade negotiations into the ethical arena of cultural justice and the rights of indigenous peoples. Only then can the hard economic policies outlined by the AU follow, namely: modernization of agriculture; acceleration of industrialization; beneficiation of Africa's enormous mineral wealth; integration of the sub-regions of Africa; and a decisive drive towards the diversification[27] of African economies.

6.4 Differential Treatment and Prioritarian Justice

Africa has high expectations concerning the principle of "special and differential treatment" (part of GATT and accepted by the WTO) and especially the hope that it will be mainstreamed into all trade negotiations and enforced in practice. For example, there are 34 African countries in the Least Developed Countries (LDC) group, and initiatives such as the Generalized System of Preferences and the EU's "Everything but Arms" have brought additional benefits to them. Although not directly related to WTO negotiations, special actions like debt relief[28] and collective efforts to reach the Millennium Development Goals are important to many African countries.

The notion of "special and differential treatment" introduces *new kinds of justice* that were previously absent or under-represented. One thinks, for example, of emerging debates about ecological justice, inter-generational justice, cultural justice[29] and participative justice.[30] Africa understands that it will never reach a point of higher integration into the global economy unless a *redefinition of distributive justice* in the context of an integrated global monetary system is accepted.

Distributive justice[31] is a form of socio-economic justice that regulates the distribution of goods and services amongst the people of a specific society, or amongst societies in a regional or global arrangement. The result of such a distribution will obviously depend on the notion of justice and the specific theory of justice adopted.

---

[27] Note the sub-title of the Economic Report on Africa: "Accelerating Africa's development through diversification" and the discussion of diversification in the report itself (ECA 2007, p. 113ff).

[28] Of the 19 countries that reached completion point in the HIPC debt relief process, 15 were from Africa.

[29] This is a form of justice not as widely discussed in the literature yet. I have found the essay by Kwenda (2003) very helpful in this regard. He argues that cultural justice is established when people are allowed unselfconscious living, i.e. they live in acceptance and appreciation of their own identity. For an analysis of the link between cultural justice, identity and globalization, read Naudé (2005).

[30] Bedford-Strohm makes the astute observation that both material and socio-cultural poverty find their origin in "fehlende Teilhabe" (1993, p. 169). People are poor because of a lack of participation in the (in)formal economy and a lack of power to influence decisions. This is one of the most urgent issues in discussions of global economic justice today.

[31] For a definition and wide-ranging discussion of different theories of distributive justice, read Roemer (1998).

Egalitarian understandings of justice will, for example, seek to spread benefits more equally than entitlement notions of justice.[32]

There is now a growing consensus that to make the emerging global monetary system moral and sustainable, special focus on disadvantaged nations and people is needed. The notion of "preferential" treatment, has over the last few decades been expressed in different terms by theologians, philosophers and economists:

In the 1960s and 1970s, Latin American liberation theologians[33] – followed later by African liberation theologians[34] – developed "the preferential option for the poor" as a prophetic critique against failed development and structural adjustment policies in Latin America and Africa.

John Rawls developed his ideas about "justice as fairness" and the priority of the least advantaged person in his remarkable book, *A theory of justice* (1971). He based this on his judgment that utilitarian ethics that simply maximizes happiness will not create just societies, and later (1999) stated that burdened societies need – at least for a specified period – special assistance in a new global order.

Joseph Stiglitz (2006) recently made a strong economic argument to replace "reciprocity for all" with the dictum of "special and differential treatment" for the poor nations of the world. In what he calls "fair trade for the poor", he suggests a reform of international trade. This reform entails that the principle of "reciprocity for and among all countries – regardless of circumstances" should be replaced by the principle of "*reciprocity among equals, but differentiation between those in markedly different circumstances*" (Stiglitz 2006, p. 83, my emphasis).

In practice, Stiglitz proposes a three-tier system of rich, middle-income and poor countries – a classification based on agreed empirical norms. The rich countries open up their markets to others in their own group, but also to the middle-income and poor countries without reciprocity, or political conditionality expected from the latter two groups. The middle-income group opens trade to all in its own group and to the poor countries without conditionality, but is not required to extend such preferences to the rich countries. In such a system, developing nations will receive "special and differential treatment", as has already happened in some bilateral trade agreements (see the EU in 2001; Stiglitz 2006:83). However, such preferential treatment should not be voluntary, but become part and parcel of WTO negotiations and enforced in fields such as agriculture, tariffs and non-tariff barriers.

The clear WTO Ministerial Declaration adopted on 14 November 2001 gave Africa at least, theoretical hope:

> We agree that special and differential treatment for developing countries shall be an integral part of all elements of negotiations and shall be embodied in the schedules and

---

[32] This difference is, for example, illustrated in the debate between John Rawls (egalitarian view) and Robert Nozick (entitlement view).

[33] The most famous proponent of this radical challenge to traditional Catholic social thought is Gustavo Gutierrez, whose classical Spanish exposition was published in English as *A theology of liberation* (1973).

[34] Well-known names are Manas Buthelezi, Desmond Tutu, Itumeleng Mosala, Allan Boesak, and womanists like Mercy Oduyoye and Isabel Phiri.

concession and commitments and as appropriate in the rules and disciplines to be negotiated, so as to be operationally effective and to enable developing countries to effectively
take account of their development needs, including food security and rural development
(paragraph 13).

We as Africans view this as a sincere commitment to and as a yardstick for the
processes and outcomes of trade negotiations.

6.5 Ubuntu as Guiding Philosophy for a New Trade Regime?

The ancient value system of traditional African societies is condensed in the notion
of *ubuntu*.[35] Whereas the Enlightenment view of the human person – power-
fully expressed by, for example, René Descartes and Immanuel Kant – focuses
on individuality and an assumed universal rationality, African philosophy rests on
the assumption of communality: *Cogito ergo sum* stands in contrast to *ubuntu* as
explained by African philosopher, John Mbiti (1969, pp. 108–109): "I am, because
we are; and since we are, therefore I am." In short: I am a person through other persons. The "other" does not stand in an accidental or a posteriori or pragmatic relation
to me, but is in fact a constitutive ontological part of my identity. My success is
invariably tied up with the promotion of communal well-being, and the criterion of
"success" is not in the first place material wealth accumulation, but the promotion
and restoration of vital force, the life-giving spirit that permeates our existence and
the cosmos of which we are a part.

If one translates this ethic from its tribal and local roots, to the emerging global
order, one realizes that what the ecological crisis and global warming recently
brought to our attention – namely that we share this finite world and we are literally dependent upon one another and cannot "go it alone" – was already embedded
in ancient African wisdom. A trade negotiating system, primarily imbued by self-
gain in the power game of win-loose-scenarios, may lead to short term "victories",
but will not yield the required social goods for sustainable economic growth in the
medium to long term.

If all countries enter trade negotiations on the premise to build one human community, they will understand that building such a community requires sacrifices,
and at times altruism instead of strict reciprocity. Furthermore, if burdened societies
(Rawls) that are in transition are treated in a special and differential way – Africa
might at one point in history also be in a position to reciprocate materially to a
greater extent than is possible at the moment.

---

[35] *Ubuntu* has been widely discussed by African and other international scholars. Mbiti (1969) is
considered to be the *locus classicus* in academic literature in this regard. Recent contributions are
by Gyekye (1996), Ramosa (1999) and Shutte (2001). Like all good notions, *ubuntu* has also been
misused and must obviously be subject to critical analysis. *Ubuntu* has in recent years also been
translated into business management and leadership literature. See for example Broodryk (2005)
and Mbigi (2005).

Despite the shortcomings of the WTO,[36] ranging from member access to asymmetric enforcement, the Ministerial Declaration does reflect this spirit of a single world community:

> We recognize the need of *all our people* to benefit from the increased opportunities and welfare gains that the multilateral trading system generates... We shall continue to make positive efforts designed to ensure that developing countries, and especially the least developed among them, secure a share in the growth of world trade commensurate with the needs of their economic development (paragraph 2, my emphasis).

As far as we keep one another to this vision, there is indeed hope.
Nkosi sikelel' iAfrika![37]

References

African Union Commission. 2004, *Strategic Plan of the African Union Commission* (3 volumes) (AUC, Addis Ababa).

Bedford-Strohm, H. 1993, *Vorrang für die Armen. Auf dem Weg zu einer theologischen Theorie der Gerechtighkeit* (Chr. Kaiser Verlag, Gütersloh).

Bhagwati, J. 2004, *In Defense of Globalization* (OUP, Oxford).

Broodryk, J. 2005, *Ubuntu management philosophy* (Knowres, Randburg).

Dunkley, G. 2004, *Free Trade. Myth, Reality and Alternatives* (David Philip, Cape Town).

Economic Commission for Africa. 2007, *Economic report on Africa 2007* (African Union, Addis Ababa).

Fage, J.D. 1988, *A History of Africa.* 2nd edition (Unwin Hyman, London).

Guest, R. 2004, *The Shackled Continent. Africa's Past, Present and Future* (Macmillan, London).

Gutierrez, G. 1973, *A Theology of Liberation.* (SCM, London).

Gyekye, K. 1996, *The Unexamined Life: Philosophy and the African Experience* (Sankofa, Accra).

Held, D., McGrew, A., Goldblatt, D. & Perraton, J. 1999, *Global Transformations. Politics, Economics and Culture* (Stanford University Press, Stanford).

Hoogvelt, A. 2002, Globalization, Imperialism and exclusion: The case of Sub-Saharan Africa, in Zack-Williams, T., Frost, D. & Thomson, A. (eds.), *Africa in Crisis. Challenges and Possibilities* (Pluto Press, London), pp. 15–28.

Isard, P. 2005, *Globalization and the International Financial System.* (CUP, Cambridge).

Kwenda, C. V. 2003, Cultural justice: the pathway to reconciliation and social cohesion, in Chidester, D., Dexter, P. and Wilmot, J. (eds.). *What Holds Us Together? Social Cohesion in South Africa* (HSRC Press, Cape Town), pp. 67–80.

Madison, A. 2001, *The World Economy: A Millennium Perspective* (OECD, Paris).

Mbigi, L. 2005, *The Spirit of African Leadership* (Knowres, Randburg).

Mbiti, J. 1969, *African Religions and Philosophy* (East African Educational Publishers, Nairobi).

Naudé, P. 2005, The ethical challenge of identity formation and cultural justice in a globalizing world. *Scriptura* 89, 536–549.

Nunn, N. 2007, Historical legacies: A model linking Africa's past to its current underdevelopment. *Journal of Development Economics* 83, 157–175.

Packenham, T. 1991, *The Scramble for Africa. 1876–1912* (Abacus, London).

Ramosa, M. B. 1999, *African Philosophy through ubuntu* (Mond Books, Harare).

---

[36] See the incisive critique of both the assumptions and actual functioning of the WTO by Australian economist, Graham Dunkley (2004, especially Chapter 8).

[37] "God bless Africa", is the first line of a pan-African hymn and is also the first line of the official anthem of the Republic of South Africa.

Rawls, J. 1971, *A Theory of Justice* (OUP, Oxford).

Rawls, J. 1999, *The Law of Peoples* (Harvard University Press, Cambridge, MA).

Roemer, J. E. 1998, *Theories of Distributive Justice.* (Harvard University Press, Cambridge, MA).

Shutte, A. 2001, *Ubuntu: An Ethic for the New South Africa* (Cluster, Pietermaritzburg).

Stiglitz, J. E. 2002, *Globalization and its Discontents* (Penguin, London).

Stiglitz, J. E. 2006, *Making Globalization Work* (WW Norton, New York).

Stiglitz, J. E. & Charlton, A. 2005, *Fair Trade for all. How Trade can Promote Development* (OUP, Oxford).

Stiglitz, J. E. & Charlton, A. 2006, "Aid for trade." *International Journal of Development Studies* **5** (2), 1–41

Thomas, H. 1997, *The Slave Trade. The History of the Atlantic Slave Trade 1440–1870* (Macmillan, London).

Thornton, J. 1998, *Africa and Africans in the making of the Atlantic world, 1400–1800*, 2nd edition (CUP, Cambridge).

UNAIDS. 2006, *Report on the Global AIDS Epidemic* (UNAIDS, Geneva).

Chapter 7
Fairness in International Trade and Investment: Latin American Challenges

Elio Ferrato and Maria Cecilia Coutinho de Arruda

7.1 Introduction

The objective of this chapter is to discuss a Latin American perspective on three topics raised by the coordination of the International Society of Business, Economics, and Ethics (ISBEE), as part of the Global Research Project on Fairness in International Trade and Investment:

1. To what extent are the workings and outcomes of the WTO perceived as fair in your region?
2. What are the main ethical issues regarding the WTO in your region?
3. What developments are there in your region to address these ethical issues?

Despite differences in the social, economic and historical formation of Latin American nations, we can assume that the data and ideas in this paper are sufficiently representative, as we have relied upon regional sources such as Economic Latin America and the Caribbean World Trade Organization (WTO), Economic Commission for Latin America and Caribbean (ECLAC), Inter-American Development Bank (IADB), and professional and academic associations and universities, among others, in twelve countries in the Region.

7.2 Fairness in International Trade

Speeches and proposals of member countries in the WTO, either poor or rich, often mention the need for fairness, justice and legitimacy. The actor, other negotiating parties, and the forum in which negotiations are taking place are factors that influence the criteria for a clear definition of fairness.

E. Ferrato (✉)
Professor of Foreign Trade, Business and Production Administration and Ethics, São Paulo, Brazil
e-mail: kandra@uol.com.br

G. Moore (ed.), *Fairness in International Trade*, The International Society
of Business, Economics, and Ethics Book Series 1, DOI 10.1007/978-90-481-8840-6_7,
© Springer Science+Business Media B.V. 2010

Thomas Franck's conception of fairness has often served as a starting point:

> ...fairness is a composite of two independent variables: legitimacy and distributive justice. Thomas Franck's Fairness discourse is the process by which the law, and those who make law, seek to integrate those variables, recognizing the tension between the community's desire for both order (legitimacy) and change (justice), as well as the tensions between different notions of what constitutes *good* order and *good* change in concrete instances (Franck, 1995, pp. 26–27).

Suranovic (2000) described seven principles to divide *equality fairness* and *reciprocity fairness*. Equality fairness includes non-discrimination, distributional fairness and golden rule fairness. Reciprocity fairness embraces positive reciprocity fairness, negative reciprocity fairness, privacy fairness, and maximum benefit fairness.

Davidson et al. (2006) describe a series of surveys related to what they call a "language" of fairness. Among several meanings, the authors indicate that "one of the most fundamental foundations for public claims about fairness in Liberal society is (in)equality. Conditional on a wide variety of contextual information, there is considerable evidence that people possess some preference for equality" (p. 997). "We are only at the very beginning of a systematic understanding of the public politics of trade policy, but it seems likely that an understanding of the politics of fairness will be central to any advance in this area." (p. 1001)

In a more concrete way, for Narlikar (2006) fairness means legitimacy of process and equity of outcomes in the context of the General Agreement on Tariffs and Trade / World Trade Organisation (GATT/WTO). Analyzing the shifts in attitudes of developing countries toward the GATT/WTO, she noticed some changes in the concepts. Different concepts may result in "claims that are mutually contradictory and yet equally legitimate" (p. 1005). Disputes between North and South may indicate these differing claims.

Brown and Stern (2007) argue that fairness in the global trading system is not to be understood as a moral principle, but as an instrumental criterion. Thus, equality of opportunity and distributive equity are conditions for fair agreements.

Our understanding is that Brown and Stern's principles to guide the relationships among WTO members should be reciprocity, most favored nation treatment and national treatment. Furthermore, the respect given to these values should be considered moral and not only instrumental. De Jasay (2006) even discusses the convergence of the terms *fairness* and *justice* whose concepts are frequently applied as synonymou*s*.

7.3 Perception of Fairness in Workings and Outcomes of the WTO in Latin America

A starting point is to look at the WTO self definition and its statement of main purposes:

> The World Trade Organization is the only international body dealing with the rules of trade between nations. At its heart are the WTO agreements, negotiated and signed by the bulk of the world's trading nations. These documents provide the legal ground-rules for international commerce. They are essentially contracts binding governments to keep their trade policies within agreed limits. Although negotiated and signed by governments, the goal of these contracts is to help producers of goods and services, exporters, and imports conduct their business" ...the system's overriding purpose is to help trade flow as freely as possible – so long as there are no undesirable side-effects. That partly means removing obstacles. It also means ensuring that individuals, companies and governments know what the trade rules are around the world, and giving them the confidence that there will be no sudden changes of policy. In other words, the rules have to be "transparent" and predictable. Because the agreements are drafted and signed by the community of trading nations, often after considerable debate and controversy, one of the WTO's most important functions is to serve as a forum for trade negotiations. A third important side to the WTO's work is dispute settlement. Trade relations often involve conflicting interests. Contracts and agreements, including those painstakingly negotiated in the WTO system, often need interpreting. The most harmonious way to settle these differences is through some neutral procedure based on an agreed legal foundation. That is the purpose behind the dispute settlement process written into the WTO agreements (WTO 2008).

The General Agreement on Tariffs and Trade (GATT) had provided the rules for the trading system since 1948. The Uruguay Round lasted from 1986 to 1994 and led to the creation of the WTO on 1 January 1995, but its trading system seemed half a century older. Whereas GATT had mainly dealt with trade in goods, the WTO and its agreements now additionally cover trade in services and in traded inventions, creations and designs (intellectual property).

A framework to address the topic Fairness in International Trade and Investments was Singer's four charges to WTO, which appear to be applicable to Latin America:

1. The WTO places economic considerations ahead of concerns for the environment, animal welfare, and even human rights.
2. The WTO erodes national sovereignty.
3. The WTO is undemocratic.
4. The WTO increases inequality; or (a stronger charge) it makes the rich richer and leaves the world's poorest people even worse off than they would otherwise have been (Singer 2002, p. 16).

These charges raise a question: How can one identify or make such a judgment about WTO? Concerning Latin America, it seems that most dispute panels and results are almost solely controlled by the WTO. According to its internal principles, some decisions may be interpreted as complying with particular interests. This can be judged as undemocratic, as it erodes national sovereignty and increases inequality. A current example of that is the Doha Round. Apparently, instead of moving forward to positive results for every country involved, it seems to go backwards, imposing that developing countries individually negotiate – as much as possible – with developed countries.

The evidence to support the first of Singer's charges to WTO is often found in the media, for instance, when the global warming risk to mankind is pointed out. Regarding Latin America, a large area of the Amazon rainforest is located in different countries. Little international support has been offered to preserve it from devastation and erosion. The WTO seems indifferent to the impact of free trade on workers' rights, child labor, the environment and health. These and other realities may indicate that WTO lacks democratic accountability, in that its hearings on trade disputes are closed to the public and the media (BBC 2008). The IADB (2007a) has raised significant issues in the health sector, which are a consequence of corruption and lack of transparency. The studies provided by the IADB (2007b) can be helpful to support strategies, policies and procedures of the WTO, related to sustainable development of Latin America and the Caribbean.

The Uruguay Round discussed the need of a fair and market-oriented agricultural trading system. This could be reached with more discipline in the areas of market access, export subsidies and internal support. Protectionism has been shown to be an obstacle to the development of the countries and the achievement of positive results with such a system. WTO should be concerned and neutral about the economic opportunities of developing countries, which have commodities to offer and are attempting to develop manufacturing industries, while developed countries tend to protect their agricultural markets, imposing the export of industrialized products. It would be a responsibility of WTO to reduce this inequality. On the other hand, Latin America and the Caribbean countries tend to adopt offensive and defensive positions on different topics within agricultural negotiations. For instance, Brazil and Argentina have proposed ambitious proposals on tariff cuts. However, China, India and South Africa have significantly supported proposals such as trade facilitation, intellectual property, and public health, special and differential treatment (ECLAC 2006).

As reported by Klapper from Associated Press (2007), in a meeting promoted by WTO involving the United States (US), European Union (EU), Brazil and India, it would be "crucial" if the WTO were to succeed in concluding a deal to liberalize the world by the end of 2007. The US and Brazil disagreed in that meeting over how far the US should cut farm subsidies as part of a global trade pact. The US indicated it was willing to limit its trade-distorting farm subsidies to $17 billion, while Brazil insisted on a figure somewhere below $ 15 billion. Critics of the subsidies say they unfairly depress international prices, making it impossible for poorer nations to develop their economies by selling their agricultural products abroad (Singer's fourth charge). The North American government has not publicly moved since offering in October 2005 to restrict its subsidies to $ 22 billion. Both the US and EU say that their agriculture concessions must be matched by lower industrial tariffs in Brazil and India. The Doha Round is already years behind schedule and may set the whole process back to 2010 as subsidy and tariff concessions were seen as unlikely in 2008, when US elections were held, and in 2009, when Indian elections are scheduled.

As per Djelic and Quack (2003), the rational choice perspective is found predominantly amongst economists and political scientists, particularly, for the latter group, in the International Relations literature. Nevertheless, some politicians and scholars of other areas seem also to be concerned about the growth of social problems caused by the lack of equilibrium in international commerce. Such a perspective tends to focus on formal and structural political and economic institutions worldwide. To a certain extent, this could explain how and why corruption is universalized and lasts so long. Despite an intense effort of the Organization for Economic Co-operation and Development (OECD), World Bank, IADB and of other organizations to eradicate it in many countries, in Latin America, corruption deeply affects the image of the Region and enables barriers to be imposed in international commerce. As a paradox, a United Nations (UN) publication (UNCTAD, 2008) indicated Latin America as an excellent region for foreign long-term investments, because Brazil is ranked 8 in the world after the United Kingdom (UK), The Netherlands, France, US, China, Singapore, and Russian Federation. Very recently, the two most famous rating Indicators, Standard & Poor's and Fitch, have elevated Brazil to Investment Grade, which is going to speed up direct investments in the country. For the time being in Latin America only Chile, Peru, Brazil, and Mexico are qualified Investment Grade. On the other hand, research reports have found, and authorities have warned, about some kinds of corruption (*Transparency International* 2007 and *Transparencia Brasil* 2007). A controversial explanation of this fact is that Latin American countries were discovered and settled by developed countries. For centuries developing countries served as a source of genuine raw material suppliers, no matter the social cost to reach the goals. According to this perspective, the creation of the WTO as an institution to mostly support the interests of rich countries can be perceived as unfair by many Latin Americans (Abramo 2007a, b).

According to its objectives and mission, the unconformity of certain procedures by the WTO can be perceived as unfair by societies, especially in the developing world. In many ways, good examples were expected from the developed countries, concerning the capacity and skills to orchestrate actions toward the developing and less developed ones. Rich countries can be, and have been shown to be, as corrupt as less developed or developing nations. In fact, the means of communication have disclosed scandals in the US, Japan, UK, Italy, France and several others countries widely perceived as less corrupt. Therefore, poverty should not be perceived as a synonym of corruption, as ethics does not necessarily mean wealth (IADB 2007b).

Therefore, the existence of irregular or unfair decisions by WTO leads developing countries to lose confidence about those who are supposed to manage based on principles of goodwill, moral equilibrium, equity and integrity (Llano 1991a, b, c).

Nevertheless, it is plausible, and it would be unfair not to recognize, that WTO has provided among countries in Latin America a certain impulse for the development of a free trade sense, especially with the assistance of the International Chamber of Commerce (ICC), based in most countries in the world, by establishing the Incoterms (2000) and Banking Regulations through Brochure 600 (ICC 2008).

7.4 Ethical Issues Regarding the WTO in Latin America

Ethical issues regarding international trade and investment can be closely related to the image of countries that have experienced economic uncertainties and political instabilities since they were created. In this regard, the Link Global Economic

Outlook (United Nations, 2007) states that the trade balances in developing countries reached the amount of 615.4 billions of US dollars against 62.9 billions of US dollars in Latin America and the Caribbean. The annual growth rate of real Gross Domestic Product (GDP) in developing countries reached 6.9% in 2007 against 5.2% in Latin America and the Caribbean, which puts Latin America behind the rest of the developing world. Aiming at change, some corruption tools have been shaped mainly by non-governmental organizations (NGOs) in several countries in Latin America. A number of politicians perceive that corruption may lead to a sad end of a career, either for those who decide to be corrupt or those who act as the corruptor. Booklets and books have been issued by individuals and NGOs, to explain the procedures to impeach mayors in city government throughout Latin America. In addition, specifically in Brazil, private initiatives are developing a sustainability program for competition among local (national and transnational) corporations, associating financial results to environmental and social targets, as a way to inhibit corruption and promote ethical development. It expresses goodwill to eliminate corruption, aiming at possibilities to progressively increase local and external trade and investments.

Contrasting situations may remain, no matter the political trends in government. In spite of all uncertainties and complexities, Latin Americans' typical spirit is described by Castells (1975) and Osland et al. (1999) as full of personal dignity, classism, personalism, paternalism, collectivism, humor and happiness. The easy-going style may hide some lack of trust and opportunism, and does not deny the stigma inherited from slavery, not only of Negroes or natives in the pre-colonial era, but also of whites composed of European immigrants, especially those not affected by the savage capitalism.

Some figures on international merchandise and services trade in Latin America can be helpful to understand these ideas. Table 7.1 offers a general view of trade operations by Latin American countries.

It is obvious that these figures indicate relevant factors that contributed to the countries' economic growth as a result of international trade. Nevertheless, social improvement still needs the boost of political measures to establish a sort of equilibrium in the respective economies, in order to diminish or eliminate severe debts that "erode national sovereignty" (Singer 2002).

Table 7.1 shows positive Account Balance in Argentina, Bolivia, Brazil, Chile and Venezuela. Other Latin American countries would have many reasons for the important debts upon the International Monetary Fund (IMF), the World Bank and other financing organizations, mainly those owned by private banks and equities in developed countries.

Again, Table 7.1 indicates that the growth itself (imports and exports) seems to be excessively high. Nevertheless, looking at the results of fifteen years, the outcomes can be considered poor and far away from ideal, especially when compared with Asian countries.

It is important to notice in Table 7.1 that most Latin American countries presented a negative balance trade during a long period of time. The results could suggest

Table 7.1 Trade development in the period 1990–2005 (in percentage, accumulated)

Countries	Imports (%)	Exports (%)	Trade Balance (*) (%)	Current account balance(**)
Argentina	510	313	−197	127%
Bolivia	264	323	+59	493%
Brazil	347	382	+35	528%
Chile	416	467	+51	218%
Colombia	363	281	−82	Negative
Costa Rica	457	495	+38	Negative
Cuba	Not registered	Estimated 159	Unknown	Not registered
Dominican Republic	507	548	+41	Negative
Ecuador	469	350	−119	Negative
El Salvador	471	470	−1	Negative
Guatemala	526	314	−212	Negative
Honduras	448	331	−117	Negative
Mexico	468	472	+4	Negative
Nicaragua	482	474	−8	Negative
Panama	253	242	−11	Negative
Paraguay	189	156	−33	Negative
Peru	371	471	+100	Negative
Suriname	183	163	20	Negative
Uruguay	279	235	−44	Negative
Venezuela	305	302	−3	+ 308%

Source: World Trade Organization (2007), adapted by the authors
(*) Trade Balance is the arithmetical difference between imports and exports per country, in the period 1990–2005
(**) Current Account Balance represents the sum Trade Balance + net factor incomes + transfer payments in the period 1990–2005

that WTO should re-visit David Ricardo's (Ricardo 1817) comparative advantage to better understand what happened to Latin America in the period 1990–2005.

Table 7.2 shows the low social and economic growth in Latin America. An important point to be observed is that no single Latin American nation presented a GNP *per capita* higher than US$ 9,000.00 in the year 2006.

It appears to be significant that about 8 million families in Latin America (out of 524 million inhabitants in the Region) can afford monthly installments of US$ 200 to cover college expenses (MEC/INEP).[1] By the way, only three Latin American universities are cited among the best 200 in the world. The University of Sao Paulo and the University of Campinas in Brazil are respectively ranked 175th and 177th positions. The National Autonomous University of Mexico occupies the 192nd (QS World University Rankings 2007).

---

[1] See www.inep.gov.br. Accessed 29 October 2009.

Table 7.2 Nominal GDP in the period 1990–2005

Countries	1990 (Millions US$)	2005 (Millions US$)	Population/ (thousands)/GNP* per capita in US$-2006	Average Growth rate 2004–2005 (%)
Central America				
Costa Rica	7.254	19.818	4.399/4,792	2.3
El Salvador	4.801	16.980	6.762/2,188	2.1
Guatemala	7.650	31.923	13.029/1,610	3.2
Honduras	3.049	8.374	6.969/1,365	4.2
Mexico	262.710	768.437	105.342/6,322	2.8
Nicaragua	3.598	4.910	5.532/843	4.0
Panama	6.077	15.241	3.288/4,749	5.5
South America				
Argentina	141.353	183.310	39.134/8,733	9.2
Bolivia	4.868	9.728	9.354/1,058	2.7
Brazil	438.228	799.413	189.323/4,021	3.3
Chile	33.507	111.339	16.465/5,873	5.9
Colombia	47.743	121.877	45.558/2,674	4.0
Ecuador	11.248	33.062	13.202/1,608	0.7
Guyana	396	786	739/858	−2.8
Paraguay	4.904	7.684	6.016/1,396	2.7
Peru	29.281	76.607	27.589/2,555	5.5
Suriname	467	1.503	455/2,343	5.1
Uruguay	8.368	16.792	3.331/6,770	6.4
Venezuela	47.028	132.373	27.191/5,429	9.3

Source: UNCTAD, 2008/CEPAL (United Nations, 2007), adapted by the authors
* Per capita gross product, at constant market prices – dollars at constant 2000 prices

According to Table 7.2, only 6 out of 19 countries achieved more than US$ 1 hundred billion of Nominal GDP in 2005. Brazil, Mexico and Argentina lead the group. Most Latin American countries depend considerably on exports of commodities in general to develop their economies. However, due to Doha Round decisions by developed countries, the barriers remain strong and seem to limit the growth of developing countries. The major reason why developing economies do not open up to the developed world is in response to those barriers. They may be procrastinating future social problems, as they open facilities for opportunism to manage countries with weak or no institutional rules. Douglas North, the 1993 Nobel Prize of Economics winner, stated: "Only countries that develop solid institutions will have progress" (North 2004).

Latin America ended 2009 with various leftist governors. Why? Singer's charges or arguments of 2002 still seem to be valid. No significant changes have occurred since then. A simple case, among others, could be added to Singer's report. In 2001, Brazil submitted a trade consultation question to the US through the WTO. No answer was received by 2008. Who is to be blamed for such a delay? Meanwhile, Brazil continued to face barriers in the introduction of certain goods in the US.

Not written down but apparently effective is that trade flow is tied up by economic interests that transcend the WTO limits of power. More bargaining articulation is given to developed nations as compared to developing ones. Speaking in financial terms, developing countries have had a very limited participation as members of the WTO. This issue is frequently summarized in the question: Does every member have the same power to vote in the sessions? If not, why? The transparency concept mentioned in the WTO purposes can become questionable, as dispute panels procedures are not described. It is not clear who is nominated to participate in a dispute judgment.

Interpretation seems to be another issue. As an example, the import of second hand tires into Brazil from other Latin American countries has been stopped by the WTO, while the EU received the exclusive right to be the only economic group to export those goods to Brazil. Apparently this is not what fair trade implies.

7.4.1 Protectionism and Barriers Suffered by Latin American Countries

Despite all efforts of developing countries to reduce tariffs, developed countries found new ways to reinforce protectionism on the basis of non-tariff barriers: sanitary, phytosanitary and environmental. A recent example is the European embargo towards Brazil, one of the most important beef exporters in the world, and the major supplier of the EU. A list of qualified sanitary farms, ready to export beef, was presented to the EU and refused. Disproportional criteria were required from some countries, characterizing a true protectionism measure to benefit Ireland. The Brazilian Government and the Associacao EuBrasil (EuBrazil Association) considered the decision a real boycott. Cristiana Muscardini, an Italian Congresswoman, sent a document to Mr. Markos Kiprianou, head of the European Health Commission, stating:

> One thing is correct: the European Union never registered a case of aphthous fever attributed to the beef imported from South America. As opposed to Ireland and the United Kingdom, Brazil currently has no registration of any case of mad cow and the beef exported to the European Union follows the standards established by the World Animal Health Organization, according to which the aphthous fever virus can not survive ... the restrictions are purely commercial and protectionist, with no scientific basis. (Muscardini 2007, our translation)

Similar controversy seems to exist in the WTO concerning the Agriculture Agreement. Constant conflicts of interest between developed and developing countries rise due to the lack of compliance with the commitments assumed in the Uruguay Round (Jank 2005; Carvalho 2007). The current ethanol case is a typical example.

> A Brazilian sector that may attract more international attention in what relates to agricultural subsidies is the sugar-alcohol production. The catalyser of this process would be a proposal

from the United States to establish a partnership with Brazil, broadening the global market for ethanol, so that this product could become a global commodity. Such a partnership foresees the involvement of other South American countries, either in the biofuel production or the consolidation of the consumer market. (Carvalho 2007, p. 88).

Jank (2005) calls attention to the circumstances that may lead to a new kind of protectionism. When the main focus of discussions and negotiations related to the Agriculture Agreement are the reduction of subsidies and tariffs, and the increase of quotas of exports, new trends seem to be consolidating the application of sanitary and phytosanitary measures to food products. The Sanitary and Phytosanitary (SPS) Agreement seems to be an efficient support for agricultural protectionism, due to the rapid results that each of these measures can generate.

Taking this into consideration, it seems strange that the WTO allows an exception to free trade as a protectionist measure, using as tools the high and legitimate interests of protecting human, animal and vegetable life and health. "Between 1995 and 2004, 204 specific trade issues related to the SPS Agreement were detected by the WTO Secretariat." (Carvalho 2007, pp. 88–89).

Several situations have been analyzed by the Agency for Solving Controversies, which belongs to the WTO. For instance, the Peruvian *sardine* generated a recent controversial issue. Its species was classified as *Sardinopus Sagax*, found in the Pacific coast of Peru and Chile. In the North Atlantic and in the Mediterranean, the common species was named *Sardina pilchardus*. Both were sold as tinned sardines. In 2001, the EU claimed that only products using *S. pilchardus* could be sold for tinned sardines. Peru's appeal was accepted in 2002 (Carvalho 2007).

It is also clear that Article X: 3 of the GATT 1994 establishes certain minimum standards for transparency and procedural fairness in the administration of trade regulations which, in our view, are not met here. The non-transparent and *ex parte* nature of the internal governmental procedures applied by the competent officials in the Office of Marine Conservation, the Department of State, and the US National Marine Fisheries Service throughout the certification processes under Section 609, as well as the fact that countries whose applications are denied do not receive formal notice of such denial, nor of the reasons for the denial, and the fact, too, that there is no formal legal procedure for review of, or appeal from, a denial of an application, are all contrary to the spirit, if not the letter, of Article X:3 of the GATT 1994 (Da Silva 2002):

> The provisions of Article X: 3191 of the GATT 1994 bear upon this matter. In our view, Section 609 falls within the "laws, regulations, judicial decisions and administrative rulings of general application" described in Article X: 1. Inasmuch as there are due process requirements generally for measures that are otherwise imposed in compliance with WTO obligations, it is only reasonable that rigorous compliance with the fundamental requirements of due process should be required in the application and administration of a measure which purports to be an exception to the treaty obligations of the Member imposing the measure and which effectively results in a suspension *pro hac vice* of the treaty rights of other Members. (Da Silva 2002).

Since 1991, Brazil has suffered such barriers in other fruits or vegetables, regarding the Sanitary and Phytosanitary (SPS) agreement. Long inspection and liberation processes either in local ports, or in the importer countries, mostly in the US characterizes the protectionism that jeopardizes the developing nations, condemning them to become only suppliers of primary goods for developed countries and going against the equal conditions preconized by the WTO (Moraes 1995):

> Despite progress, SPS measures remain significant barriers in many cases, in part driven by Brazil's implementation of the harmonized phytosanitary standards of the Southern Cone Phytosanitary Committee (COSAVE). Brazil prohibits the entry of poultry products from the United States, alleging lack of reciprocity. The issue, however, should not be reciprocity, but rather the fulfillment of WTO obligations regarding sanitary and phytosanitary decisions, which dictate that such determinations shall be based only upon sufficient scientific evidence. Brazilian legislation bans the importation of beef produced with growth hormones; however, beef imports from the United States have been allowed on a waiver basis since 1991. (Da Silva 2002).

The Doha Round still does not include this issue in the agendas of the WTO meetings. The complexity of SPS measures, as well as the stages of application and requirements to be followed, seems to bring more difficulties to negotiations, mainly with the EU (Da Silva 2002).

Negotiations around the SPS Agreements can be polarized by developed countries, which reflect the consumers' always more severe requirements concerning quality and control. The developing countries interpret these measures as dissimulated trade barriers (Thorstensen 2003; Carvalho 2007).

7.4.2 Sustainable Development and the Environment

The sustainable development concept has become a development paradigm in the last decade with special interest in multilateral organizations, governments, development agencies, NGOs and private sector, in many areas, but mostly in health and organic products. Protection of the environment generated several multilateral agreements and conventions. Some of them are:

- (b) necessary to protect human, animal or plant life or health; (...);
- (g) relating to the conservation of exhaustible natural resources if such measures are made effective in conjunction with restrictions on domestic production or consumption. (GATT 1947, Art. XX, pp. 27, 28)

The WTO is not and has no intention to be an environmental protection agency. Nevertheless, in its area of competence promoting the relationship between trade and environment, its policies are limited to the commercial objectives, and to the significant impact of the environmental aspects upon the trade activities (WTO 2004). In this sense, members do not expect that the WTO offers answers to the environmental issues. They do believe that the trade and environmental policies are mutually complementary:

> In reaching these conclusions, we wish to underscore what we have not decided in this appeal. We have not decided that the protection and preservation of the environment is of no significance to the Members of the WTO. Clearly, it is. We have not decided that the

sovereign nations that are Members of the WTO cannot adopt effective measures to protect endangered species, such as sea turtles. Clearly, they can and should. And we have not decided that sovereign states should not act together bilaterally, plurilaterally or multilaterally, either within the WTO or in other international *fora*, to protect endangered species or to otherwise protect the environment. Clearly, they should and do (Da Silva 2002).

Thus, the WTO is not involved with environmental legislations, but with the intensity of laws and rules that may interfere in the trade of products, meaning to balance environmental concerns and free trade. Extreme protectionism exists in some developed countries that mostly encourage developing nations to adopt free trade. With this practice, developing countries find difficulty in accessing the market of products and services that compete with those of the developed countries (Carvalho 2007).

Even though some Latin Americans perceive the current WTO president as positive and fair, nonetheless, it is generally believed that the WTO is dominated by unfair neo-liberal economic attitudes. Certainly, almost nothing has been changed, in the sense of putting into effective practice the written rules. For instance, contracting parties agree that there is a need for positive efforts designed to assure that less developed contracting parties secure a share in the growth in international trade commensurate with the needs of their economic development (Carvalho and Barbieri, 2008).

Details of the WTO definition, mission and principles indicate outstanding humanitarian and economic concerns. However, what is observed in Latin America is that the WTO administrators treat certain issues with an exclusive economic power bias, or allow politics to influence and guide some resolutions and conclusions. In this sense, Singer's four charges to WTO may be perceived as applicable and may be used, as per analogy, in limited circumstances, as related to the local power in towns and cities in Latin America.

A group of Latin American authors of books and booklets denouncing corruption in different spheres declares that a permanent supervision and monitoring of public administrators' lives is an ethical way to lead the political system into justice. It impels organizations to be honest and fair both internally and abroad. This requires available information, which is expensive and time consuming. One publication refers to the case of Ribeirao Bonito, a town of Sao Paulo State, in Brazil. Founders of the "Friends of Ribeirao Bonito" organization, monitoring the acts of public local administrators, led the mayor to be impeached from governance of the town. He was sued, and several judicial processes were started, implicating him in various sorts of crimes. This case reflects the abuse of power by corrupted politicians to the detriment of the system. The population supports many private and non-governmental organizations in Latin America, to avoid the proliferation of corruption, which is deeply perceived as a cancer that destroys any society. Because of the stigma of corruption in the Region, Latin Americans are more and more reluctant to comply with immoral ways to do business.

Most countries in Latin America have their own ethics institutions, generally established in the form of a non-governmental organization, which independently monitor private and state enterprises. The Asociacion Latinoamericana de Etica, Negocios y Economia (Latin American Association of Business, Economics, and Ethics, ALENE)[2] was created in 1998, and the most active members live in Argentina, Bolivia, Brazil, Chile, Ecuador and Peru. Its regular meetings enable it to maintain the objective of questioning and discussing ethical issues in governments and companies in the Region. Other organizations in Latin America are very active and dynamic, aiming mostly at corporate social responsibility and sustainability. It is often seen that socially and environmentally responsible enterprises attract investments, as corporate codes of ethics are perceived as a clue that the organization is ready to start a substantial negotiation.

7.4.3 Moral Norms Framework

De George (1993) states that moral norms in international business can be universally formulated, despite different interpretations related to characteristics of different societies:

> Some general ethical norms apply to any business operating anywhere. These norms are universally applicable because they are necessary either for a society to function or for business transactions to take place. They are widely held, and everyone is expected to live by them and up to them; they are obvious, common sensical, and available to all. If they were arcane or difficult or available only to an intellectual elite, they could not serve as basic norms governing all human interactions. (De George 1993, p. 19)

Fairness in international trade and investments can be observed through prohibition against arbitrariness in commerce, truthfulness, transparency, and respect for properties, citizens, companies and governments. The WTO could certainly be the sphere to assure that these ethical values are present in all rules and agreements.

> We can speak similarly about exercising fairness in business dealings. If there were not some minimum level of trust between buyer and seller on international level, just as on the national level, business transactions would prove impossible ... lack of fairness undermines the systems and works against the norm of efficiency so important to the workings of a free market. (De George 1993, p. 21)

According to this perspective:

> ... these general ethical norms apply to all businesses in all countries and across all borders; they do not depend on one's ethical theory (p. 21) ... The reason why the norms apply no matter which of the basic ethical theories one adopts is that of these theories attempt to justify these norms, which are pretheoretic. (De George 1993, p. 199)

Just as it is expected that multinational companies operate with integrity abroad as they do in their home country, so too governments should be careful when negotiating through multilateral or bilateral agreements. De George (1993) calls

---

[2] See www.alene.org Accessed 31 October 2009.

attention to differences that may occur in doing business in the international scenario:

- Absence of many legal and other restraints that constrain American business at home;
- Varying outlooks, needs and practices of foreign societies and of multinational corporations from those countries;
- Presence of corruption of governmental and other levels within some societies that far exceeds the corruption found in the United States (which has its fair share);
- Economic power between the largest of the multinationals and the smallest and the frailest of the less developed countries in which they sometimes operate (De George 1993, p. 22).

These same procedures should be applied to the decisions of the WTO. Mahoney (1999) encourages organizations to develop a climate of compliance with the approved procedures. It not only facilitates ethical behavior, but encourages individuals to act in ways which on occasion may not be foreseen by these established procedures. In this sense, the virtue ethics can bring out more than any other ethical theory applied to business activities. "There is no substitute for the integrity, including the trustworthiness, loyalty, and moral courage of the individual person working within the company and for its best interests" (Mahoney 1999, p. 258). This rationale is applicable to all persons involved with the WTO, if the goal is to reach the common good.

7.5 Developments in Latin America to Address the Ethical Issues

Based upon Elkington's triple bottom line model, and the SustainAbility assumptions, a Brazilian sustainability index was created in 2006, as a joint effort of BOVESPA (Sao Paulo Stock Exchange), Fundacao Getulio Vargas (Center of Studies on Sustainability of the Business School in Sao Paulo) and other organizations. Over 200 large companies filled out questionnaires, and a ranking of the 20 most sustainable was published in *Revista Exame*, a leading business magazine in Brazil. The publication of these results has served as benchmarking for enterprises – including state owned corporations – willing to become more transparent and eliminate organizational corruption, which indicates deep commitment with social and environmental responsibility, transparency and corporate governance. In 2007, these companies were: Accor, Acesita, Amanco, Aracruz, Arcelor, Basf, Brasken, Caterpillar, CPFL, Elektro, IBM, Itau, Mapfre, Natura, Philips, Promon, Banco Real, Serasa, Suzano, and Unilever.

These reports are submitted once a year, aiming to measure sustainability in its strategic, economic, financial, environmental and social aspects. At times ethics is understood as one more characteristic of sustainability, while ethicists stress that it has to be the basis, the essence of the process.

It is expected that within ten years similar contests will attract more than five hundred companies in the whole Region, also called *The Latin American Continent*. It will imply more transparency and less corruption in a generalized context, where governments will be involved in the process in a natural manner. From 2010 onwards, Brazilian companies expanding IPO's in the Stock Exchange will have to adapt themselves to the International Financial Reporting Standards, corresponding to the Sarbanes-Oxley procedures in the US. Their true commitment with ethics and sustainability will then be clear.

Just as the criticism of WTO measures was brought up by this Latin American Panel, expecting immediate effective changes for the good, in terms of actions versus goals, WTO deserves the compliments from this Panel for some positive efforts regarding the Trade-Related Aspects of Intellectual Property Rights (TRIPS) in the last few years. Correa (2000) shows that TRIPS contain elements which whenever adequately applied allow a certain equilibrium in its implementation. For example, the agreement establishes in its preamble the recognition of the basic objectives of political policies of national systems for the protection of the intellectual property, including the objectives of technological development.

The 7th Article, referring to objectives of the agreement, declares that the protection to these rights may contribute to the promotion of the technological innovation, the transfer and diffusion of technology, in mutual benefit of producers and users of technological knowledge, in a way conducive to the social and economical welfare and a balance between rights and obligations.

The 8th Article establishes among the agreement principles that members, by formulating or amending laws and rulings, may adopt necessary measures to protect public health and nutrition, as well as to protect the public interests and sectors of vital interest for its social economical development. It also determines that measures may be adopted in order to avoid the abuse of proprietors of those rights or in order to avoid practices that limit in an unjustifiable way the commerce or affect adversely the transfer of international technology. Among those measures, Correa (2000) cites the parallel import admissibility, according to the international principle of exhaustion of rights, contemplated in the 6th Article of TRIPS; the non-patentability of substances existent in nature, plants, animals, and the compulsory license. The preamble, objectives and principles of the agreements administered by WTO are frequently used by the Controversy Solution Agency to mitigate conflicts.

Two relevant points are to be recommended to those responsible for TRIPS at WTO:

1. The question of technology transfer as a promise by TRIPS still remains a critical blank to be filled out (Barbieri and Chamas 2008)
2. Latin American countries find limited capacity to develop and to deal with many details in terms of intellectual property and commerce. It is imperative that urgent investments in human resources and in capabilities in intellectual property be made, so that those countries may be in condition to analyze and propose public policies concerning economic, technological, and industrial development. In a more intensive and continuous basis, they could influence the global debate.

7.6 Final Considerations

Singer points out the importance of the WTO:

> Even those who accept the general argument for the economic benefits of a global free
> market should ask themselves how well a global free market can work in the absence of any
> global authority to set minimum standards on issues like child labor, worker safety, the right
> to form a union, and environmental and animal welfare protection. (Singer 2002, p. 103).

An honest, transparent, egalitarian, and fair global leadership could lead nations to discuss their ethical dilemmas in the light of social and economic justice. It should not be overlooked that even in developing countries there are intellectuals aware of crises and trends in political, economic, and social arenas. It seems to be the case of the Doha Round: why are the negotiations of the Doha Round moving backwards, instead of forwards? This might happen because the US and the EU have a common understanding about settling agribusinesses, according to their respective interests: the US, by cutting down subsidies; the EU, by defining less or lower tariffs. In a related step, developing countries as Brazil, Argentina, Mexico, among others, are pressured to make more concessions in the manufacturing industry, services, and, nowadays, in the environmental area as well. It means that developed countries offer a little, as compensation for the higher prices charged. Up to a certain level, the developing countries ask themselves whether it is worthwhile to negotiate.

The agribusiness market is a good example of these trends: many countries have already cut import tariffs to combat inflation. As food prices are high, they reduce the duties to allow cheaper imports. Currently, the situation has reached a point in which the reduced import duties became higher than what the Doha Round may offer.

For Latin Americans, it seems clear that global negotiation brings results, provided that there is an effective agreement. Such an agreement will possibly be implemented within perhaps ten years. This means that the tariff cutting or subsidies will not happen all of a sudden. This is why Argentina states that the country has already earned what it had to earn in agribusiness. Indeed, the reduction of tariffs has already happened. In this context, why should Latin Americans accept the price to expand its market for foreign industrial and consumer products?

This is the most common picture perceived in the Region. Developed countries agree among themselves and pressure the emergent. Developing countries like Mexico, Argentina, Brazil, among others, have the feeling that they do not need to make concessions in other areas to obtain worldwide agribusiness openings, which necessarily occur due to the increase of food prices. What could then be expected? Will the Doha Round negotiations be settled by 2010? Hopefully they will. Significant movements seem to be influencing the trends: Mexico or Brazil joining G8, active participation in G20, intensive agreements through Mercado Comun del Sur (MERCOSUR), or Southern Cone Common Market (MERCOSUR 2008).

Rich countries manipulating the poor has led Latin Americans to think that they can be cheated by the First World with the consent and approval of the WTO.

This cannot be considered positive in institutional terms, which is aiming at the preservation of good customs and at friendly relationship among peoples.

If trade or commerce were the only reason for creating the WTO, maybe GATT and other mechanisms might have been enough. Development should be pursued as an objective, as sustainability becomes the order of the day (Carvalho 2007). Consensus in multilateral agreements, characteristic of WTO, will occur only if the nation-members aim at the same target. Barriers, tariffs, antidumping, anticorruption and several other practices will make sense only if there is a fair trade in the international context. This requires a high level of ethical commitment on all sides and respect to the economic vocation of each country. Growth without development does not lead to sustainability. Narlikar (2006) emphasizes the significant role of India and Brazil as large developing countries in WTO and concludes, as follows, that her paper:

> ... has traced the process through which notions of fairness, as advanced by developing countries, have evolved in the WTO since the early days of the GATT. It is still too early to asses the effectiveness of re-introducing the fairness-as-equity discourse into the WTO, but the strategy of challenging the institution on its own terms by framing issues in conformity with its underlying norms seems to have already generated some success. Perhaps the biggest indicator of the new-found sensitivity to the concerns of developing countries is the name of the new round, the Doha *Development* Agenda. Paragraph 2 of the main Ministerial Declaration states: *The majority of WTO member are developing countries. We seek to place their needs and interests at the heart of the Work Programme adopted in this Declaration.* (p. 1028).

A lack of greater development outcomes in developing countries can be the result of the policy of preferences. On one side, trade may enable a unidirectional economic growth and development. On the other side, each country may adopt its own trade and investment policies and strategies, in line with its development needs (Ochieng 2007).

Thanks to Latin American idealists with ethical principles in business, corruption possibly will reduce power in the medium and long run (Paladino et al. 2007; Schmidt 2000). Similarly, with the same degree of effort, rich countries must change the image for fair business doers in the short run. Initiatives as the sustainability index will reinforce the need of changes in enterprises and in society. This should occur in such a way that investments, production, and trade serve as levers for prosperity, to the benefit of all Latin Americans.

Hayes and Moore (2005, p. 3) point out that, according to FINE,[3] an informal network that involves several institutions in Europe, an acceptable definition of Fair Trade is: "Fair Trade is a Trading Partnership, based on dialogue, transparency and respect, that seeks greater equity in international trade." So far, this concept seems to mean more for trade among enterprises than among nations. Under the Latin American point of view, provided WTO works under these guidelines, life would

---

[3] FINE (2008). An informal network that involves Fairtrade Labelling Organizations International (FLO), the International Federation for Alternative Trade (IFAT), the Network of European World Shops (NEWS!) and the European Fair Trade Association (EFTA).

be better for all, because it would bring and support a real development among countries worldwide.

The objective of this chapter was not to offer a deep analysis of actions taken by the WTO regarding Latin America, but to raise discussions on the proposals made by the Coordination of the ISBEE Congress. However, future studies can add contributions from other Latin-American perspectives, mainly in what is related to ethics in the Region. Similar or different research projects or surveys are strongly encouraged, so that information can be shared and compared with other countries. Interesting findings may emerge.

The intention here was not to offer a one sided criticism of the WTO, but to raise issues that may improve the image of an institution created by governments, aiming at the improvement and development of countries in the whole world.

Acknowledgement The authors are deeply grateful to Professor Geoff Moore for his comments and contribution, while coordinating the panel on Fairness in International Trade and Investments, during the Fourth ISBEE World Congress in Cape Town, South Africa, 2008 (International Society of Business, Economics, and Ethics). The reviewers' comments were also extremely useful.

The authors also express their gratitude toward national and international institutions in different Latin American countries, which dedicated time and attention to providing adequate information. Without it, the ideas here registered might have been understood as emotional.

Abbreviations

BOVESPA	Bolsa de Valores do Estado de Sao Paulo (Sao Paulo Stock Exchanage)
ECLAC	Economic Commission for Latin America and Caribbean
EU	European Union
GATT	General Agreement on Tariffs and Trade
GDP	Gross Domestic Product
IADB	Inter-American Development Bank
ICC	International Chamber of Commerce
ISBEE	International Society of Business, Economics, and Ethics
MEC/INEP	Instituto Nacional de Estudos e Pesquisas Educacionais Anísio Teixeira – Ministério de Educação
MERCOSUR	Mercado Comun del Sur
NGO	Non-Governmental Organization
OECD	Organization for Economic Co-Operation and Development
UK	United Kingdom
UN	United Nations Organization
UNCTAD	United Nation Conference on Trade and Development
US	United States of America
WTO	World Trade Organization

References

Abramo, C. W. 2007a, O Que Fazer. *Folha de S. Paulo*, Feb. 8. http://www.transparencia.org.br/index/htm. Accessed 30 April 2008.

Abramo, C. W. 2007b, Parlamento Capturado. *Folha de S. Paulo.* April 12. http://www.transparencia.org.br/index/html Accessed 30 April 2008; http://www.deunojornal.org.br/materia.asp?mat=151640 Accessed 30 April 2008.

Barbieri, J. C. and Chamas, C. I. 2008, O Acordo Sobre Direitos de Propriedade Intelectual Relacionados ao Comercio (TRIPS) e as Politicas Publicas de Saude e de Defesa da Biodiversidade. *REAd (Review of Administration)*, *Edicao* 59, 14 (1), Jan-Apr.

BBC News 24, 2008. http://news.bbc.co.uk/1/hi/world/europe/copuntry_profiles/2429503.stm Accessed 10 Mar 2008.

Brown, A. G. and Stern, R. M. 2007, Concepts of Fairness in the Global Trading System. *Pacific Economic Review* **12** (3), 293–318.

Carvalho, A. 2007, *Rotulos Abientais Oganicos como Ferramenta de Acesso a Mercado de Paises Desenvolvidos.* Unpublished doctoral dissertation, Escola de Administracao de Empresas de Sao Paulo da Fundacao Getulio Vargas, Sao Paulo, SP, Brazil

Carvalho, A. and Barbieri, J. C. 2008, Comercio: 60 Anos de Controversias. *Pagina 22* 17 Marco, 32–35.

Castells, M. 1975, *The Urban Question: A Marxist Approach* (Edward Arnold, London).

Correa, C. M. 2000) *Intellectual Property Rights, The WTO and Developing Countries* (Third World Network, Penang, Malaysia).

Da Silva Neto, O. C. 2002, *D-Goods – Technical Barriers to Trade.* WTO http://www.tralac.org/scripts/content.php?id=321 Accessed 8 April 8 2008.

Davidson, D., Matusz, S., and Nelson, D. 2006, Fairness and the Political Economy of Trade. *The World Economy* doi: 10.1111/j.1467-9701.2006.00832.x

De George, R. T. 1993, *Competing With Integrity in International Business* (Oxford University Press, New York, NY).

De Jasay, A. 2006, When Fair Is Not Just and Just is Not Fair. *The Independent Review* XI (2), 165–176.

Djelic, M. L. and Quack, S. 2003, *Globalization and Institutions: Redefining the Rules of the Economic Game.* In G. M. Hodgson (Series Editor) (Edward Elgar Publishing Limited, Northampton, MA).

ECLAC 2006, *Latin America and the Caribbean in the World Economy* 2005–2006 (ECLAC/UN Division of International Trade and Integration, Santiago, Chile), October.

Franck, T. 1995, *Fairness in International Law and Institutions* (Clarendon Press, Oxford).

GATT 1947, The General Agreement on Tariffs and Trade – *GATT 1947.* http://www.wto.org/english/docs_e/legal_e/gatt47_02_e.htm Accessed 13 November 2009.

Guia Exame 2007 de Sustentabilidade. The List of 20 Company-Models of Corporate Social Responsibility in Brazil (Sustainability). *Revista Exame* (Editora Abril, Sao Paulo, Brazil), December.

Hayes, M. and Moore, G. 2005, *The Economics of Fair Trade: A Guide in Plain English.* http://www.fairtraderesearch.net Accessed 6 February 2008.

Inter-American Development Bank – IADB 2007a, Health Technical Note 03/2007. May. http://www.iadb.org/sds/publication/publication_4640_e.htm Accessed 30 April 2008.

Inter-American Development Bank – IADB 2007b, *Toward Sustainable and Equitable Development. Sector strategies for Latin America and the Caribbean: An overview.* http://www.iadb.org/sds/publication/publication_3635_e.htm Accessed 30 April 2008.

International Chamber of Commerce – ICC 2008, *Banking Regulation Brochure.* UCP 600 training online. Access 31 May 2008. www.iccwbo.org/uploadedFiles/ICC/ICC_Home_Page/pages/ICC_2008.pdf

Jank, M. 2005, Agricultura, in V. Thorstensen and M. Jank (eds.). *O Brasil e os Grandes Temas do Comercio Internacional* (Ed. Aduaneiras, Sao Paulo, Brazil) Chap. 2, pp. 37–70.

Klapper, B.S. 2007, The WTO Is Running Out Of Last Chances For Trade Talks. *The Associated Press*. 22 June 2007. http://www.iht.com/articles/2007/06/22/business/trade.php Accessed 31 May 2008

Llano, C. 1991a, *El Empresario y Su Accion* (McGraw-Hill/Interamericana de Mexico, Mexico, D.F.).

Llano, C. 1991b, El Empresario y Su Mundo (McGraw-Hill/Interamericana de Mexico, Mexico, D.F.).

Llano, C. 1991c, El Empresario Ante La Responsabilidad y La Motivacion (McGraw-Hill/Interamericana de Mexico, Mexico, D.F.).

Mahoney, J. 1999, Moral courage in business, in Enderle, G. (ed.). *International Business Ethics: Challenges and Approaches* (The University of Noter Dame Press, Noter Dame, IN), pp. 249–259.

MERCOSUR 2008, – *Mercado Comun del Sur.* http://www.mercosur.int Accessed 10 April 2008.

Moraes, R. 1995, *Celso Furtado: O Subdesenvolvimento e As Ideias da CEPAL* (Editora Atica, Sao Paulo, Brazil).

Muscardini, C. 2007, In M. Bizzotto (ed.). *Para Brasil, Embargo A Carne E Arbitrario.* BBCBrasil.com Brussels. http://www.bbc.co.uk/portuguese/reporterbbc/story/2008/01/080130_embargocarnereacao_mb_bg.shtml Accessed 8 April 2008.

Narlikar, A. 2006, Fairness in International Trade Negotiations: Developing Countries in the GATT and WTO. *The World Economy*, Doi: 10.1111/j.1467-9701.2006.00833.*x*

North, D. 2004, Statement. In C. Mano. Eles Controlam o Mercado. *Portal Exame*. November 3.

Ochieng, C. M. O. 2007, The EU-ACP Economic Partnership Agreements and the 'Development Question': Constraints and Opportunities Posed by Article XXIV and Special NS differential Treatment Provisions of the TWO. *Journal of International Economic Law* **10** (2), 363–395.

Osland, J., Franco, S., and Osland, A. 1999, Organizational Implication of Latin Culture: Lessons for the Expatriate Manager. *Journal of Management Inquiry* 8 (2 June)(Sage Publications, Newbury Park, California), pp. 219–234.

Paladino, M., Debeljuh, P., and Delbosco, P. 2007, *Integridad*. 1st Ed. (Emece Editores, Buenos Aires, Argentina).

QS University Ranking. http://www.topuniversities.com Accessed 29 October 2009.

Ricardo, D. 1817, *The Principles of Political Economy and Taxation* (J.M. Dent & Sons, New York), 1911 (1st publication).

Schmidt, E. 2000, *Etica y Negocios para America Latina*. 3rd ed. (Universidad del Pacifico, Lima, Peru); OXY.

Singer, P. 2002, *One World: The Ethics of Globalisation* (The Text Publishing Company, Melbourne, Australia).

Suranovic, S. M. 2000, A Positive Analysis of Fairness with Applications to International Trade. *The World Economy* 23, 283–308.

Thorstensen, V. 2003, *OMC: As Regras do Comercio Internacional e a Nova Rodada de Negociacoes Multilaterais*. 2nd edn. (Ed. Aduaneiras, Sao Paulo, Brazil).

Transparencia Brasil 2008, http://www.transparencia.org.br/index/html Accessed 30 April 2008.

Transparency International: 2007, The Global Coalition Against Corruption. http://www.transparency.org/ Accessed 30 April 2008.

United Nations Conference on Trade and Development – UNCTAD 2008, *UNCTAD Handbook of Statistics 2006–07* (UNCTAD, Geneva, Switzerland) p. 438. http://www.unctad.org/en/docs/tdstat31_en.pdf Accessed 30 April 2008.

United Nations 2007, *Link Global Economic Outlook* (Development Policy and Analysis Division/UN, New York, NY) November, p. 42. Accessed 30 April 2008. http://www.un.org/esa/policy/link/addisababa07/linkgeo_fall07%20final.pdf

World Trade Organization – WTO 2004, *Avaliação do Impacto de Sustentabilidade Comercial (SIA) do Acordo de Associacao em Neegociacao entre a Comunidade Europeia e o MERCOSUL, Síntese final e Estudos Setoriais. Retalorio Inicial (Proposta de Consulta). (Original: Sustainability Impact Assessment of WTO Negotiations)*. The University of

Manchester, London, UK. www.sia-trade.org/mercosur Accessed on 13 November 2009; www.sia-trade.org/.../OVERVIEW_INCEPTION_summary%20(PORT).pdf Accessed on 13 November 2009; http://www.wto.org/english/res_e/statis_e/its2007_e/its2007_e.pdf Accessed 30 April 2008.

World Trade Organization – WTO 2008). http://www.wto.org Accessed 30 April 2008.

Chapter 8
Fairness in International Trade and Business Ethics: A Japanese Perspective

Iwao Taka

8.1 Introduction

The following questions were raised by the FITI project. Therefore, the purpose of this chapter is to answer all those questions.

1. To what extent are the workings and outcomes of the World Trade Organization (WTO) perceived as fair in your region/continent?
2. What are the main ethical issues regarding international trade and investment (or alternatively the WTO) in your region/continent?
3. What developments are there in your region/continent to address the above ethical issues?

In order to answer those three questions, in this chapter, we will refer to the following six points:

(1) Formal Position of the Japanese Government on the WTO
(2) From the WTO-Centered to the Bilateral EPA Approach
(3) A Typical Ethical Issue for Japan: Protecting Rice Farming
(4) Reconsideration over Globalization and the WTO: Poverty Reduction
(5) Initiatives by the Japanese Government: MDGs and TICAD
(6) Initiatives by Leading Japanese Corporations: Education and Basic Infrastructure

With regard to the first question, "To what extent are the workings and outcomes of the WTO perceived as fair in Japan?" we will answer by referring to point (1) and (2) at Sections 8.2 and 8.3. As for the second question, "What are the main ethical issues regarding international trade and investment (or alternatively the WTO) in Japan?" we will pick two ethical issues, (3) protecting rice farming and (4) poverty

I. Taka (✉)
Professor of Business Ethics, Reitaku University, Kashiwa, Japan;
Visiting Professor, Kyoto University, Kyoto, Japan
e-mail: itaka@reitaku-ac.jp

G. Moore (ed.), *Fairness in International Trade*, The International Society
of Business, Economics, and Ethics Book Series 1, DOI 10.1007/978-90-481-8840-6_8,
© Springer Science+Business Media B.V. 2010

reduction, each of which is discussed at Sections 8.4 and 8.5. In order to answer the last question, "What developments are there in Japan to address the ethical issues?" we will introduce initiatives taken (5) by the Japanese Government and (6) by leading Japanese corporations at Sections 8.6 and 8.7.

8.2 Formal Position of the Japanese Government on the WTO

The first question is "To what extent are the workings and outcomes of the WTO perceived as fair in Japan?" In order to answer this question, we will highlight the formal position of the Japanese Government on the WTO and EPAs as the following two sections.

8.2.1 Free Trade and the WTO Are Indispensable for Development

Like other developed countries, the Japanese Government basically has seen that the WTO and its Agreement are necessary and desirable for developing the global economy. In accordance with the preamble of the Agreement Establishing The World Trade Organization, *The 2007 Report on Compliance by Major Trading Partners with Trade Agreement* published by the Ministry of Economy, Trade, and Industry (METI) of Japan describes the objectives of the WTO Agreement as raising living standards, ensuring full employment, growing income and effective demand, and expanding the production of and trade in goods and services (METI 2007a: 247).

Japan has long benefited from the free trading system based upon the GATT. Thanks to this system, after World War II, it miraculously revived out of the devastating situation it faced, and has grown up to be one of the biggest economies in the world. Because of this, Japan is likely to think that free trade is an indispensable basis for nations' economic development, and is a very effective activity to get nations out of poverty. With regard to solving poverty issues, this way of thinking is very much like a conclusion of the WTO secretariat study published in the year 2000: It says, "trade liberalization helps poor countries to catch up with rich ones," and "faster economic growth helps to alleviate poverty" (WTO 2000). The Japanese Government basically agrees with this conclusion.

8.2.2 Provisions on Exemptions Are Necessary

Due to this, the Japanese Government supports the WTO's fundamental principles like Most-Favored-Nation Treatment, National Treatment, and General Prohibition of Quantitative Restrictions, because those principles are very clear and simple to understand, and are designed to remove various barriers for the purpose of promoting international trade.

But at the same time, when Japan was at the earlier developmental stage, it took various protective measures such as import control, restrictions on foreign investment, and supports for technological developments of private corporations (Oxfam 2002: 231–232). Therefore, while welcoming the free trading system, the Japanese Government also shares understanding over the necessity of exceptions to those fundamental principles. Namely, it considers that the fundamental principles should not be enforced to all nations at once and uniformly (Oxfam 2002: 233). Especially when developing countries have not yet fostered enough abilities to fulfill their trade obligations, Japan believes that the WTO Members (Members) should provide them with a special status (METI 2007a: 249).

For this reason, the Japanese Government appreciates the fact that the WTO considers not only traditional matters but also new issues such as environmental protection and developing countries (METI 2007a: 247). As for environmental consideration, the WTO allows "the optimal use of the world's resources in accordance with the objective of sustainable development," which makes it possible for each country to protect and preserve the environment in a way consistent with their needs and concerns at different stages of economic development. As for consideration for developing countries, the WTO expects developed countries to make efforts to ensure that developing countries, especially the least developed countries, enjoy a share of the growth in international trade (METI 2007a: 251; Urata et al. 2007: 26).

8.2.3 List of Annexes

Up until the Uruguay Round (from 1986 to 1994), the GATT had concentrated on introducing tariffs to trade in all goods (except for agricultural products). Its main strategy had been (1) to replace quantitative restrictions with tariffs, and then (2) to gradually reduce tariff rates through negotiations on a reciprocal basis. In other words, before the Uruguay Round, it was not so complicated for Members to understand how the GATT worked. At the same time, because Members did not raise serious questions on agricultural policies of developed countries, the GATT worked in favor of industrialized countries. But this picture started to change drastically during the Uruguay Round.

On the one hand, developing countries began to criticize the agricultural policies of developed countries, insisting that import restrictions on agriculture products should be replaced with tariffs, tariff rates should be reduced, and export subsidies and domestic support should be abolished as early as possible. On the other hand, developed countries proposed that the WTO Agreement include agreements designed to liberalize services (GATS) and designed to protect intellectual property rights (TRIPs), expecting to enter services market in developing countries, and to prevent developing countries from using intellectual properties free of charge.

GATS and TRIPs were the last things developing countries wanted to include so that they strongly opposed this proposal. But since developed countries did not make any concession on this proposal, in the end, in exchange for GATS and TRIPs, developing countries requested to add agreements on agriculture and textiles, hoping

Table 8.1 Contents of the WTO agreement

AGREEMENT establishing the World Trade Organization (Marrakesh Agreement)
ANNEX 1
ANNEX 1A: Multilateral Agreements on Trade in Goods
(b) Agreement on Agriculture
(d) Agreement on Textiles and Clothing
ANNEX 1B: General Agreement on Trade in Services (GATS)
ANNEX 1C: Agreement on Trade-Related Aspects of Intellectual Property Rights (TRIPs)

that those sectors of developed countries would be liberalized in a way consistent with GATT basic rules. What is more, developing countries urged the developed countries to introduce provisions of Special and Differential Treatment (SDT) to most of the WTO agreements. Therefore SDT provisions are now spread across almost all the agreements.

The result of compromising and coordinating processes between developed and developing countries is now clearly reflected in Annex 1 (Table 8.1). In response to developing countries' requests, ANNEX IA now includes new agreements like Agreement on Agriculture and Agreement on Textiles and Clothing. In response to developed countries' requests, ANNEX IB (GATS), and IC (TRIPs) are newly created.

Even if the Japanese Government formally supports the WTO and its purpose, we have to admit that from the beginning of its establishment, the WTO has grappled with complicated issues, many of which are extremely controversial and mutually exclusive (METI and Keidanren 2007: 5). At the same time, because the WTO decision-making process is consensus-based, and because the Membership has rapidly increased to over 150, it has been getting more and more difficult for Members to reach an agreement within the WTO framework.

8.3 From the WTO-Centered to the Bilateral EPA Approach

Japan had long supported multilateral negotiations within the GATT and WTO frameworks, and had assumed that regional efforts for Free Trade Agreements (FTAs) are rather undesirable for fair development of the global economy (Urata et al. 2007: 112). It had believed that the multilateral approach is much better than the FTA case-by-case approach, simply because the former minimizes distortions in international trade, applies the same rules to all Members non-discriminately, and thereby reduces transaction costs as far as possible. Put differently, the latter makes market transactions very complicated, requires strenuous efforts to coordinate rules set out among different trade partners, and thereby makes transaction costs very expensive.

During the 1990s, however, notifications on establishing FTA to the WTO rapidly increased. Entering the 21st century, this number continued to rise, and finally reached 210 in the year 2006 (rising from 27 in 1990). The establishment of the single market within the European Economic Community (1992), the agreement to promote the ASEAN Free Trade Area (1992), and the inauguration of the NAFTA (1994) were part of this sharp increase in number (METI 2007a: 515). In this context, Japan began to reconsider its long-standing position toward the multilateral negotiation approach. What made the Japanese Government decisively change its approach is a failure of the Seattle WTO Ministerial Conference in 1999, which revealed how difficult it was to promote multilateral trade negotiations only within the WTO framework (Urata et al. 2007: 112; METI 2007a: 517).

8.3.1 Shifting to Bilateral Economic Partnership Agreements

After the Seattle Conference, in fact, many countries accelerated their efforts to establish FTAs, so as to eliminate tariff and non-tariff barriers between contracting countries, and to establish new rules in areas of investment, competition, services, and intellectual property rights. Seeing this new trend, the Japanese Government also started to establish Economic Partnership Agreements (EPAs) with a number of countries (METI 2007a: 517).

Needless to say, the METI thinks, "the efforts toward multilateral trade policies in the WTO and the efforts for bilateral agreements in EPAs are complementary to each other," and "under the WTO framework, EPAs are positioned as an exception" (METI 2007a: 516; Urata et al. 2007: 20–23). But at the same time, it strongly believes that there are many advantages of bilateral EPAs over WTO multilateral negotiations. That is, even if contracting parties have difficult issues, which have not been resolved within the WTO framework, by considering actual economic conditions of each country, they could find realistic solutions in a flexible and constructive manner (METI 2007a: 517).

Thinking this way, Japan initiated its first negotiation with Singapore in January 2001. Since then, it has been making bilateral EPAs with a number of countries (Urata et al. 2007: 113; METI 2007a: 518). So far, EPAs with Singapore, Mexico, Malaysia, Thailand, and the Philippines already came into effect. EPAs with Indonesia, Brunei, and Chile were signed. Negotiations with Switzerland, Gulf Cooperation Council, India, Vietnam, Korea, China, Australia, and others are underway (METI 2007b: 226–227).

8.3.2 Five Characteristics of Japan's EPAs

There are five characteristics of Japan's EPAs. These are as follows:
(a) It places emphasis on eliminating non-tariff barriers such as complicated customs procedures;
(b) Most of Japan's EPAs have taken a form of bilateral co-operation. Making use of know-how accumulated through Overseas Development Assistance (ODA) programs in the past, the Japanese Government has been responding to various requests from partners in the fields of trade, investment, competition, human resources, services, intellectual property, and environment. Such co-operations

are believed to contribute to improving trade and investment infrastructure of
contracting partners;

(c) Japan's EPAs aim to facilitate the movement of people from partners (mainly
Asian countries) to Japan. In fact, it plans to accept more skilled workers from
Singapore, the Philippines, and Indonesia (Urata et al. 2007: 110–111);

(d) The main purpose of establishing EPAs with Mexico and Chile is to make it
possible for Japanese corporations to catch up with American and European
counterparts, which have taken advantage of RTA or FTA with Latin American
countries. Now that EPAs with Mexico and Chile have started, Japanese corporations can do business on an equal footing with those non-Japanese competitors
(Urata et al. 2007: 115);

(e) Japan regards EPAs with ASEAN countries as a hub of a broader free trade
network, which will cover India, China, Korea, Australia, and New Zealand
(Urata et al. 2007: 81–109).

8.3.3 Is the WTO Effective and Fair?

With those movements in mind, we simply conclude that the Japanese Government
views that (1) at least to some countries, the outcome of the WTO does not seem
fair enough, and because of this, (2) the WTO is not functioning effectively (METI
2007c: 5). Based upon this observation, Japan has shifted its approach from the
WTO-centered multilateral negotiations to the bilateral EPAs.

Nonetheless, even if the Japanese Government thinks the WTO is not functioning effectively, as far as the Dispute Settlement Body (DSB) is concerned, Japan
believes that the WTO is basically working in a fair and balanced manner. Under
this Dispute Settlement Mechanism, Members have an equal right to take a case to
the DSB (Takikawa 2005: 22–24). Discussed in this forum are a variety of issues
such as technical barriers to trade, antidumping measures, export subsidies, countervailing measures, trade in services and the like. In fact, since its establishment in
1995, the WTO has settled 361 cases as of March 2007 (MTSD 2007: 3).

Like other member countries, when faced with difficulties in trade with
Members, Japan has also resorted to this mechanism (MTSD 2007: 3). In the case of
EPAs, however, even if there is an agreement on a dispute resolution mechanism, we
cannot expect this mechanism to work as effectively as the DSB. Yet, when parties
are truly dissatisfied, in the end, they could bring cases to the WTO as its Members.
Thanks to existence of this system of the DSB, EPA partners are likely to make
some compromises, before going to the WTO panel. Seeing this practical merit, the
Japanese Government feels that the DSB and its mechanism are basically useful,
effective, and fair for all the WTO Members (METI and Keidanren 2007: 12).

8.3.4 Is the Outcome of Japan's EPAs Fair?

By mentioning that the DSB seems to work in a fair manner, we have suggested
that part of the WTO "process" is fair. But this does not mean that the "outcome"

Table 8.2 Is WTO fair?

	A View of the Japanese government	A View of NGOs or developing countries
Process of the WTO	*At least, the DSB process is Fair*	*Probably Unfair*
Outcome of the WTO	*Not Working*	*Not Satisfactory*

of activities by the WTO is also fair (Table 8.2). In order to evaluate the outcome, probably we would need to have a couple of decades to observe the full effects. Yet, most of us cannot wait so long. Although we cannot definitely conclude that the outcome of the WTO is not fair, at this point of history, one thing is very clear. That is, NGOs and developing countries insist that the outcome of the WTO is not satisfactory (they might also think that the process has not been fair, either).

If we assume that the outcome of the WTO is not fair, then how about the outcome of Japan's EPAs? In comparison with European EPAs with African, Caribbean and Pacific countries, Japan's EPAs have not been severely criticized yet in Japan. According to Geoff Moore, in Europe there has been a "Stop EPAs campaign" run by NGOs for a number of years (see Moore's chapter later in this volume). As far as Japan's EPAs are concerned, we have not seen radical campaigns led by Japan's civil society. To be sure, there have been opposing activities organized by farmers, hog-raisers, and other agricultural stakeholder groups. But their main concern is not on fairness of EPAs but on protection of their vested interests.

Nonetheless, outside of Japan, globally acting environmental NGOs have been criticizing Japan, saying that Japan's EPAs include a provision for transferring hazardous wastes between contracting countries. Although Japan ratified the 1989 Basel Convention on the Control of Transboundary Movements of Hazardous Wastes and Their Disposal, it has not ratified the 1995 amendment, because this amendment prohibits all the transnational movement of wastes even if its purpose is to recycle wastes and to reduce an environmental impact. Whatever reasons the Japanese Government gives, those NGOs have been attacking Japan's EPAs from the viewpoint of the environmental impact. Environmental News Service describes this as follows (http://www.ens-newswire.com/ens/mar2007/2007-03-14-02.asp):

> SEATTLE, Washington, March 14, 2007 (ENS) -Since 2002, Japan has been laying the groundwork for a plan to liberalize and promote toxic waste trade among Asian countries in violation of an international treaty, claims a hazardous waste watchdog group based in Seattle. The Seattle-based Basel Action Network, BAN, filed a formal complaint against Japan on Monday concerning what BAN calls Japan's 'intent to create toxic waste colonies around Asia.' BAN says that Japan is utilizing bilateral trade agreements concluded with Singapore, the Philippines, Malaysia, and Thailand that eliminate tariffs on hazardous wastes such as pharmaceutical wastes and waste oils containing PCBs to promote trade in these substances.

We do not know the credibility of this news (Taka 2006: 227–236). But if this information is not one-sided, then we have no choice but to say that the outcome of Japan's EPAs is not fair.

8.3.5 Is the Process of Japan's EPAs Fair?

Then how about the process of Japan's EPAs (Table 8.3) (EPA Team, 2007: 380–381)? As far as the process is concerned, we might be able to say that it could be fair. Three reasons are worth referring to. First, in the case of Asian countries, Japan did not tempt contracting partners with ODA. The decade in which Japan intensively provided them with ODA was the 1990s. At that time, Japan did not have any plan to form EPAs with them. Second, in the case of Latin American partners, they were far better than Japan at making a Free Trade Agreement. Mexico especially had already accumulated experiences of establishing FTAs. Therefore, making full use of such experiences, Mexico entered negotiations with Japan. Because of this, Japanese experts confess that through a series of negotiations Japan learned a lot from Mexico (EPA Team, 2007: 70–82). Third, when Japan started to explore possible co-operations with a contracting partner, Japan tried to understand developmental stages of the candidate. In other words, placing oneself in the partner's shoes, and taking their conditions into account, Japan has offered an EPA model suitable for the contracting partner. This is why Japan has always taken a form of bilateral EPAs.

Needless to say, those reasons might not be enough to convince all the contracting partners that the process of Japan's EPAs is fair. Despite such possibilities, we would like to mention that at least the Japanese Government feels that the "process" of EPAs is fair for most of its trading partners. The main reason why it feels so is that so far trading partners have not shown clear indignation and have not made substantial complaints against Japan. If the view of the Japanese Government reflects the reality, we could say that the "process" of EPAs is fair. Yet even if this conclusion is correct, this does not imply that the "outcome" of Japan's EPAs is also fair. Although the Japanese Government assumes that the outcome of EPAs is also fair, the actual outcome could be much different from this assumption (MOFA 2005b: 8).

To sum up, as far as officially published documents are concerned, firstly we conclude that the Japanese Government thinks that the WTO is not working effectively (because some Members feel that the outcome and process of the WTO are not fair). And this is why the Japanese Government has shifted its focus from the WTO to EPAs. Secondly, we could say that the government believes that the process of Japan's EPAs is fair on the whole, but that in the latter case this belief is contested. These are the answers to the first question of the FITI project.

Table 8.3 Is Japan's EPA fair?

	A view of the Japanese government	A view of contracting partners	A view of NGOs
Process of Japan's EPAs	*Fair*	*Probably Fair*	Unknown
Outcome of Japan's EPAs	*Probably Fair*	Unknown	*Unfair*

8.4 A Typical Ethical Issue for Japan: Protecting Rice Farming

The second question is "What are the main ethical issues regarding international trade in Japan?" In order to respond to this question, we shed light on two issues. The first one is a very sensitive issue for Japanese people, and the second one is also extremely important for the global community.

8.4.1 Issues of Agriculture

GATT Article XI does not admit any restrictions other than duties, taxes or other charges, simply because other restrictions are basically against the WTO basic principles. The WTO assumes the imposition of tariff as the only method to control trade. Following this principle, the Uruguay Round and Doha Round have been exploring various possibilities in reducing tariff rates on agricultural products and in abolishing other restrictive measures.

For example, Members have been in discussion over the modalities, which contain general rules and formulae for cutting tariffs and trade-distorting subsidies. Within this framework, Members are given flexibility in determining where to reduce tariffs significantly and where to make lesser tariff cuts, as long as such an approach is not against the tariff reduction formula in the modalities (ICTSD 2002: 17).

The general ideas evident in the modalities are (1) Tariff reductions should be progressive with deeper cuts in higher tariffs. (2) Linear tariff reductions should be applied at different rates to developed countries and developing countries. For instance, in the case of the lowest tariff band range, reduction rates could be from 25 to 70 percent for developed countries and from 15 to 50 percent for developing countries. In the case of the highest range, reduction rates could be from 40 percent for developed countries and from 30 percent for developing countries. (3) Members should be given a right to decide "sensitive products," and set lower tariff reductions on sensitive products (Blandford and Josling 2006: 9; MAFF 2008a: 14).

As we can imagine from these general ideas, interests of Members are so complicated that fulfilling demands of all the parties requires strenuous efforts for Members to achieve and needs seemingly an unlimited number of years to discuss (Maeda 2007).

8.4.2 High Tariff Rates on Agricultural Products

Taking into account results of the Uruguay Round (1993 Agreement on Agriculture), and in response to criticisms from agricultural exporting countries (G20), Japan gave up its long-standing import restrictions, replaced them with the imposition of tariffs on agricultural products. As far as rice is concerned, tariffs were introduced to import rice with the minimum access obligation, in which Japan has to import a certain quantity of rice with no tariffs (Takikawa 2005: 115). But the

Japanese Government is said to maintain protective tariffs on import rice exceeding the predetermined quantity (e.g., 778 percent tariff on polished rice, 568 percent on unpolished rice, 252 percent tariff on wheat) (MAFF 2008a: 1–4; MAFF 2008b: 7). Because of this, we have to admit that basically Japan has not changed its stance of protecting rice and rice farmers for a long time. The reasons why the Ministry of Agriculture, Forestry, and Fisheries (MAFF) of Japan consistently supports this stance are as follows.

In 2000, agricultural negotiation among Members started to explore the General Framework designed to overcome sensitive issues for the Doha Round (WTO 2001). Before entering details of this round in December 2000, the MAFF formally made five proposals, stating that, "Agriculture is the foundation of society in every country, and provides a variety of functions that are beneficial to the society. As there are differences in the natural conditions and the historical background from one country to another, the diversity and coexistence of agriculture among various countries need to be preserved." After this introduction, five proposals were made (MAFF 2000):

> "(i) Consideration of the multifunctionality of agriculture; (ii) Ensuring food security, which is the basis of the society in each country; (iii) Redressing the imbalance between rules and disciplines applied to agricultural exporting countries and those applied to importing countries; (iv) Consideration for developing countries; and (v) Consideration for the concerns of consumers and civil society. These five points reflect the general consensus of the people of Japan, which itself is the biggest net food-importing country, having imports equivalent in amount to the consumption of 75 million people."

8.4.3 Mutli-functionality

In relation to the first point, GATT Article XX on General Exemptions shows instances in which Members could be exempted from GATT basic rules. It describes that if it is necessary to protect human, animal or plant life or health, or if it is related to the conservation of exhaustible natural resources, Members are allowed to adopt policy measures that would normally be inconsistent with GATT principles.

With those exemptions in mind, the MAFF thinks that life in Japan's rural areas is heavily dependent upon rice farming in an economic and cultural sense. And it believes that rice farming has made sustainable use of natural resources, and through this activity, rice cultivation has long maintained the landscape and natural environment of rural areas. That is, the MAFF feels that fulfilling the minimum needs of rural areas' life, and protecting the natural environment meet the conditions of GATT Article XX.

Reflecting this, Japan's Basic Law on Food, Agriculture and Rural Areas (Article 3) stipulates, "In consideration of the importance of maintaining the stability of the people's lives and the national economy, the multiple roles that agriculture plays through stable production in rural areas, from the conservation of national land, water resources, and the natural environment to the formation of a good landscape and maintenance of cultural tradition, in addition to its conventional role as a primary food supplier shall be fulfilled sufficiently for the future" (MAFF 1999).

8.4.4 Food Security

With regard to the second point, food security, the MAFF places emphasis on the fact that Japan is the biggest net importer of agricultural products, and that its degree of self-sufficiency in foods is the lowest among the major developed countries. As far as agricultural products are concerned, in the year 2004, Japan's total importation was US$ 41.5 billion, while its exportation US$ 1.9 billion. This means, Japan's agricultural trade was in the red, and still remains almost the same. The gap between importation and exportation, 39.6 billion dollars worth of the net importation, is the largest in the world (the second biggest net importer is the UK, whose net importation was US$ 20.2 billion in 2004) (MAFF 2008b: 3).

In order to deal with this unstable situation, the Basic Law on Food, Agriculture and Rural Areas (Article 2) states "(1) In consideration of the fact that food is indispensable in maintaining human life and important as a basis for healthy and fulfilled living, a stable supply of good-quality food at reasonable prices shall be secured for the future. (2) In consideration of the fact that there are certain unstable factors in the world food trade and supply/demand, this stable food supply to the people shall be secured with the increase in domestic agricultural production as a basis, together with an appropriate combination of imports and stockpiles" (MAFF 1999).

The MAFF has long believed that in every country, agricultural products are extremely important and indispensable for people's life, and therefore, the supply of foods must be guaranteed. But Japan does not have a reasonable ability to supply foods to its people. Therefore, if something serious happens to the supply of agricultural products, Japanese people might starve within a year or so. To be sure, GATT Article XI prohibits quantitative restrictions not only on importation of products but also on exportation of products to other countries.

Yet, in 2008, for the purpose of keeping agricultural products for their own people, exporting countries (in the case of rice, India, Vietnam) reduced the export of their products to other countries. We understand that such a governmental intervention is a rational action or rather an obligation any government has to take for the benefit of its people. Seeing this situation, however, the Japanese Government sensed a crisis, and accordingly it insisted on the necessity of ensuring food security far more seriously than previously.

8.4.5 Other Factors: Environmental Impact and Food Safety

Currently environmentalists have begun to refer to another factor. That is, they assert the necessity of reducing the total emission of carbon dioxide, using the words, "food mile" or "food mileage," which is defined as the aggregate product of a food item's weight and transportation distance. Although food mileage is just one factor in the total environmental impact, proponents are insisting that by reducing food imports from a great distance, societies could reduce carbon dioxide emissions.

In addition to this, citizens and consumers began to avoid buying imported foods, with concerns over food safety. Even if exporters explain that the production process is safe, and free from toxic chemicals, they are now very skeptical about overseas safety standards and labeling practices. To be sure, extremely protective measures taken by a government are against the Technical Barriers to Trade Agreement. But if exporters' explanations are not based upon scientific data, and products do not meet basic requirements of the international safety standard, non-tariff restrictions imposed by a government would be acceptable. This is because ensuring food safety is another obligation each government has to take.

8.4.6 Protecting Rice Farming

On the surface, the first point (multi-functionality) seems plausible and justifiable, because liberalization of rice importation could destroy not only the lives of people in the rural areas (on the whole, the less advantaged people in Japan), but also the culture and natural environment of the countryside of Japan. The second point (food security) is also important, since further importation of agricultural products could threaten the food security of Japan. Third, buying more foods from domestic suppliers contributes to reducing carbon dioxide emissions, and lastly food safety is an indispensable obligation every government has to take, so as to ease concerns of citizens and consumers.

Although those reasons seem persuasive, if we look at them from the viewpoint of GATT's basic principles such as the General Prohibition of Quantitative Restrictions, we have to admit that Japan's logic is inconsistent with the sprit of a free trading system. In addition, from the perspective of agricultural exporting countries, Japan's logic could be seen to be self-centered. For Japan, this is a very difficult ethical dilemma between increasing import from developing countries and protecting interests of the less advantaged people in Japan, because they seem mutually exclusive. For now, although we do not know how to handle this situation, Japan has been exploring possibilities of overcoming this dilemma. We will return to Japan's initiative in this regard at Section 8.6.

8.5 Reconsideration of Globalization and the WTO: Poverty Reduction

Importation of rice is a difficult issue for Japan. Therefore, we have reviewed this issue and described reasons why the Japanese Government has long protected rice and other sensitive agricultural products. From the size of the Japanese economy, however, we cannot confine our focus to just a domestic agricultural issue. With a broader perspective, we have to highlight other ethical issues, which are extremely important for the global community. So what is the most important global issue? We believe that it is the issue of poverty reduction.

8.5.1 The Ultimate Purpose of Globalization in the Original Position

What is the ultimate purpose of globalization? We believe, that it is not to maximize profits of some private corporations, that it is not to benefit specific countries or regions, and that it is not to develop certain industries. Whatever globalization has been actually bringing about, or no matter how difficult the issues that globalization has caused, its ultimate purpose must be to benefit all countries, every race, and all citizens. In other words, its purpose must be to make the world a better place to live, to share the merits of trade among Members, to alleviate poverty, and to get poor nations out of desperate situations.

This belief should be established theoretically. To this end, we utilize a concept of "the veil of ignorance" and the "rational person in the original position," which John Rawls once introduced. As is well known, he tried to identify fundamental principles of justice, from the viewpoint of a rational person on the original position, a person behind a veil of ignorance. The veil of ignorance is a hypothetical situation where a person does not know his/her place in society, his/her strength in comparison with others, which income class he/she belongs to, which generation he/she belongs to, etc. Rawls assumed that if this rational person with no information of his/her place in society tried to derive ideal Principles of Justice, the rational person eventually would come to an ideal set of principles (Rawls 1971: 11–22).

For example, Rawls assumed that in the original position, natural talents distributed in a society are regarded as a common asset for a society, and an individual's talent is regarded as just a part of a common asset. Because of this, the rational person thinks that advantaged persons with talents may gain benefits only if their conduct would improve the situation of the least advantaged in the society. This is the core part of the Difference Principle.

But unfortunately this principle does not explain to what extent a situation of the least advantaged should be improved. To be sure, whatever principles we propose, and no matter how carefully those principles are applied, it could be almost impossible to show clearly how much the situation should be improved. Therefore, we do not intend to define here how much it should be improved. We would rather simply confirm what is the ultimate purpose of globalization, from the viewpoint of the rational person behind a veil of ignorance.

In order to do this, (1) we suppose that a rational person knows at least the gaps between the situation of the most developed countries and the situation of the least-developed countries at the global level, and gaps between the situation of the most advantaged class of people and the situation of the least advantaged class of people at the national level. Then, (2) we assume that this rational person does not know which group of countries and which class of people he/she belongs to. And finally, (3) we check why this rational person joins the movement for globalization, on the grounds that there should be a substantial motive to join.

When those conditions are given, we believe that this rational person eventually comes to think that the ultimate purpose of globalization is to narrow gaps by improving the situation of the least-developed countries and the situation of the least advantaged class of people. Stated another way, with this definition, all parties in the global community are expected to contribute somehow to poverty reduction internationally and domestically.

8.5.2 Criticism Against the WTO

If we define the goal of globalization like this, a number of NGOs and developing countries might continue to attack the WTO and its outcomes. It is because they believe that the WTO is acting as an agent for influential corporations, and does not consider the interests of the poor seriously (Sachs 2005: 355). Although we do not know whether their criticism is correct or not, at least we have to face the fact that they are likely to insist that both the process and the outcome of the WTO are neither acceptable nor fair (Oxfam 2002: 217, 221).

For example, the Third World Traveler insists, "Every ruling of the WTO proves that the institution is fundamentally flawed, designed to place corporate profits above the need to protect our environment, our health and our democracy" (Third World Traveler). We can easily find similar critical articles on the web. A typical one is on the ZNET. In one article, the author (Vodovnik) quotes the following communiqué (communiqué of Subcomandante Marcos), which was addressed to the civil society at the time of the WTO Ministerial Conference in Mexico in September 2003:

> In complex equation that turns death into money, there is a group of humans who command a very low price in the global slaughterhouse - the indigenous, the young, the women, the children, the elderly, the migrants, all those who are different. That is to say, the immense majority of humanity. This is a world war of the powerful who want to turn the planet into a private club that reserves the right to refuse admission. ... All of us are given the option of being inside this zone (club), but only as servants. Or we can remain outside of the world, outside life. But we have no reason to obey and accept this choice between living as servants or dying. ... Brothers and sisters, there is dissent over the project of economic globalization all over the world. Those above, who globalize conformism, cynicism, stupidity, war, destruction and death. And those below, who globalize rebellion, hope, creativity, intelligence, imagination, life, memory and the construction of a world that we can all fit in, a world with democracy, liberty and justice. We hope the death train of the World Trade Organization will be derailed in Cancun and everywhere else (Ziga Vodovnik, "WTO Derailed," December 2004, p. 3).

We refrain from making comments on this communiqué. But from the rhetoric and tone of the communiqué, one thing is very clear. That is, there exists a deep-rooted suspicion on the side of radical NGOs or bellicose activists, and in the future, this suspicion might trigger severe violence and in a very extreme case, it might mistakenly justify acts of terrorism against developed countries or multinational corporations, even against citizens in developed countries. Needless to say, all who believe that human rights should be respected and protected never tolerate any form of terrorism, whatever reasons exist.

8.5.3 The Ultimate Purpose of the WTO

Then how should we define the purpose of the WTO? This institution was established in 1995, so as to liberalize unnecessary regulations and so as to develop the global economy. Usually, we define its purpose as developing the global economy through the liberalization of trade in goods and services. Yet, we would like to define it here in a different manner. As long as the WTO is a means of globalization, its purpose should also be the alleviation of poverty. It is because, as noted above in relation to globalization, in the original position, any rational person, who knows the gaps between developed and least-developed countries, and who does not know which group of countries he/she belongs to, will eventually come to conclude that the main reason why a country should join the WTO is to alleviate poverty at the global as well as the national levels, and to make the world a better place to live.

At Section 8.3, we referred to both the process and the outcome of the WTO, the process and outcome of Japan's EPAs, and then discussed them in terms of fairness. Now that we have defined the purposes of globalization and of the WTO like this, the process of the WTO or the process of EPAs becomes less important than the outcome. The outcome here means how much poverty has been reduced. In other words, even if the process of alleviating poverty was agreed upon among Members, if this process is not contributing to poverty reduction, soon Members will raise a question on the process, and begin to insist upon changing the process, in a way to make it easier to achieve the purpose (the outcome). Although we do not intend to ignore the importance of the process (rule-making process, decision-making process, monitoring process, dispute settlement process, etc.), once we adopt this definition of poverty reduction, the outcome eventually becomes far more important than the process.

8.5.4 How to Make Use of Globalization

There exist criticisms against globalization and the WTO, saying that globalization does not reduce poverty. According to Ann Harrison, there is not enough evidence on the relationship between globalization and poverty reduction. But we witness that one way or another globalization has steadily reduced poverty in the past 50 years (Harrison 2005: 3, 32–33). According to Jeffrey Sachs, a head of the UN Millennium Project, two generations ago, a half of the world population lived below the poverty line (1.08 US$ a day, usually rounded down to 1.00). At that time, no one could imagine that solving the poverty issue was achievable. But one generation ago, that proportion declined to 1/3. And now it has reached 1/6. It means even if globalization has been causing problems, it has been somehow reducing poverty (Sachs 2005: 289).

On account of this, just criticizing the WTO, multinational corporations, and globalization might not contribute to solving the poverty issues. Of importance seems to be finding out creative ways to make full use of the merits of globalization for getting the poorest out of a desperate situation and helping poor countries start their own sustainable development. Then how do we alleviate poverty in the world? Regarding this question, Sachs suggests that if a small percentage of GNP of developed countries, which consists of 1/6 of the world population, is invested in basic infrastructure (transportation, electricity, water supply, soil development, hygiene, epidemic prevention, medical care) and human resources (education) of the poorest countries, extreme poverty would disappear within a decade (Sachs 2005: 227).

Amartya Sen also places emphasis on basic infrastructure and education. For him, poverty means the deprivation of basic human capabilities rather than the low level of incomes. Although he assumes low income as one of the major causes of poverty, he does not think that low income is identical with poverty. Coupled with low income, other causes such as physical handicaps, illness, isolation, or lack of information place people in poverty or a desperate situation. With this in mind, instead of simply saying that income should be increased, Sen insists that the human environment should be improved in a way to make it possible for people to demonstrate their potential and capabilities (Sen 2000: 87–110). For this purpose, he emphasizes the importance of infrastructure such as healthcare and basic education. Since Sachs regards basic infrastructure and human resources as key factors to alleviate poverty, we could say that both of them agree on the same requirements for poverty reduction.

In order to respond to the second question, "What are the main ethical issues regarding international trade in Japan?" we have suggested that typical issues are (1) protection of rice farming and (2) poverty reduction. The last question required us to ask how Japan has been addressing this identified issue. We feel that Japan has engaged in a number of initiatives especially in the fields of basic infrastructure and human resources at the level of government and at the level of private corporations. And we believe that those initiatives have somehow contributed to poverty reduction in the world, mainly in the Asian region. Having TICAD (Tokyo International Conference on African Development) in May 2008, and facing the world food crisis, Japan is about to make the best use of its own experience and its experience in Asia for poverty reduction in Africa.

8.6 Initiatives by the Japanese Government: TICAD and MDGs

At Section 8.4, we described how Japan has been exploring possibilities of overcoming the dilemma between the interests of Japanese farmers and the interests of agricultural exporting countries. In this section, first of all, we will see agricultural initiatives taken by the Japanese Government in Africa. Although those initiatives promised in the TICAD process might not directly overcome that dilemma, they could contribute to poverty reduction, the ultimate purpose of globalization. Then, secondly, we will overview Japanese initiatives relating to the Millennium Development Goals (MDGs), and describe initiatives in the TICAD process, which also constitute a major part of the MDGs. We regard all those initiatives as developments in Japan to address the two major ethical issues.

8.6.1 World Food Crisis and TICAD IV

In April 2008, the World Bank explained that the price of all staple food had risen by about 80 percent in the past 3 years. Experts list a number of reasons. One of the plausible reasons is environmental challenges to convert agricultural land into biofuel production. For example, in the US, the government has encouraged farmers to switch their land from food supply to energy supply, and in Europe, the European Union plans to boost biofuel production. Seeing such changes, other countries like Argentina, Brazil, Canada and Eastern Europe have been diverting foods into biofuels.

As a result, in 2008 the price surge on staple food hit the poorest, especially Sub-Saharan Africa, very hard, and the world itself fell into a food crisis. But just criticizing biofuels does not solve problems of food shortage and climate change simultaneously. From the viewpoint of food security, we had better explore other creative ways to solve the problem. Thinking this way, the Japanese Government has initiated several initiatives in this regard.

In May 2008, hoping to make the 21st century "the Century of African Growth," Japan held TICAD IV (the Fourth Tokyo International Conference on African Development), which received the attendance of representatives from 52 African countries, including 36 heads of state, and major international organizations (MOFA 2005a: 5). At the end of the conference, it adopted the Yokohama Action Plan, which covers a variety of initiatives in the next 5 years. One of them is on Agriculture and Rural Development of Africa (TICAD 2008a). Regarding this initiative, this action plan lists three actions for Japan to take in Africa. That is, (1) To enhance capacity to increase food production, (2) To improve access to markets, and (3) To support sustainable management of water resources. Let us review the first and the third actions.

8.6.2 Boosting Rice Production in Africa

As for the first action (Increasing food production), Japan's then Prime Minister Yasuo Fukuda stated that, "In order to fully ensure growth in Africa, the development of agriculture is extremely important, as some two-thirds of the total population of Africa is engaged in it. As Africa seeks to achieve its own Green Revolution, I would like to put out a call for action, aiming to double the current rice production output of 14 million tons over the next ten years" (TICAD 2008b).

Since Africa's current food self-sufficiency is around 50 percent, having dropped from 96 percent two decades ago, the food price surge dealt African countries a severe blow. In order to make the impact of food shortages smaller in the long run, agricultural productivity of Africa should be enhanced as early as possible (TICAD 2008b). Keeping this belief in mind, in the past Japan has provided technological supports as a part of MDGs (MOFA 2005a: 9), and from now through the TICAD process, it will offer more concrete support to the production of New Rice for Africa (NERICA), which could grow even in harsh climate conditions (TICAD 2008a).

To proceed with this action, the Japanese Government newly created an international organization in October 2008 (the headquarters is located in Nairobi), so as to analyze ways to increase rice production and to select nations as recipients of assistance.

8.6.3 Sustainable Management of Water Resources

With regard to the third action, then Prime Minister Fukuda also emphasized the necessity of sustainable management of water resources. Focusing on water management, Japan has long offered "comprehensive assistance that covers provision of drinking water and sanitation, improvement of water productivity, water pollution control, disaster mitigation and water resources management." It is said that in quantitative terms, "Japan has been the largest contributor in the water supply and sanitation sector. Its assistance accounted for 41 percent of the global total in the five years from 1998 to 2002" (MOFA 2005a: 13).

Based upon such experiences in the past, Japan now plans to promote further "development, rehabilitation and maintenance of water resources management infrastructure to contribute to the joint efforts aiming at expanding the irrigated area by 20 percent in 5 years" (TICAD 2008a). In this regard, for example, Japan organizes a new technical assistance team of water specialists known as W-SAT (Water Security Action Team), which works with people in Africa, in drilling new wells, fixing broken water supply pipes, etc. (TICAD 2008b).

As mentioned before, Japan's policy on rice import has long been criticized. But in the past Japan has made constructive use of its own experiences in the field of agriculture for poverty reduction overseas, and now intends to utilize them far more seriously than ever for the benefit of Africa. What is more, the Japanese Government facilitates research and development on the next generation of biofuels, and plans to share the results with poverty-stricken countries. Currently, it has been studying possibilities to use crop waste such as straw for production of biofuels. It might be too early to predict anything at this point. But if such efforts bear fruit, Japan's initiative would surely contribute to solving problems of food shortage and global climate change simultaneously. To sum up, by challenging agricultural, environmental, and global issues with firm determination, Japan expects the global community to show some understanding over Japan's own policy on agriculture. At any event, those agriculture-related initiatives toward Africa could be regarded as some of the developments to address the issue of protecting rice farming in Japan.

8.6.4 Major Initiatives Related to Millennium Development Goals (MDGs)

Then how has the Japanese Government been responding to the global ethical issue, poverty reduction? Needless to say, supporting African agriculture is a part of the poverty reduction initiative. But from the broader perspective, we want to see Japan's MDG activities, and then characterize its basic stance toward poverty reduction.

According to a report published by the MOFA, during the 1990s, Japan's ODA toward basic education, basic health, nutrition, water and sanitation, was at its highest levels in terms of volume among the DAC (Development Assistance Committee) member countries (MOFA 2005a: 1–2). Since Japan believes that education plays a critical role in human development and nation-building, it has used a large portion of ODA for education (MOFA 2005a: 10). It also believes that without a safety-net for people's lives, any country cannot maximize the use of people's experiences, skills, and know-how in their society. Coupled with this reason, Japan has long supported activities to fight HIV/AIDS, Tuberculosis and Malaria. For example, as far as combating Malaria is concerned, Japan had provided 10 million special mosquito nets to African countries by the year 2007 (MOFA 2005b: 9).

Although there have been a variety of MDG initiatives like these, Japan has always placed a great importance on economic infrastructure. The main reason comes from its own and East Asian experiences. The same report describes, "Japan's ODA to East Asia and the Pacific, which accounted for about 60 percent of its total, played an important role in supporting the development efforts of the countries in the region." "Based on this experience as well as its own experience after World War II, Japan has placed an emphasis on the provision of economic infrastructure in its ODA. The development of infrastructure in the developing countries in areas such as transportation, energy, and water is essential for promoting private sector activities and economic growth. Japan's ODA for infrastructure development in East Asia, together with relevant capacity building, has been instrumental in facilitating growth in the region. Japan's ODA for economic infrastructure between 1990 and 2003 totaled 66.9 billion dollars – by far the largest among the DAC member countries" (MOFA 2005a: 8).

8.6.5 Mobilizing Private Sector and Japan's ODA Policy

The Japanese Government basically thinks that in order to promote economic growth, the private sector should be mobilized as effectively as possible. Namely, it considers that if the private sector is at the centre of strategy, eventually poverty will be reduced, and then MDGs will be achieved accordingly. From 1990 through 2001, average GDP growth rate of East Asia and the Pacific region was 7.5 percent, which led to a reduction of nearly 200 million people out of poverty. During the same time period, the total amount of ODA provided to this region was about 78 billion dollars. This amount was less than the total provided to Sub-Saharan Africa, which received about US$ 110 billion. Taking this data into account, Japan insists that how ODA is utilized is extremely important for countries' economic development (MOFA 2005a: 7–8). A lesson Japan learnt from its own development is, at the early stage of economic development, to concentrate as much investment as possible on infrastructure such as transportation, energy, and water, which eventually encourages the private sector's investment (MOFA 2005a: 5).

Table 8.4 Industrialized countries' debt ratio (%)

Year	1995	2000	2005	2007
Japan	87.7	137.1	173.1	177.6
USA	70.7	55.2	61.8	61.8
UK	52.4	45.7	46.7	49.0
Germany	55.7	60.4	71.1	69.9
France	62.6	65.2	76.1	74.6
Italy	121.8	121.0	120.4	121.0
Canada	101.6	82.1	70.8	66.3

*Calculation based upon OECD Data originated by the Ministry of Finance of Japan

Although Japan provided the largest ODA in the 1990s, we have to admit that it has been reducing ODA and, in 2007, it finally dropped to 5th place in terms of the total amount of assistance. Since it is still the second-largest economy, the international community might have doubt as to the seriousness of Japan's commitment to poverty reduction. While we understand such a criticism against Japan, it might need to be set in the context of Japan's financial situation.

To be frank, the Japanese Government has serious trouble with a towering budget deficit. As of March 2008, it accumulated about US$ 5.5 trillion of debt, and the ratio of accumulated governmental bonds to Japan's GDP reached almost 180 percent (see Table 8.4). This ratio is the worst among the industrialized countries, and its debt is still mounting. Because of this, Japan is now searching for a new and sustainable way of managing itself, which also enables Japan to keep taking international responsibilities in a consistent manner.

But even if Japan is suffering from a towering budget deficit, it has to make the best efforts to support developing countries as effectively as possible. For this reason, Japan is exploring three directions to go forward. First, it is steadily shifting its emphasis from Asia to Africa, since some of the Asian and the Pacific countries have already succeeded in achieving economic growth. Second, it intensively applies financial support like ODA to specific fields. As noted above, since Japan assumes that economic infrastructure is important, it tends to concentrate on construction of transportation networks and the like. Third, it also supports fundamentals such as finance, trade insurance, livelihood protection, and human resources, because if those fundamentals are not provided, the private sector might not be mobilized.

8.6.6 Establishing Economic Infrastructure in the TICAD Process

From the viewpoint of these directions, let us describe the initiatives in the TICAD process. First of all, at the Opening Address, Mr. Fukuda emphasized, "The time has come for the countries of Africa to adopt as their own a model that led to success in post-war Japan and many other Asian countries." Then, secondly he described the importance of economic infrastructure. That is, "In particular, the experiences of

Table 8.5   Contents of TICAD IV Yokohama Action Plan

Preamble
I. Boosting Economic Growth
(a) Infrastructure
(b) Trade, Investment and Tourism
(c) Agriculture and Rural Development
II. Achieving MDGs
(a) Community Development
(b) Education
(c) Health
III. Consolidation of Peace, Good Governance
IV. Addressing Environment/Climate Change Issues
V. Broadening Partnership

Japan and other Asian countries tell us that improvements in transportation infrastructure play a critical role in attracting private investment." Because of this, as we see in the Contents of the Yokohama Action Plan (see Table 8.5), this formal document starts with "Infrastructure," aiming at "Boosting Economic Growth."

This "Infrastructure" section covers (1) Regional transport infrastructure, including roads and ports, (2) Regional power infrastructure, (3) Water-related infrastructure, (4) Enhanced involvement of regional institutions, and (5) Promotion of public-private partnership (PPP) in infrastructure. Placing extreme importance on (1) Regional transport infrastructure, Japan believes that missing links in transportation networks should be connected as early as possible.

As concrete measures, Japan plans to "Provide financial and technical assistance for the planning, construction and improvement of regional transport corridors and international ports," "Support capacity building for the management and maintenance of regional infrastructure," and "Promote facilitation of cross-border procedures such as One Stop Border Post (OSBP)" (TICAD 2008b). As far as OSBP is concerned, since building roads, linking roads, and connecting roads with ports are not enough to achieve its original purpose, the Action Plan touches upon the necessity of training officials at OSBP, on the ground that better customs and immigration procedures would contribute to making cross-boarder transportation more efficient and less time-consuming (TICAD 2008b).

By establishing and improving such economic infrastructure, Japan hopes the private sector will increase its investment, and transfer technologies and managerial know-how to Africa, thereby creating more job opportunities in the continent. As for fundamentals, Japan plans to reinforce trade insurance, and to launch the Facility for African Investment within the Japan Bank for International Cooperation (JBIC), the purpose of which is to finance businesses in African countries and to guarantee the financing provided by Japanese banks for businesses in Africa. It is said that financial assistance for Africa through the JBIC will be on a scale of US$ 2.5 billion over the next 5 years. Through such public-private collaborative initiatives, Japan plans to double private investment in Africa (TICAD 2008b).

8.6.7 MDG Initiatives in the TICAD Process

As in the Yokohama Action Plan, there are many other initiatives such as agriculture, community development, education, and health. At TICAD IV, Japan promised to gradually double the amount of ODA, currently around US$ 0.9 billion (excluding debt waivers), to US$ 1.8 billion over 5 years (this does not include debt waivers). Japan plans to use a large portion of ODA for alleviating issues in those areas. Among them, basic education is given great importance.

As his philosophy, then Prime Minister Fukuda mentioned, "For Japan, a country with virtually no underground resources to speak of, the most important type of resources is human resources. First, we give our children a thorough education. Then, we make them self-reliant. On that basis, they live in harmony together with others, pooling their abilities to deal with any difficulties that their friends might face. This is the principle of "self-reliance and mutual cooperation." This is almost the same as the founding philosophy of TICAD, namely "ownership" and "partnership." Where there is no "ownership," which respects self-reliance, neither sustainable development nor growth is possible" (TICAD 2008b).

With this premise, the Yokohama Action Plan refers to the importance of basic education - expansion of access and quality, on the ground that in order to eradicate extreme poverty, access to education should be provided securely and equally. In this regard, Japan has pledged to "Support construction and rehabilitation of school buildings and related infrastructure," and to "Provide assistance to train and retain primary and secondary school teachers and support the establishment and expansion of teacher training systems and organizations" (TICAD 2008b). For example, Japan plans to build about 1,000 primary and secondary schools in Africa within 5 years to come. This plan will provide around 400,000 students with 5,500 classes to study. Since it is reported that teachers are not well trained in Africa, Japan will offer training programs to 300,000 instructors of science and mathematics, including 100,000 African teachers.

In order to answer the third question, what developments are there in Japan to address the ethical issues, we have seen governmental initiatives such as agricultural contributions, efforts toward MDGs, and promises at the TICAD IV. We assume that all these initiatives led by the Japanese Government could be regarded as developments to address the agricultural (food security) and global poverty issues.

8.7 Initiatives by Leading Japanese Corporations: Education and Basic Infrastructure

The governmental initiatives are just a part of the developments in Japan to address ethical issues. Other stakeholders are also addressing those issues. Among them, multinational corporations are especially important in the context of global issues. Therefore, with the intent of supplementing our answer to the third question, we would like to review contributions made by major Japanese corporations.

8.7.1 Contributions Corporations Can Make

MDGs might be understood as goals to be pursued by governments. Nonetheless, this does not mean that corporations are not expected to help in alleviating world poverty. On the contrary, No. 8 of MDGs expects the private sector to cooperate. In fact, corporations have very competitive technology, know-how, skilled and talented staff, well-organized networks, and ways to operate with high efficiency. Therefore, if they cooperate with governments and others, extreme poverty might be reduced far more effectively than if governments work alone.

According to our research, Japanese NGOs and the mass media believe that the WTO widens the income gap within a country. NGOs also suggest that the WTO does not bring benefits to all countries. This is in clear contrast to the perceptions of officials at Business Federations and business people. In spite of such perception gaps among different Japanese stakeholders, all the stakeholder groups believe that multinationals can play an important role in solving global issues as good partners. Reflecting this shared belief, Japanese corporations have long been involved in Corporate Social Responsibility (CSR) activities. Therefore, in this section, we would like to see what initiatives leading Japanese corporations have taken so as to address the poverty issue.

Needless to say, there must be a variety of ways to alleviate poverty. But here let us confine our focus to major contributions in the fields of education (human resources) and basic infrastructure, because the Millennium Project assumes that those two fields are especially important for poor countries to achieve sustainable development. In addition to this, although there are a number of corporations involved in such activities, it is impossible to refer to all of them. Therefore, we would like to introduce only a few typical examples.

8.7.2 Improvement of Educational Environment

As we have seen at Section 8.6, the Japanese Government places a stress on basic education, promoting a variety of programs such as constructing schools, offering training to instructors, etc. Interestingly, Japanese corporations have also been proceeding with similar programs in various countries. Three cases are worth referring to.

First, in South Africa, with six NGOs and educational institutions, Toyota has participated in a training program for teachers and administrators. Before starting this program, they came to the conclusion that in South Africa, a large number of students are not academically prepared for high schools or vocational schools, and it is because teachers themselves are not sufficiently trained (Neighbors 2005: 10). Taking this conclusion very seriously, they launched the training program for the purpose of helping South Africa improve its educational environment.

Second, an initiative of Mitsui & Co. is also worth mentioning. In Thailand, through its subsidiary (Mitsiam International), Mitsui & Co. has taken part in the Doi Tung Development Project, a national project. The purpose of this project is to alleviate rural poverty, by helping villagers master how to manufacture their own local products. In fact, this project has successfully provided them with job opportunities and effectively eradicated illicit activities related to drug production. In addition to this national project, as an independent initiative, in 2006, Mitsui & Co. launched the Library Gift Project, believing that reading is a key to develop promising people in Thailand. In this project, they selected the poorest and the most underprivileged 10 elementary schools, visited all the 10 schools so as to understand their real needs regarding a library. Based upon their inquiry and analysis, it has donated a library suitable for each of those elementary schools.

Lastly, an initiative in Sub-Saharan countries by Sumitomo Group four corporations is also noteworthy. Since they believe that the educational environment for children is a key element for poverty reduction in Africa, and this is a practical way for them to contribute to MDGs, Sumitomo Chemical, Sumitomo Trust & Banking, Sumitomo Life Insurance, and MSIG (Mitsui Sumitomo Insurance Group) joined the elementary school construction project organized by World Vision. So far they have built elementary schools equipped with a dining hall and teachers' accommodation in Tanzania, Kenya, Uganda, and Zambia. The school construction project of the Japanese Government could be considered an imitation of this Sumitomo Group's initiative.

8.7.3 Improvement of Basic Infrastructure

As the Japanese Government has contributed to poverty reduction by improving conditions of health, safety, agriculture, and land use, Japanese corporations have also engaged in similar activities. Let us review three typical contributions Japanese corporations have made in this regard.

First, in poverty-stricken communities of the Philippines, Toyota Motor and its charitable foundation have conducted the so-called Medical and Dental Outreach Program. The program has taken place twice a year. By 2006, more than 75,000 people had received medical attention through this program. According to a report published by Toyota, most of the patients might have otherwise never received care from medical professionals. Usually parents bring children for treatment of a parasitic disease. And when it is necessary, physicians perform simple surgery at the outreach sites (Neighbors 2006: 24–25).

Second, Sumitomo Chemical's contribution in the field of healthcare might be well known. It is said that each year, about 300 million people contract Malaria and one million die of it. In order to challenge this tragedy, Sumitomo Chemical has participated in the roll back Malaria campaign and has supplied its original mosquito nets (Olyset nets) to poor villages through UNICEF and WHO. While the company offered manufacturing know-how to a Tanzanian company free of charge, it has also been expanding the production capacity in response to increasing needs for the nets. So far Sumitomo Chemical has supplied 30 million nets to the global community. The Olyset net is said to be very effective in preventing Malaria. For example, in 2006 the company donated 330,000 nets to the Millennium Promise, one of the influential NGOs, and this donation is believed to save and protect over 500,000 people from Malaria.

The last one is a very brave and far-reaching initiative. The president of Yamanashi Hitachi Construction Machinery, a very small company, has been making strenuous efforts to return fertility to land and safety to children in poor countries devastated by wars. According to a report, currently about 110 million antipersonnel landmines are in place around the world. If people try to find all of them following the established procedure, it will take more than 100 years. Shocked by this reality, Mr. Kiyoshi Amemiya, president of the company, launched a landmine clearance project to improve the situation where many civilians, especially children, become victims of those mines. Keeping a strong belief that without cultivable and fertile land any country cannot support itself, he has devoted his life to developing special bulldozers and to clearing the land of many countries with his inventions.

We have indirectly suggested that in order to mitigate criticisms against the WTO and the business community, multinationals have to make social contributions. But as far as corporations introduced here are concerned, we cannot see such motives in a clear manner. They seem to have engaged in global challenges and promoted philanthropic movements, just because of a very strong sense of corporate social responsibility. In other words, they take poverty as one of the most important ethical issues, and have proceeded with their self-setting missions. Regarding the third question of the FITI project, we believe that a series of those initiatives taken by leading corporations could be also noteworthy developments by the business community.

8.8 Summary and Closing Remarks

8.8.1 Answering the First Question

In this chapter, we have discussed a number of issues so as to answer three questions of the FITI project. As for the first question, we described the formal position of the Japanese Government. In a nutshell, it considers that a part of the WTO process (DSB) is fair and effective, but it sees that the WTO has not been working effectively, because the outcome of the WTO does not seem fair enough to some Members. This is the main reason why Japan has shifted its position from a WTO-centered to a bilateral EPA-driven strategy. When it comes to the perceptions of ordinary Japanese, we found that most of them (except for NGOs) are likely to consider that the WTO is working in a fair manner. One of the interesting points is that every stakeholder group in Japan including NGOs feels that corporations and civil society could work together as good partners.

8.8.2 Answering the Second Question

With regard to the second question, we identified two ethical issues as the most important and challenging issues.

First is protection of rice farming in Japan. From the viewpoint of life in rural areas, natural environment, sustainable management of water resources, cultural traditions, and food security, the Japanese Government has long protected rice farming. On the other hand, agricultural exporting countries have urged Japan to import more agricultural products, and reduce tariff rates on them, including rice.

Second is poverty reduction, especially alleviation of extreme poverty in the least developed countries. Given the size of its economy, Japan has to take this responsibility far more seriously than ever. It is suggested that so far Japan has made contributions mainly to the development of East Asia and the Pacific. Now that many countries in this region have began to develop economically on their own, even if poverty remains in some areas of this region, it is clear that Japan has come to a point to shift its focus from Asia to Africa.

Before answering the third question, we defined the ultimate purpose of globalization and the WTO, from the viewpoint of a rational person on the original position. That is to reduce both the gap between developed and developing countries at the global level, and the gap between the most advantaged people and the least advantaged people at the national level. With this definition in mind, we explained typical initiatives led by the Japanese Government and by major Japanese corporations.

8.8.3 Answering the Third Question (1): Protecting Rice Farming

As for the first ethical issue, protection of rice farming in Japan, through the TICAD process, the Japanese Government has started to make the best use of Japan's experiences in rice production for the benefits of Sub-Saharan Africa. Faced with the food shortage crisis, Japan has facilitated the development of NERICA, and explored possibilities of producing the next generation of biofuels. By committing itself to those initiatives, Japan expects WTO Members to understand its policy on rice and its contributions to rice harvesting in poor countries, even if such contributions do not solve clearly the dilemma between the requests of agricultural exporting countries and the interests of domestic rice farmers.

8.8.4 Answering the Third Question (2): Poverty Reduction

With regard to the second ethical issue, poverty reduction, like other developed countries, Japan has also engaged in MDGs from the beginning. Based upon its own experience and its experience in East Asia, the Japanese Government will input more resources into the infrastructure of Africa. As one of the major initiatives through the TICAD process, Japan plans to connect missing links in transportation infrastructure. It strongly believes that by improving market access, the private sector would eventually be mobilized. On top of that, the Japanese Government has initiated the primary and secondary school construction project, and offers training programs to instructors of science and mathematics in Africa.

In addition to those governmental initiatives, major Japanese corporations have also addressed the second issue. As we have seen, when it comes to the development of a country, Japanese people are likely to place great importance on education. Following that belief, in the field of education, the private sector has offered training programs to local teachers and administrators, has provided libraries to elementary schools in the most underprivileged areas, and has constructed primary schools in the least developed countries. Many corporations have also made contributions in the fields of health and security. For instance, some have supplied mosquito nets to fight Malaria, and others have made strenuous efforts to clear anti-personnel landmines so as to make the war-devastated land safe and cultivable. All of them, including governmental initiatives, could be regarded as developments in Japan to address these global issues. This is the answer to the last question the FITI project raised.

8.8.5 Remaining Issues

We have seen initiatives to achieve poverty reduction. All those initiatives, whether government-led or private sector-led, are basically voluntary not obligatory. As long as those voluntary-based initiatives are working well, we might not need to consider other ways to assist. But at the end of this chapter, we would like to mention a little bit about a new movement, which might give us some ideas, when we think of making the world a real global community. This is the so-called "global taxation" movement. A typical example is to impose a tax on airline tickets for achieving MDGs, mainly for funding the global fight against diseases like HIV/AIDS, Tuberculosis, and Malaria.

TRIPs came into effect in 1995, which prohibited pharmaceutical manufacturers from producing generic medicines without authorization of the patent right holders. As a result, the price of quality drugs like HIV-related drugs became very expensive. To be sure, developing countries can still manufacture or import cheap generic drugs, if they invoke the compulsory license procedure within the TRIPs framework. But even in those countries there are still many people who cannot afford quality drugs. As one of the effective ways to alleviate this situation, the global tax was introduced and imposed on airline tickets. On the basis of this taxation system, UNITAID, an international drug purchase facility, negotiates prices for those drugs on behalf of poor patients. Seeing this mechanism working well, NGOs began to explore possibilities to impose global taxes on other activities or sectors such as speculative money transactions, carbon dioxide emissions, etc.

It is clear that in this taxation system there are many difficult issues such as how to maintain fair taxation among industries or among taxpayers, how to distribute tax revenues among recipients in a fair manner, and how to govern this taxation system in a responsible and accountable manner. Despite those complicated issues, we feel that at least, this mechanism designed to contribute to MDGs might be useful, since it could work on an obligatory-basis. Imposing taxes on individuals not on countries is also a very interesting point. If we take into consideration the fact that even in developed countries there are many poor people, and even in developing countries there are wealthy people, imposing global taxes on individuals could be rational and practical. With those reasons in mind, we conclude by suggesting that the global taxation movement would be worth examining further.

References

Blandford, D., and Josling T. 2006, "Options for the WTO Modalities for Agriculture," *IPC Discussion Paper*, May.

EPA Negotiation Team (EPA Team) at the Ministry of Foreign Affairs (MOFA) of Japan 2007) *Commentary on FTA and EPA Negotiations* (Japanese), ed. by Watanabe T., Nihon Keizai Hyoronsha.

Harrison A. 2005, "Globalization and Poverty" (draft for NBER), October.

ICTSD 2002, "Agriculture Negotiations at the WTO: Modalities Phase Outlook Report," Geneva Switzerland, April.

Maeda, K. 2007, "WTO Agricultural Negotiations and Importing Rice (Japanese)".

MAFF 1999, Basic Law on Food, Agriculture and Rural Areas, July. http://www.maff.go.jp/soshiki/kambou/kikaku/NewBLaw/BasicLaw.html

MAFF 2000, "Negotiating Proposal by Japan on WTO Agricultural Negotiations (Japanese)," December. http://www.maff.go.jp/wto/wto_nihon_teian_e.htm

Ministry of Agriculture, Forestry and Fisheries (MAFF) of Japan 2008a, "The Current Movements over the WTO Agricultural Negotiations (Japanese)," the Japanese Government. http://www.maff.go.jp/j/kokusai/taigai/wto/pdf/wto_meguru.pdf

MAFF 2008b, "The Current Movements, Appendix (Japanese)," the Japanese Government. http://www.maff.go.jp/j/kokusai/taigai/wto/pdf/ref_data.pdf

Ministry of Economy, Trade and Industry (METI) of Japan 2007a, *The 2007 Report on Compliance by Major Trading Partners with Trade Agreement* (Japanese), the Japanese Government.

METI 2007b, *White Paper of International Trade* (Japanese), the Japanese Government.

METI 2007c, "About the 2007 Report (Japanese)," the Japanese Government.

METI and Keidanren 2007, The WTO and FTA Seminar (Tokyo) held by the METI and Keidanren on February 23. http://www.wto.org/english/tratop_e/dda_e/dohaexplained_e.htm

Ministry of Foreign Affairs (MOFA) of Japan 2005a, *Building Global Partnerships for Development* (Japanese), September.

MOFA 2005b, *Initiatives of Japan towards 2015* (Japanese), the Japanese Government, March.

Multilateral Trade System Department (MTSD) of the METI 2007, "Summary of 2007 Report (Japanese)," the Japanese Government.

Neighbors 2005, *Worldwide Philanthropic Activities at Toyota*, Toyota Motor, Vol. 1.

Neighbors 2006) *Worldwide Philanthropic Activities at Toyota*, Toyota Motor, Vol. 2.

Oxfam International 2002, *Rigged Rules and Double Standards: Trade, Globalization, and the Fight Against Poverty*, Oxfam GB.

Rawls J 1971, *A Theory of Justice* (The Belknap Press of Harvard University Press, Cambridge).

Sachs JD 2005, *The End of Poverty: Economic Possibilities for Our Time* (Penguin Books).

Sen A 2000, *Development as Freedom* (Anchor Books).

Taka I 2006, *Uncompromising Integrity* (Japanese), Nikkei Shinbun.

Takikawa T 2005, *WTO Laws: Practices, Cases, and Policies*, (Japanese) Sanseido.

TICAD 2008a, TICAD IV Yokohama Action Plan, May 30.

TICAD 2008b, Address by Prime Minister Yasuo Fukuda at the Opening Session of the Fourth Tokyo International Conference on African Development (TICAD IV), May 28.

Urata, S., Ishikawa, K., and Mizuno, R. 2007, *FTA Guidebook 2007* (Japanese), JETRO.

The World Trade Organization 2000, "Free trade helps reduce poverty, says new WTO secretariat study," June 13, press/181. http://www.wto.org/english/news_e/pres00_e/pr181_e.htm

The World Trade Organization 2001, " The Doha Declaration explained," http://www.wto.int/english/tratop_e/dda_e/dohaexplained_e.htm

Chapter 9
Fairness in International Trade and Investment: North American Perspectives

Frederick Bird, Thomas Vance, and Peter Woolstencroft

9.1 Introduction

North Americans have adopted a number of different views with respect to what they consider fair in relation to international trade and investment. These differences reflect the distinctly different histories of the United States, Canada, and Mexico; the varied roles that international trade plays in these countries; markedly different social and economic positions of groups within these countries; and varied political and economic interests. Within each country typically different positions regarding fairness in international trade have been taken by small and large businesses, farming groups, trade unions, consumers, and different regions. In spite of these differences, Canada, Mexico, and the United States have joined together in the North American Free Trade Agreement (NAFTA), which has been both widely applauded and criticized. All three countries are members of the World Trade Organization (WTO).

In the initial part of the chapter we review recent developments with respect to trade. We note the way that the multi-lateral trade arrangements associated with the WTO have modified how regional bi-and-tri-lateral agreements have been interpreted in ways that have at times promoted the interests of smaller countries. In the second part of the chapter we discuss four typical normative views that North Americans have taken with respect to international trade and investment. In addition to a traditional and currently resurgent protectionist stance, the other major view, which we refer to as the liberal fair play position, has championed both international trade and fairness in such trade based on notions associated with procedural justice. This mind set has not only at times influenced official government policies, especially in the United States, but also informed the negotiations that led to the creation of the General Agreement on Trades and Tariffs (GATT). While likewise championing international trade, a third perspective, has called for greater attention to concerns for distributive justice and fair outcomes. Finally, while not being

F. Bird (✉)
Research Professor, Department of Political Science, University of Waterloo, Waterloo, Ontario, Canada; Distinguished Professor Emeritus, Concordia University, Montreal, Quebec, Canada
e-mail: fbird@uwaterloo.ca

G. Moore (ed.), *Fairness in International Trade*, The International Society
of Business, Economics, and Ethics Book Series 1, DOI 10.1007/978-90-481-8840-6_9,

overtly protectionists, a number of North Americans have raised serious questions about the ways current trading relations endanger the environment and aggravate inequalities.

These differing interests and views of international trade and the fairness of this trade – national, sectoral, and normative – do not seem to be simply resolvable, either by invoking overarching principles or common interests. However, adopting a normative perspective in parts three and four, we argue that fairness is best approached not by trying to overcome these different interests and values but through open and reciprocating political processes that enable these differences to be voiced, acknowledged, and debated and thereby encourage compromises to emerge. In addition, we identify five fundamental affirmations, which seem to be both important for these inevitable ongoing debates and ones that these diverse points of view can embrace as basic despite their differences. In the last two parts of the chapter, we outline these views calling particular attention to views of commutative justice and issues associated with abusive transfer pricing.

Since its birth in 1995, the WTO, successor to the GATT, has grown rapidly – from an original 76 members to its current roster of 152, with approximately 30 additional "observer governments" making strides toward full membership (WTO, 2008). Membership growth has been accompanied by an expanding agenda. While GATT restricted itself to commercial trade issues, the WTO's initial mandate was wider; and since then it has had to deal with myriad issues, especially pertaining to the environment and human rights, trade in services and intellectual property rights, unknown in the pre-WTO period. Some see the emergence of the WTO as the embodiment of globalization and economic liberalism (Hart, 2002: 434–7). Others see the WTO as not just a trade liberalizing vehicle but one that is oriented towards privatization of services – for example, health and education – that heretofore had been the prime responsibilities of governments; that is, they argue, the WTO's agenda has come to include more than issues related to trade and investment; it has come to include a number of more value-laden and thus contested social, economic, and political objectives (McDougall, 2006: 64–5).

9.2 Bilateral and Multilateral Trade Relations in North America: Recent Developments

North Americans have adopted a number of quite different views with respect to whether, and to what degree, current international trade practices are fair or unfair. The Mexican, Canadian, and American governments frequently hold different views on these matters, even though all three countries are members of the North American Free Trade Agreement (NAFTA). In each country various groups have defended positions associated with fair trade, protectionism, economic nationalism, bilateralism, and free trade. In the first part of this chapter, we examine issues of fairness in international trade largely from a Canadian perspective. We begin with recognition of the asymmetrical relationships between the three large countries that constitute North America.

9.2.1 Three Asymmetries

North America is a complex social, economic, and political entity, characterized by growing commonalities and also great differences. Since the 1980s two overall themes have been evident in discussions about the future of North America. First, since the 1988 Canadian-US Free Trade Agreement (CUSFTA) and NAFTA (signed in 1994), which created the world's largest trading bloc, there has been increasing interest in – and debate about – the desirability of North American economic integration. For many, increasing economic integration leads to more and more political integration, desirable or not. At the same time, heightened consciousness of three asymmetries between Canada, Mexico, and the United States raises questions about how future economic and political arrangements will be structured.

First, by measures of gross economic activity, the three countries of North America rank in the top 15 of the world's economies. However, the United States, the world's largest economy (with about one-quarter of the world's economic activity), exercises far greater economic power in the world than do Canada, ranked eight (less than 1 percent of the world's economic activity) and Mexico, ranked 15 (International Monetary Fund, 2008). Further, the United States – the world's leading political and economic power – overwhelms its northern and southern neighbours in many other respects, such as population, per capita purchasing power, and annualized growth rates. For example, Canada's market is only 9 percent of the US market.

Second, Canada and the United States clearly represent developed economies, a small subset of all the world's economies in terms of numbers, at the same time as they constitute a large fraction of the world's economic activity, with both countries belonging to the G8. Mexico, by contrast, clearly falls into the category of developing countries, which number many and are slowly growing in economic weight. Differences between developed and developing countries underlie much of the protracted and failed Doha development round of negotiations. The differences between these countries in terms of per capita income or overall economic activity have not decreased over the past several decades.

The third asymmetry pertains to the role of international trade in each nation's economy. Global international trade is immensely important for both Canada and Mexico (respectively, trade-to-GNP ratios in 2006 being 70.1 and 65.1), but less important for the United States, with a ratio of 28.1, the lowest of states in the Organization for Economic Co-operation and Development (OECD Statistical Abstracts).

As shown in Table 9.1, there are important differences in trade patterns within North America. For both Canada and Mexico, trade with the United States is of signal importance, representing for each country over 85 percent of its global trade. Trade between the United States and its neighbours commands less weight, though Canada is the leading destination for American exports and Mexico the third.

Regular meetings between the leaders of Canada, Mexico, and the United States speak to the continuing importance of intra-regional issues, with trade and investment being prominent but security issues assuming great importance, principally

Table 9.1 Percentage of all merchandise imports and exports between Canada, Mexico, and the United States, 2007

	Exports to			Imports from		
	Canada	Mexico	USA	Canada	Mexico	USA
Canada		1.1	79.3		4.2	54.2
Mexico	2.6		89.5	2.3		59.9
USA	21.4	11.7		15.7	10.6	

Source: World Trade Organization, International Trade Statistics, 2008

driven by the attacks on the United States on September 11, 2001. The three countries signed in 2005 the "Security and Prosperity Partnership of North America" (SPP). Its purpose was twofold: to develop trilateral agreements on security issues and to provide for economic cooperation and information sharing. Both Canada and Mexico are apprehensive that American security issues will lead to hardening of America's two borders with economic consequences more severe for Canada and Mexico than for the United States. Indeed, some see the United States in the post 9/11 period turning away from its long-standing and public commitment to trade liberalization in favour of "strategic power" and "economic power" (Staples, 2007).

The idea of "asymmetrical dependency" best captures the dynamics of the economic relations between the three countries in that one – the United States – is much less dependent on the other two than are the latter two dependent upon the United States (Baldwin, 1980: 471–506).

9.2.2 North America and the WTO

In general, Canada and the United States have supported trade liberalization in both the GATT and WTO eras. Mexico moved toward support of trade liberalization in the 1990s. The United States, again in general, has justified trade liberalization in terms of enhancing choice and spurring economic growth through competition and comparative advantage. Canada and Mexico, conscious of size differentials between themselves and the United States and desirous of protecting social, economic, and political institutions, have perceived competitive pressures and economic weight as potentially disrupting, if not destroying, "Canadian" or "Mexican" ways of doing things.

North American debates about trading arrangements and governments pivot on two questions. The first concerns whether regional or global trading agreements are preferable. The second pertains to the relationship between society (advocacy groups, interest groups, and political parties) and governments.

In the case of Canada, after over a century of political argumentation about the desirability of "free trade" with the United States, the signal event clearly was the 1998 CUSFTA. The voluminous literature on the agreement contains two significant points. First, an important motivation for the Canadian government to enter into negotiations with the United States was the fear of ascendant protectionist forces, especially in the U.S. Congress. Canada was perceived to be especially vulnerable in the absence of formalized trade arrangements. Second, in an age of concern about fossil-fuel reserves and security of supply, coupled with price uncertainties, the United States will be increasingly looking for Canada to meet its future energy needs (Council on Foreign Relations, 2005). The growing interdependence between the Canadian and American economies makes it very difficult for the Canadian government to interfere with the flow of energy to the hungry American market. Mexico, for its part, was interested in a trade arrangement with the United States in order to establish itself as a secure and attractive destination for investment monies. Canada joined what became NAFTA in order to protect its interests in any agreement reached between the two countries to the south.

Multi-lateral trade arrangements highlighted, of course, by the WTO provide a telling contrast with the regional trade arrangements found in North America. The WTO – in its stated objectives – clearly is oriented toward trade liberalization on the basis of general rules. That is, very much embedded in the WTO system is the establishment and implementation of policies, procedures, and practices that allow for free, smooth, and predictable trade flows, all of which should be reflected in international trade law. Five principles constitute the WTO's framework for trade policies; they are:

non-discrimination;
reciprocity;
binding and enforceable commitments;
transparency; and
"safety valves" which allow governments, under certain conditions, to restrict trade.

The premise, then, of the WTO is that unencumbered international economic exchanges will be beneficial to all countries. Let us turn to the case of North America, primarily through an examination of the American and Canadian cases, the two countries having had a long history of commercial relations, to understand the differences between regional and multilateral trade arrangements.

The two North American trade treaties, in comparison with the European Community and the WTO, have one important distinguishing feature, namely the lack of overarching institutional structures. Free-market proponents of the trade agreements did not appreciate the need for supranational political institutions. Those looking for such institutions were confronted with the clear unwillingness on the part of the United States to contemplate the possibility and the fear on the part of Canada and Mexico that they, singly or jointly, could and would not be heard in such institutions. Simply, trade arrangements did not change political ones, with the United States happily pursing its tradition of unilateralism and Canada and Mexico relying on bilateralism for the furtherance of their interests (Pastor, 2001). Indeed, the three governments, in the course of the NAFTA negotiations, "seemed to be haunted by the specter of the European Union" and its many institutional forms which incorporated many of the executive, legislative, and judicial functions of government (Clarkson, 2008: 51).

Another telling feature of the North American trade agreements is the organization of dispute resolution mechanisms (DRM). In the case of NAFTA, provision is made for governments to attempt to resolve disputes about interpretative matters through discussion and negotiation. Failing such agreement, the matter is transmitted to ad hoc bilateral panels for arbitration. These panels are low-level in that they lack enforcement mechanisms, thus allowing governments to follow decisions as they wish. A similar low degree of institutionalization is evident in regards to the settlement of disputes about anti-dumping or countervailing duties. While Clarkson argues that NAFTA trade disputes have been successful in attenuating somewhat the power differences between the United States and its two neighbours, he points to an important condition: Washington has accepted decisions when there is little domestic opposition, but "bi-national panel rulings have not managed to discipline American government behaviour on issues of major domestic salience" (Clarkson, 2008: 81). On critical matters, then, the trade agreements do not appreciably alter the asymmetrical power relations in North America.

What does the WTO mean for North America? That question leads to consideration of the WTO and its two decision-making features. First, decisions are to be made consensually. Second, the current (and now failed) negotiations were a "single undertaking". This means that instead of negotiations proceeding sequentially from issue to issue or from sector to sector, all issues proceed simultaneously and must be resolved before the negotiations have concluded. Failure in one part is a failure in all parts.

The fundamental decision-making rules of the WTO are highly contentious. The requirement for consensus is problematic in small groups as it encourages "hold-out" behavior; (some) participants, knowing the norm, take hard positions, calculating that others will concede at least some critical points. Within larger groups, the likelihood that negotiations will be successful would seem to be quite low. A compounding institutional factor that contributes to the low probability of success is that states vary enormously in their approval processes, highlighted by the United States, where the Senate must approve any international commitments. Assertive domestic political interests may trump what American negotiators have accepted. American leaders have spoken glowingly about the desirability of trade liberalization. However, many cases that have gone before the WTO concerning American actions and laws have been resolved in ways that have been favorable to economic interests in the United States.

The "single-undertaking" requirement has been interpreted by many to be inordinately demanding and inevitably destructive of success. The "utilitarian" interpretation of states and interests says that negotiations take place within the context of each state trying to maximize its gains and minimize its losses. Two predictions follow from this perspective: first, that there will be collapsed negotiations because of the unwillingness to make the compromises necessary to reach consensus; second, the agenda of western industrialized nations – the liberalization of trade in its many forms – will not be matched by the full opening of their markets to the produce and products of developing countries because of the heavy weight that they bring to negotiations; in other words, the asymmetries between the developed and developing countries work to the advantage of the former.

A contrary view, cogently argued by Robert Wolfe (2008), sees the negotiating context of the WTO in positive terms. His "constructivist" perspective is predicated on the assumption that actors enter negotiations, not with interests in mind that perhaps will be begrudgingly trimmed in light of their bargaining strategies, but in a context "in which contracts and treaties furnish a framework for an ongoing relationship of the relationship, not a precise definition of the relationship." Arguing processes lead actors to contemplate reasons for positions – for all actors, not just theirs—and to think about ways to reach agreement in light of what they have learned. In other words, the institution of trade negotiations embodied in the WTO system will not only reflect power politics but also the reasoned accommodation by actors of interests through the interpretation, understanding, and appreciation of the reasons for stated positions. The constructivist perspective, as compared to the underlying "power" politics of utilitarianism, is consistent with the idea of procedural fairness.

From the perspective of Canada and Mexico, the WTO represents their best hope of arriving at trade and investment agreements that do not reflect the strong asymmetries that exist in North America. In utilitarian terms, regional or bilateral agreements will reflect the weight of the United States. (And, indeed, some commentators see an emerging interest on the American side in the marginalization of the WTO in favor of bilateral trade agreements.)

Three important cases point to the importance of the WTO for Canada. The first originated in the WTO ruling in 1997 that "content requirements for magazine advertising were illegal, raising the prospect that quotas and subsidies protecting Canadian culture would be stripped away" (Byers, 2007: 113). In the subsequent decade the Canadian government worked energetically to move the WTO to accept that cultural industries are separate from other economic sectors despite American objections that choice by consumers and the profits of its large corporate entertainment sector were threatened.

The second case comes from the agricultural sector. Agriculture is not ordinarily identified as being caught up in globalizing forces, yet, as Coleman and his colleagues (2004) point out, it is very much at the centre of the interaction between myriad actors – states, transnational corporations, global institutions (including the WTO), international non-governmental organizations (NGOs), and social movements – and the intersection between issues of intellectual property (especially genetically-modified seeds), food supply and security, biological diversity, and environmental protection and enhancement. The linkages between the state, the market, and agricultural producers are also variable, as is exemplified by the comparison between Canada and the United States. One important difference is the existence in Canada of a number of marketing boards which have monopoly buying and selling powers whereas in the United States producers operate in the open market (although subsidies, as in many countries, are an important element of the agricultural economy). Agriculture is one of Canada's leading value-added economic sectors, with wheat constituting an important export product, thereby competing under the auspices of the Canadian Wheat Board with American producers. The difference between the Canadian and American approaches in support of their agricultural industries is that there "is a perception in the American wheat industry that the Canadian Wheat Board (CWB) is structured in such a way as to ensure it will not operate in accordance with commercial considerations – that is, in the interests of free market competition" (Froese, 2008: 2).

The United States challenged the Canadian system at the WTO by arguing that the Canadian Wheat Board, a state-trading enterprise (STE), acted as a monopsony. By being the single buyer and seller of wheat, it alleged that the CWB undercut the workings of competitive markets. However, the issue was more than just a matter of economic outcomes, but, rather, one that reflected different approaches to the role of government in the economy (Froese, 2008: 5). In 2004, the WTO ruled, for the most in favour of Canada, and on the central issue of the legality of the marketing board supported Canadian arguments.

The third case concerned the softwood lumber industry in Canada. It paralleled the agriculture issue in one sense as Canadian practices related to stumpage fees (how Canadian governments sell harvesting rights on crown land, which constitute over 90 percent of Canada's forestland) were seen by protectionist-minded American competitors, who work within a market-system, as leading to an unfair competitive advantage; however, the issue was more complex, as American consumers, benefiting from lower Canadian prices for softwood, were an interest not at play in the dispute about the CWB's impact on global wheat pricing. The issue was also more protracted, running for about 25 years and going through many FTA, NAFTA and WTO dispute settlement mechanisms (Anderson, 2006: 586).

One point is especially pertinent in light of the foregoing discussion of fairness in trade and investment. As the American case failed in the course of going through various dispute settlement mechanisms, the response of the United States government was to seek solutions outside of NAFTA – that is, through a negotiated settlement between the Canadian and United States governments (Gagne, 2003). The long-term goal of Canadian governments in pursuing formalized trade agreements with the United States had been institutionalization of the dispute settlement mechanisms, which would have the effect of depoliticizing disputes. Although the eventual decision – rendered by a WTO panel – was mixed, nonetheless it was a victory for the Canadian government inasmuch as a solution to the impasse was found. At the same time the panel supported the basic contention of the US government that stumpage fees amounted to a subsidy for Canadian softwood exports (Williams, 2008). On the whole, American economic power and pressures were undercut by the WTO. Tellingly, however, with the American government refusing to accept judgments from both NAFTA and WTO panels, the Conservative government of Canada bowed to the American demand for a negotiated settlement, which in its details contradicted WTO rulings (Clarkson, 2008: 83).

In constructivist terms, large-scale negotiations promise the possibility of balancing interests given the WTO's two overriding principles – that of non-discrimination and most-favoured-nation (in which trade concessions to one must be extended to all). The constructivist perspective presumes that learning (and attendant appreciation and understanding) will function to balance the weight of state interests.

Clearly multi-lateral trade relations, like those embodied in the WTO, function to serve the interests of relatively large economies like Canada's and Mexico's in their relationships with the much larger economy of the United States.

9.3 Several North American Normative Perspectives on Fairness in International Trade and Investment

In part one, we have examined several active political positions which North Americans have adopted with respect to achieving what proponents of these several movements have regarded as fairness in international trade. We have in particular examined the practical impact of the multilateral approach on trading issues between the United States and Canada. In part two, we will examine several normative perspectives articulated by North Americans on how to foster fairness in multilateral trade. While all parties invoke basic principles of fairness, they do so in quite different ways.

9.3.1 Protectionism and the Prevailing Liberal Views of Fair Play

In order to protect what Alexander Hamilton regarded as its infant industries, the early American Republic adopted a protectionist perspective towards international trade. Tariffs served both as a means of fostering domestic businesses and industries as well as a reliable means of raising public revenues. This position remained dominant until sometime during the New Deal years of the 1930s as Americans began to develop what we are here labeling as the liberal fair play view of fairness with respect to international trade. As they negotiated a number of bilateral treaties in the thirties and forties and as they took the lead in championing multilateral approaches to trade in the post world war two years, American governments sought to encourage the expansion of foreign trade in keeping with certain basic principles of fair play. Several principles have remained basic to the notions of fair play with regard to international trade throughout the subsequent years.

One, the initial assumption emphasizes the importance of free choice. Accordingly, trading arrangements ought to be established so that firms and nations can freely negotiate the terms of their exchanges. The traditional rules and tariffs restricting these choices should be liberalized in due course. Two, countries should proceed with these negotiations in keeping with the principle of non-discrimination such that all nations would be treated the same in keeping with a general set of rules. Often referred to as the "most favored nation" principle, this standard requires that the same basic rules and procedures be followed in negotiating trading relations with any and all other countries. Finally, three, it was assumed that these liberal market exchanges only became viable to the extent that contracts and property rights were adequately guaranteed in law. These principles of fair play have been typically justified in utilitarian terms. Thus, as governments created opportunities for free market negotiations and exchanges, it has been widely argued that they thereby also fostered arrangements that favored constructive wealth creation.

Based on these normative beliefs, American governments from the 1930s onward negotiated dozens of bi-lateral treaties to liberalize trade. In the post World War Two years they proposed establishing an International Trade Organization and when this effort failed, they joined with other countries in efforts to promote the General Agreement on Tariffs and Trade (Zampetti, 2006).

The liberal ideas of fair play assume that governments should and would proceed to work to liberalize trading rules with other countries, thereby enhancing the opportunities of domestic exporters and investors. In exchange the government would make concessions that provided opportunities for foreign firms to sell imports domestically so long as imports in no way injured the opportunities of domestic firms. Liberal notions of fair play were thus closely connected with assumptions about reciprocity. Opportunities would be extended mutually on something like a tit for tat basis so long as these arrangements did not put domestic businesses at a decided disadvantage.

Similarly with liberal ideas about equal opportunity, these beliefs about fair play focus on the conditions that allow for open, rule-regulated, competition. Ideas of fair play do not focus on whether outcomes are just or not. Rather, this perspective seeks to allow for and support the free choices of individuals and firms: it assumes that individuals and firms will compete on the basis of their own self-interest; it seeks to identify and reinforce impersonal rules that will facilitate the expansion of trade; and it assumes that public good will be maximized by fostering this kind of self-interested competition.

This view of fair play is limited in several important ways. One, it is assumed that, while governments ought to restrain their intrusive efforts to over-regulate commerce, they will nonetheless act to provide the legal and political infrastructures that facilitate and protect free market exchanges (Finn, 2006). Two, the beliefs about fair play presuppose as well that governments will act constructively in several different ways to support domestic enterprises as these firms enter into competition in international markets: by protesting against what seem like unfair competition by others, by offering subsidies for industries especially threatened by foreign competitors with cheaper labor markets, and by keeping them well informed of technological and even economic innovations. Three, additionally this liberal fair play approach assumes a national not global perspective. This view has been used progressively to liberalize trading relations within particular industries and sectors but only to the extent that reciprocating relationships can be developed with other countries. Where this kind of mutual adjusting and repositioning has been resisted both by other countries and national enterprises, for example, with respect to a wide range of agricultural products, then these trading relations have not been correspondingly liberalized.

Liberal views about fair play in international trade have been widely embraced. They have been articulated and defended as economic common sense. Along with some protectionists' sentiments voiced in defense of domestic workers, in practice these views have shaped much of American international trade policy since the

Great Depression. These views have also influenced American policies with respect to the proper role of the World Bank, the International Monetary Fund, and the General Agreement on Tariffs and Trade. To a large extent, Mexican and Canadian economic liberals adopt similar views.

Over the years different groups have interpreted and expressed the core set of basic liberal standards of fair play somewhat differently. While some neo-liberal defenders of these principles have set forth their views in ways that seemed to suggest that international trading markets were almost free standing institutions, other more traditional liberals have called for greater attention to the important roles that governments, their laws and regulations, trade agencies, and central banks, have played in creating and maintaining these institutions. Because of these variations, the liberal views of fair play have often seemed vague if not amorphous.

9.3.2 The Liberal Search for Distributive Justice

Typically, North Americans have dissented from this liberal position by supporting some form of trade protectionism. Whether in defense of particular industries, in the name of national self-determination, on behalf of domestic workers and their wages, or in protest against the environmental damages of international businesses, many North Americans at both ends of the political spectrum have assumed genuine fairness would be best achieved through tariffs and subsidies in support of the farmers, laborers, and businesses of their own countries. However, there have also been those who criticized the liberal fair play position in hopes of achieving a more just although still liberal system of international trade. Basically, these liberal dissenters argue that the fair play ideas as they have been put into practice have been applied in ways that been both inconsistent and excessively doctrinaire. They argue further, that the fair play liberals have not given sufficient attention to whether the actual experiences of fair play trading arrangements have worked in practice to occasion outcomes – patterns of distribution—that were also fair.

Joseph Stiglitz and Andrew Charlton have recently published an articulate statement outlining an alternative liberal approach in defense of international trade with greater focus on achieving practical outcomes that were just for all. We will use their account as a contemporary expression of liberals who especially signal the importance of distributive justice. Stiglitz and Charlton set forth their ideas in a book *Fair Trade For All: How Trade Can Promote Development*. They mount a number of criticisms of the fair play ideas, which they refer as the "classical model." This model erroneously assumes, they argue, full employment in all countries engaging in trade. It assumes as well that local markets everywhere work effectively, overlooking in the process how the absence of effective legal, regulatory, and physical infrastructures distorts markets. Further, they argue that the fair play model overlooks the historical fact that industrializing nations as well as new nations have traditionally used tariffs both to develop their national industries and to raise public revenues. Stiglitz and Charlton note as well that the fair play model fails to take account of the often excessive costs involved in instituting and implementing fair trade practices.

Finally, and in some ways, most importantly, because of its national bias and its continued commitment to protect certain industries, the fair play doctrine has allowed liberal-minded politicians to defend the continued existence of international trade-restricting tariffs, subsidies, and regulations with respect both to trade in agricultural products and services (Stiglitz and Charlton, 2005).

In keeping with their reading of Rawls' *Theory of Justice* (1970), Stiglitz and Charlton insist that a fair system of international trade ought to be one that not only operates in terms of liberal principles of free choice to liberalize trading arrangements but also works to the advantage of the least advantaged peoples (Stiglitz and Charlton, 2004). That is, the situation of developing countries ought to be improved and not aggravated as a result of way the rules governing international trade are interpreted and applied. Stiglitz and Charlton make a number of proposals.

First, they set forth in principled terms guidelines on thinking about the "Special and Differential Treatment" for which developing countries supposedly qualified in keeping with the charter that established the WTO. In practice the language of "special and differential treatment" has been used to extend the deadlines by when developing countries have to comply with a number of the WTO regulations. In addition, Stiglitz and Charlton propose a couple of basic principles with respect to market access. These guidelines are as follows. One, countries with larger economies and larger per capita incomes should establish no barriers to trade arriving from countries with smaller economies and lower per capita incomes. Two, in order to help their own economies to grow, countries with smaller economies and lower per capita incomes can impose tariffs on goods and services arriving from countries with larger economies and higher per capita incomes. Stiglitz and Charlton defend these standards as being procedurally fair because they apply the same to all countries and fair in keeping with norms of just distributions because these standards would both foster increased trade, which is advantageous to all, and would especially help the poorest countries to enter into trading relations in ways that would facilitate their own development.

Second, Stiglitz and Carlton argue that a system of international trade only becomes genuinely fair when all countries have comparable capabilities to participate in this system. Here the authors are focusing on practical matters. For example, all countries, they argue, should have equivalent opportunities to assess the consequences for their own economies when alternative trading arrangements are being discussed. The WTO ought, therefore, to provide the research services that would help each country to gain a good sense of the economic impact of alternative regulations and trading regimes. Additionally, each country ought to be able to call upon relevant legal and accounting services so they are not disadvantaged in trade negotiations and dispute resolution conferences. If the least developed countries cannot afford these services, then by some means these services ought to be made available for them. In practice the prevailing fair play model overlooks these discrepancies, which greatly disadvantage poorer countries.

Third, Stiglitz and Charlton make a number of specific recommendations with respect to the items discussed as part of the Doha Round of international trade negotiations. Their aim here is to identify in general terms some modification in overall systems of rules governing international trade which would both foster increased liberalization of trade and do so in ways that would especially benefit poorer countries. Thus, with respect to the proposed General Agreement on Trade in Services (GATS), they observe that poorer countries would especially benefit from changes that would allow the temporary migration of low skilled laborers, who typically send home remittances that greatly help their home economies. Stiglitz and Charlton support as well proposed broad changes in the rules governing international agricultural trade that would reduce tariffs and price supports for agricultural products currently employed by the industrialized countries. They go on to note that while these proposed changes are consistent with the general support for free trade, they are likely to produce uneven benefits for poorer countries, helping larger producer countries while raising food prices for consumers. They suggest some more specific reforms, such as reducing tariffs for all tropical products, which are overwhelmingly produced by poorer countries, as well as cotton. Stiglitz and Charlton suggest specific foci for liberalizing trade in industrial goods, namely reducing the tariffs for low-skilled manufactured goods from developing countries. By retaining these tariffs, industrialized countries penalize developing countries from developing their own value-added industrial processes. Stiglitz and Charlton propose that developing countries might focus greater attention on how they might use existing non-tariff barriers for their own purposes. By and large dumping duties, countervailing duties, and safeguards have been used by the large industrialized countries to the disadvantage of poorer countries. However, these authors note that in a number of cases developing countries might well use these devices to their own advantage. Finally, these authors examine the domestic costs involved in adjusting to more liberalized trading arrangements. They offer a number of practical suggestions on how to reduce and manage these costs.

As they make these proposals, Stiglitz and Charlton adopt a pragmatic posture. Although they work to find principled justifications for the rules and policies they propose, they demonstrate their own conviction that justice is often found in the impact of detailed rules and practices on actual outcomes. A just and fair system of international trade, while based upon universal principles and arrived at through fair procedures, should also produce results that can be judged to be fair. Producing these results often requires directing attention to assessing likely impact of proposed changes, effects of alternative institutional arrangements, and consequences of overlooked details.

9.3.3 Questions, Criticisms, and Dissent from Non-liberal Perspectives

Beginning in the late 1990s, a large number of North American labour and civil society groups came together in a loosely organized anti-globalization movement in opposition to the Multilateral Agreement on Investment (MAI) proposed by the OECD. Canadian groups had been energized by the protracted debate over the signing of CUSFTA, which had been a central issue in the 1988 Canadian federal election. The movement's success in derailing the MAI led to them next targeting the WTO. With slogans such as "No New Round: Turn Around," the WTO was described by its opponents as a vehicle promoting the interests of large, multinational business enterprises. Led by Global Trade Watch in the United States and the Council of Canadians in Canada, hundreds of civil society organizations and trade unions organized protests at the third ministerial meetings of the WTO in Seattle in 1999. More than 1500 organizations world-wide endorsed a statement entitled "Shrink or Sink" opposing trade liberalization (often simply equated with globalization) and calling for a trimmed-down WTO. The protests, sometimes violent, succeeded in shutting down the WTO talks. The failed Seattle talks meant that trade discussions would occur "in an increasingly competitive environment where newly emboldened developing states would seek greater concessions from wealthy states, while civil society group agitated to bring their agenda of accountability, transparency, legitimacy, equity, and representation to the bargaining tables" (Ayres and Macdonald, 2007: 27). In 2000 more than 100 civil society groups met in Boston over four days to map out next steps in the anti-globalization movement. Led in part by North American groups, the movement staged protests in Genoa, Prague, and Quebec City over the next couple of years. Consistent with the long tradition of protectionist thinking in North America, the anti-globalization movement warned of the destruction of local and national economies by unfettered trade between high and low wage states. This movement also was energized by the view that trade liberalization initiatives downplayed a wide range of environmental issues as well as the plight of developing countries, and put economic efficiency ahead of basic needs, social justice, and communitarian values.[1]

These critics raised serious questions about current patterns of international trade and investment. For example, there is a deep and wide-spread suspicion that current systems of global trade are designed primarily for the benefit of large corporations. These systems, many North Americans argue, put the economic interests of large businesses ahead of human needs, varied cultural values, and even citizen's rights. These critics maintain that the current international trade arrangements favor the copyright entitlements of pharmaceutical companies over health needs of AIDS patients in developing countries, support economic growth over democratic involvement, and work to advance the success of businesses over environmental concerns (McMurtry, 1998; Saul, 2005; Daly and Cobb, 1989; Korton, 1996). These critics point to the ways trade and investment policies tend to reflect very much the successful influence-playing of large, powerful, organized business groups to the disadvantage of civil society and trade labor movements (Gawande and Hockman, 2006).

Other North Americans especially interested in the condition of the working classes have opposed the liberalization of trade in products and services because they believe that these liberalizing moves have directly and unfairly aggravated

---

[1] This description of the loosely-organized oppositional movement to economic globalization is from Alain Roy (2010).

domestic unemployment and reduced the real wages of thousands of workers. Certainly the steady growth in the number of workers hired conditionally on part time and/or temporary contracts has taken place during the eighties and nineties as international trade has steadily grown. Additionally, large numbers of Canadians and Mexicans have been especially suspicious of the role played by the United States both within NAFTA and the WTO unfairly to further its interests to the disadvantage of its neighboring trading partners.

This deeply-rooted divergence of views with respect to fairness in international trade is not likely to diminish if left to its own devices. Any proposals regarding fairness in international trade are likely to meet with challenges if not opposition. This fact makes it very difficult to arrive at a common position within or among the nations of North America. Comparable differences of view exist among the other nations and peoples of other continents.

9.4 Open Political Processes and Fundamental Considerations

Given the asymmetrical relations among these countries, decidedly different views regarding the importance of international trade, and different assumptions regarding fairness in trade, it is not likely that we can identify a set of first principles that will provide common reference points for transcending these differences. However, it may be possible to move forward towards more common trading arrangements by first acknowledging these differences and then considering their implications. Ultimately, this may lead to consensus about several elements that need to be considered as basic and fundamental as people think about current international trade patterns and ways to reform them.

In the paragraphs that follow, we discuss five considerations that are relevant to the ongoing highly value-laden – and typically ideologically informed – debates over international trade, debates that variously invoke the values of fair play, distributive justice, and respect for local interests, civil society, and the environment. We do not argue that these five basic considerations will overcome differences in normative views. Rather, we do contend that these considerations can gain assent from opponents as well as proponents and, further, that they can serve as mediating values to foster possible compromises regarding fair trading relations. We discuss four of these considerations in this part of the essay and the fifth consideration in the last part of this essay.

One: Any workable approach to establishing greater fairness in international trade needs to be flexible and respective of local traditions and institutions. Dani Rodrik, a Harvard economist, makes a strong economic argument for this point. He notes that national economies have developed using quite different policies. Countries that have been able to develop have done so because they have found ways to marshal their own energies, utilize their own institutions, and draw upon their own resources in effective ways (Rodrik, 2007, Chapters 1, 2, 3, and 8). The WTO, therefore, ought to utilize its energies not to harmonize these differing policies of trading countries but to facilitate negotiations and exchanges between countries that will inevitably approach trade and development in different terms. The efforts to create what fair play liberals refer to as a level playing field operate to ignore, under-value, and/or treat these national cultural and institutional differences as problems to be overcome rather than assets to be respected.

An equivalent argument can be made in more strictly ethical terms. Humans have crafted and followed diverse ethical traditions associated with their religions, ethnic traditions, political beliefs, legal practices, and cultural values. They are most likely to arrive at common moral understandings as they seek to address specific historically contingent issues – such as, banning land mines or managing intractable debts of the least developed countries—and as they explore ways of fostering civil, reciprocating, communications across these differences (Bird, 1996).

Two: Any viable system of fair international trade must be articulated in terms of institutions that make markets possible as well as market principles themselves. Fair play liberalism tends to take these institutions for granted focusing attention instead on procedures and principles. Dani Rodrik addresses this point as well, while defending liberal economic ideas as basically sound. In order for markets to work effectively, he argues, governments and civil societies need to establish and maintain a range of political, legal, economic, and social institutions that provide a variety of infrastructural supports for markets. These include not only the identification and protection of property, the definition and enforcement of contracts, and the delineation and maintenance of rules of competition, but also establishing and protecting systems of credit as well as currency exchanges.

In addition, markets are unable to operate freely and effectively when governments are not able to provide public order and security. Markets work best where governments are also able to support educational systems that help prepare citizens to take places in the work force and to provide social insurance safety nets to assist workers in managing the economic insecurity associated with economic cycles and volatile labor markets (Rodrik, 2007, Chapters 4, 5, and 6). Dan Finn, an American theologian and economist, has made a comparable argument in ethical terms, calling attention to what he refers to as "The Moral Ecology of Markets." (Finn, 2006, Chapters 6, 7, and 8). The freedom of markets, he explains, is made possible by sets of fences that protect markets from diverse threats. Liberals and conservatives disagree about the number and nature of these threats and how the protective fencing ought to be best established. Although they often presume their existence, liberals and conservatives don't disagree on the need for some kinds of institutions and regulations to establish and protect markets. With these observations in mind, we can correspondingly argue that international trade regimes should minimally operate in ways that do not undermine the capacity of national governments to provide the requisite infrastructural and institutional supports for effective market operations.

Three: In a fair system of international trade each country should be able to exercise basic bargaining power on its own behalf. As we observed above, Stiglitz and Charlton have directed attention to this point. The WTO was established as a multiparty arena in which countries would negotiate with each other to establish rules for international trade, would develop particular trading arrangements, and would raise and settle disputes about trade. Inevitably, some countries exercise more power in these negotiations because they control access to certain vital resources (oil or certain manufactured goods, for example, or certain valued currencies), they have larger economies, their economies are less dependent on foreign trade, and/or they can variously influence the positions other countries take. For all of these reasons, the United States, for example, wields disproportionate power compared, for example, to Mexico or Canada. These variations in effective power are, in large part, inevitable outgrowths of historical developments. However, in spite of these differences, each country should be well-equipped and empowered to represent its vital interests. That means, at a minimum, that each country should have access to accountants, economists, and lawyers to represent and defend its interests adequately. Most of the less and least developed countries have not been in position to well-represent their own interests by means of effectively prepared lawyers, accountants, and fact-finders in many trade negotiations and dispute resolution sessions. At a minimum, a fair system of international trade should move to reduce this basic inequality.

The rationale for this position is well-articulated by the basic ethical standards associated with commutative justice. This approach to justice, articulated traditionally by both Aristotle and Aquinas, has not recently received as much attention as the several well known and widely discussed efforts to define and defend standards for distributive justice and procedural justice. Ideas of commutative justice call for fair exchanges based on free choice, full disclosure of all relevant information, and adequate support for the systems of institutions and rules that make these exchanges possible. Commutative justice is associated with reciprocal but not necessarily equal and symmetrical relations. It is possible to develop and to sustain reciprocating, mutually satisfactory, but unequal relationships between parents and children, masters and servants, public officials and citizens, professionals and their clients, as well as employers and employees. Although asymmetrical, these relationships remain reciprocal and fair so long as both parties can initiate interactions and help set agendas; both remain responsive to the voiced interests of the other; and both agree to end negotiations only when both consent. Ideas of commutative justice, rightly and broadly understood, have considerable relevance for international trade.

These ideas indicate how countries should approach and engage in negotiations, that is: on the basis of full disclosure, with neither party being forced to take positions to which they do not freely consent. Further, trading relationships should support and not undermine the institutions that make these trading relationships possible. Correspondingly, these relationships should support and not undermine the administrative capacity of national governments to establish the rules and institutions that make international trade possible. Most importantly, from the perspective of commutative justice, each party engaging in exchanges judged to be fair should be equivalently able to state its cases, bargain, raises complaints, and make appeals. Negatively expressed, a party unable to exercise this minimum level of capacity lacks the corresponding ability to state and choose positions based on full access to relevant information. Many of the standards associated with commutative justice accord well with the focus of fair play liberalism on free choice, reciprocity, and full disclosure. Commutative justice, however, calls for greater efforts to insure that those engaged in negotiating exchanges can do so with basic capabilities to state and defend their positions (Bird, 2006).

Four: A fair system of international trade ought to be well integrated with national and regional and local systems of trade: that is, it should support and not undermine less distant patterns of commerce in so far as the latter are effective and efficient. Fairness calls for a fitting balance between local and distant trade. Ordinarily, trade initially develops locally. Within specific locales, districts, provinces, countries, and regions, trade and commerce grow. Most trade is not in the beginning distant. Local trade in turn fosters local economic development as well as the development of local infrastructures. These include not only physical infrastructures like roads, canals, water systems, sewage systems, and electrical systems but also the economic, social, and legal infrastructures that occasion, support, and protect the development of local markets. Local trade in turn helps to develop webs of interactions between individuals, enterprises, and communities involved. People enter into exchanges, which in turn are seen as being in the interests both of each and all who participate in these exchanges.

In a number of places the emphasis on the value placed on local trade has been expressed in WTO documents. Thus, the document on intellectual property rights allows countries to override patent laws in order to protect the health and security of their population. Moreover, as part of the final efforts to arrive at an agreement with respect to the Doha round of negotiation, trade ministers agreed in Hong Kong (CRS, 2006) countries could act to restrain international trade in order to protect the food security, the livelihoods of workers, and the rural economies of their people (CRS, 2008).

Countries often engage in distant trade in order to enhance local trade. They seek out items not available locally – technologies, fuels, minerals, spices, produce, skilled workers, low-cost supplies, etc. They seek to sell items in order to obtain foreign exchange values, with which they can purchase items otherwise not available locally. Within reasonable measures, it has been acceptable for countries to institute tariffs in order to protect infant industries and local trade against the threat posed by international businesses and trade. Most of the industrialized countries protected their industries as they were developing. The fastest growing Asian countries all protected their infant industries. For the most part the African and South American economies more clearly grew as they followed import substitution policies in the sixties and seventies than when they later abandoned these policies (Rodrik, 2007, Chapter 1; Chang, 2007, Chapters 2, 3; Wade, 1990).

Anti-dumping regulations have been instituted in part to protect local trading arrangements from being undermined by foreign enterprises selling products at costs below normal market value. By WTO rules countries may judge that foreign products are being sold at "dumping" prices" if they can demonstrate that products sold at these prices meet the following criteria: One, foreign products sold at these prices put their own domestic industry at risk and, two, the foreign firms are selling at below market value. Countries, which judge that they have been harmed by sales at "dumping" prices, can then impose anti-dumping fees in order to protect and compensate domestic firms. For the most part, anti-dumping rules have been used without any clear pattern by some of the larger economies – the USA, India, the EU, Argentina and South Africa—against other large economies – China, the EU, the USA, and Japan—as well as some smaller countries like Taiwan and South Korea. Potentially, developing countries might make much greater use of anti-dumping rules, especially to protect their local agricultural industries in foods and agricultural by-products.[2]

9.5 Fairness and Transfer Pricing

A fair system of international trade should especially work to counter and limit a set of questionable, deceptive, and often illegal trading practices – including corruption, abusive transfer pricing, and false pricing – that utilize public trading systems for private advantage. While we contend that all three warrant attention from the WTO, we choose to highlight abusive transfer pricing of internationally traded goods and services for several reasons. One, developing countries probably lose as much or more by these practices than by the skewed rules with respect to international trade in agriculture goods and by-products. Two, the continued poverty of the least developing countries, reinforced by these practices, occasions and undergirds political instability in these areas (Collier, 2007). Three, these practices result in market distortions with corresponding miss-information about actual supplies of, and demand for, items in question. Finally, these practices help to accentuate the excessive and politically unaccountable influence of off-shore financial centers (Baker, 2005; Ramos, 2007).

What is a transfer price? As firms become decentralized in operation, transactions occur between segments as well as with external entities. Transactions between a given segment of a firm and a party outside the firm are readily priced by the prevailing market forces of supply and demand. However, transactions between autonomous segments within a firm are more difficult to manage and are often subject to significant distortion by firm management (see Desai et al., 2006; Kozlow and Abaroa, 2006). The amount charged in these within-firm transactions is referred to as the transfer price (Garrison et al., 2006).

The transfer price directly affects the allocation of profit to the segments; a higher transfer price results in greater costs for the purchasing segment, reducing income for that segment. For a firm operating internationally, the incentives and a mechanism (i.e. transfer pricing) are in place for firm managers to shift income to low tax

---

[2] Anti-dumping rules will remain controversial because of the difficulties and disagreements associated with standards and processes used to determine "normal market value." Market values clearly vary. It seems illegitimate to use market prices in other industrialized countries to determine whether or not firms in developing countries are selling products at "dumping" prices. Nonetheless, industrialized countries have invoked these kinds of standards. It would seem to be much fairer if dumping prices were determined in relation to the actual local costs of production (Stiglitz, 2007, 2006).

Scenario One – 100 units at $10 per unit

	Segment A	Segment B	Corporate
Revenue	$-	$1,000.00	$1,000.00
Costs	$1,000.00	$-	$1,000.00
Effect on Income	$(1,000.00)	$1,000.00	$-
Tax Rate	20%	30%	
Effect on Taxes	$(200.00)	$300.00	$100.00

Scenario Two – 100 units at $1 per unit

	Segment A	Segment B	Corporate
Revenue	$-	$100.00	$100.00
Costs	$100.00	$-	$100.00
Effect on Income	$(100.00)	$100.00	$-
Tax Rate	20%	30%	
Effect on Taxes	$(20.00)	$30.00	$10.00

Fig. 9.1 Transfer price illustration

regimes, thereby avoiding tax obligations in a high tax regime (see Dean et al., 2008, Kuschnik, 2008). This is illustrated in Fig. 9.1 where Segment A buys from Segment B at different prices in the two scenarios. All else equal, because the tax rate is higher where Segment B operates, a lower transfer price yields a reduced tax burden for the corporation (i.e. $10 versus $100). Empirical evidence presented in the accounting and tax literatures is consistent with this occurring in practice (e.g. Swenson, 2001; Clausing, 2006).

A global issue. There is significant evidence that transfer pricing is a global issue of importance to business managers, accounting firms, governments and advocacy groups. Neighbor and Owen (2002) report that in 2001, 60 percent of world manufacturing trade was comprised of transactions involving transfer pricing. All four major accounting firms (Deloitte, Ernst & Young, PricewaterhouseCoopers and KPMG) have significant operations dedicated directly to transfer pricing activities and several publish strategy guides (Deloitte, 2007; PricewaterhouseCoopers, 2006; KPMG International, 2008).

Ernst & Young publish a biennial survey of multinational enterprises focusing on transfer pricing. In the 2007–2008 edition, 850 firms were surveyed and nearly 40 percent of respondents reported that transfer pricing was the single largest tax issue to be faced (Ernst & Young, 2008). In addition, 75 percent believe that transfer pricing will be "absolutely critical" or "very important" in the next two years and over half have been subjected to review by a revenue authority since 2003 (Ernst & Young, 2008). Finally, over half of those audited were subjected to a transfer price adjustment as a result of the review, suggesting either broad confusion around complying with transfer pricing regulation or deliberate manipulation. In addition to management concerns, various inter-government organizations around the globe are involved with the orchestration of international trade. All of these organizations, to greater or lesser degree, take a position or advocate policy on transfer pricing – World Customs Organization (WCO), Organization for Economic Cooperation and Development (OECD), WTO, United Nations (UN), United Nations Conference on Trade and Development (UNCTAD), World Bank, European Commission and many others. Taken together, these results suggest that transfer pricing is an especially important global issue.

North American perspectives. Exposure to transfer pricing as a significant issue is, of course, correlated with the prevalence of trade conducted by multinational firms in the home country. As a result, for North American firms, those in the United States and Canada have a disproportionate interest in transfer pricing policy relative to Mexico. This is supported by the Ernst & Young survey findings (2008). Managers in Canada and the US report that transfer pricing is critical or very important at 96 percent and 73 percent, respectively. Just 56 percent of Mexican firm managers respond similarly.

More than 80 percent of Canadian and US firm managers reported being subject to an audit by a revenue agency since 2003. Just 8 percent of Mexican managers responded similarly. The global average was 52 percent, suggesting that within the North American region, the experiences with respect to transfer pricing are extreme. A recent survey on North American transfer pricing issues published by PricewaterhouseCoopers (2006) observes that the transfer pricing situation in North America is relatively stable, as compared to the rest of the world. This is reflective of the fact that US law has incorporated transfer pricing policy in some form since 1928 (Kuschnik, 2008). In contrast, in many developing countries the transfer pricing rules are less than a decade old (O'Brien and Oates, 2008). The overall complexity of the transfer pricing problem is increasing in North America, as in the rest of the world (see PricewaterhouseCoopers, 2006; Taylor, 2008; Dean et al., 2008).

Conditions are similar in Canada and the US. Both countries have seen regulatory changes in the mid-1990s to address various issues such as pricing of services and intangibles as well as an increase in audit frequency and intensity (O'Brien and Oates, 2008; PricewaterhouseCoopers, 2006). This is consistent with the Ernst & Young survey data, which reports that 84 and 92 percent of Canadian and US respondents expect to be audited again within two years (2008). As of 2003, the US requires contemporaneous data from both sides of each transaction, increasing the need for, and benefit from, greater multinational coordination and information sharing.

Mexico is unique among North American countries at this point. Transfer policy is relatively new (PricewaterhouseCoopers, 2006) and is being developed in a manner consistent with OECD policy (as opposed to US and Canadian policy, the origin of which predates the OECD Guidelines). The Ernst & Young survey results are consistent with a system that is under development and is moving toward the global position (2008). For instance, few respondents report being audited (8 percent), however, nearly half expect to be audited within the next two years and over half consider transfer pricing to be an issue of significant importance (Ernst & Young, 2008). The first legal challenges to transfer pricing audit decisions and adjustments are beginning to reach the courts in Mexico (PricewaterhouseCoopers, 2006), so an increase in litigation and legislation is likely on the horizon.

Ethical dimension. The majority of the writings on transfer pricing are centered on whether it occurs (see Clausing, 2006; Desai et al., 2004), the mechanics of complying with the legal requirements (see O'Brien and Oates, 2008), and on the wisdom of tax avoidance as a business practice (see Dean et al., 2008). However, evidence supports the assertion that transfer pricing has resulted in enormous transfers of wealth from developing to industrialized countries. Baker estimates that the amount of taxes correspondingly lost to developing countries per year amounts to tens of billions of dollars (Baker, 2005). Abusive transfer pricing practices without question violate standards associated with distributive, commutative, and procedural justice, yet very little discussion of the ethical components of the behavior is to be found.

One notable exception is Hansen et al. (1992) who directly address the question of whether transfer pricing is an ethical dilemma. They begin by making the case that tax avoidance is appropriate and is consistent with existing regulations. As a result, firm managers making internal decisions that do not violate existing law are simply being smart managers minimizing costs. Further, maximizing profits is a morally defensible policy that is the ultimate social responsibility of the firm (Friedman, 1970). This position is consistent with the perspective (often tacitly) championed in the existing literatures. The authors then present the "moral ethical view" to contrast the "tax ethical" view that dominates the discourse:

> This common principal, which is the heart of ethical action, is the willingness to sacrifice one's self interest for the well-being of others. This ethical principle does not preclude the pursuit of profits by an organization. In planning, controlling, and making decisions, however, managers should always consider the impact of their actions on others, both within the organization and without. Thus, the objective of profit maximization should be constrained by the requirement that profits are achieved through ethical means. (Hansen et al., 1992: 684).

The authors then make a key distinction: profit maximization and tax avoidance are certainly acceptable; however, altering the transfer pricing arrangement from what it "normally" would have been to avoid paying taxes that would have been due is ethically untenable. In other words, they conclude that "tax avoidance does not provide an exemption from ethical behavior" and that there needs to be more concern with "what is right than with technical compliance with the law" (Hansen et al., 1992). That is, the pursuit of profit must be tempered by accountability to a more general standard of well-being.

The fact that transfer pricing practices within a firm can have far-reaching effects, including shifts in government tax receipts, is certainly not disputed. The notion of tax avoidance simply being appropriate business practice dominates the discourse. The necessary consequence of this practice – the ability or inability of the revenue agencies to provide funds to support the well-being of the community represented by that government – is rarely directly addressed.

The role of the WTO. This global concern and the involvement of myriad parties are leading to tremendous complexity in transfer pricing policy. OECD Guidelines, including the position that an arm's length standard – the price that would have been negotiated had the buyer and seller been independent entities – should be applied, currently dominate (Wundisch, 2007; Dean et al., 2008; van Hilten, 2002); however, there is disagreement about the scope and applicability of the Guidelines (van Hilten, 2002). Further, the proscription that an arm's length transaction approach be applied does not suit a great many transactions where an arm's length price cannot be determined, leaving open the question of what firm management should do in these instances (Kuschnik, 2008).

In a piece designed to prompt debate around the political strategies related to transfer pricing, Wundisch (2007) argues that the variation in policy, and the unilateral action taken by individual governments, is costly to economic trade by creating confusion and increasing risk. Kuschnik (2008) asserts that cooperative work environment among nations would be of great assistance in addressing transfer pricing challenges. The common thread is that in a matter of global concern, global cooperation as opposed to unilateral action is the key to resolving these issues.

Taken together, the overall picture of transfer pricing is one of global significance, ethical considerations and complexity. As such, it may be that the WTO is in a relatively unique position to weigh in on future transfer pricing policy; however, the Organization for Economic Cooperation and Development (OECD) currently sets the global tone in terms of transfer pricing standards (Kuschnik, 2008) while the WTO is largely silent on the issue. The OECD has 30 members, dominated by developed nations in Europe, but "shares expertise" with more than 100 additional nations (OECD, 2008). By contrast, the WTO has 152 members, including significant numbers of developing economies. Given the need for broad international membership as well as international cooperation, it would seem that the WTO would be a natural body to take a forceful role in shaping transfer pricing policy going forward. Raymond Baker argues that the WTO should "place honest pricing firmly on its agenda, because false pricing distorts free and fair trade and moves more illicit money across borders than any other single mechanism." (Baker, 2005: 349).

A number of people have urged the WTO to become the champion for human rights and environmental concerns – issues already covered by other global institutions, like the International Labor Organization and varied international associations working for sustainable development, climate controls, and bio-diversity. Given its current difficulties, the WTO may or may not have the ability to take up these concerns. In the meantime, it remains both the special and central mandate of the WTO to work to foster and facilitate the international trading relationships and, therefore, to identify and limit trading activities that directly undermine transparent rule-regulated trading like the practice of abusive transfer pricing. Further, the parties involved and the tax structures implicated make this one of the most daunting issues facing international trade. It is this very degree of complication, combined with the potential economic significance of transfer pricing policy, that make the topic appropriate for inclusion when discussing the WTO and the ethics of international trade, regardless of the region of the globe under consideration.

9.6 Conclusion

Many people and countries have benefitted as international trade has expanded during the second half of the twentieth century. After surveying the history of international trade since primitive times, William Bernstein concludes that this post Second World War expansion of trade has often worked especially to the advantage of poor households, both as consumers and producers. The proportion of the world population that was impoverished declined during these years, especially in the sixties and seventies (Bernstein, 2008, chapter 14). Moreover, those countries least connected with these systems of international trade remained the most poverty-stricken (Group of Lisbon, 1995; Legrain, 2003). However, internationally, regionally, nationally, and locally, all systems of trade produce winners and losers. As the often-cited essay by Stolper and Samuelson make clear, at any particular point in time and in ways likely to change over time, the benefits of expanding trade are likely to extend to certain but not all sectors of any one society. At varying times and in different countries, they argue, some but not all of those whose incomes and wealth derive from land, capital, and/or labor are likely to benefit (Stolper and Samuelson, 1941). Any system of trade is, therefore, likely to seem unfair to some. While NAFTA and the WTO have probably helped to occasion some plant closures and job losses, these trading arrangements have also in modest ways helped to nudge up the average levels of employment and wages in all three countries. Nonetheless, for complex reasons, related in large part to domestic taxation policies and salary practices, the overall levels of benefits have been decidedly skewed in all three countries with the well-to do gaining proportionately and decidedly much more in terms of opportunities, wealth, and income.

North Americans have correspondingly adopted a range of positions with respect to international trade. Because of the asymmetrical relations between them, Mexico, Canada, and the United States have developed different views of fairness in international trade. Additionally, within each country, citizens have supported varied positions regarding foreign trade. Protectionist sentiments have been fueled both by economic nationalists and by those who in the name of environmental concerns and human rights have opposed economic globalism. In so far as they seek to enhance international trade, many citizens, industry representatives, and politicians have favored bi-lateral or regional trade agreements as being both more easily established and maintained. As the Doha round of multilateral negotiations faltered, North American governments at the same time were taking steps at establishing varied bi-lateral and regional agreements with other Western Hemisphere countries as well as with countries in Europe and Asia. Nonetheless, at the same time the governments of these countries have generally supported efforts to expand and liberalize international trade through the WTO.

As they have argued for and against expanding and liberalizing the rules governing multilateral trade, North Americans have readily invoked ideas of self-interest as well as ideas of justice, which they have in turn variously formulated in relation to concerns for fair procedures, fair distributions, and/or fair exchanges. Notions of fairness have correspondingly been invoked to stress the importance of rules, transparency, proportionality, equity, absence of corruption, absence of discrimination, and due process. Ideas of fairness have been referred to in order to call for both the fitting balance between rewards, risks, efforts, and investments as well as impartial and impersonal deliberations and adjudications. While some have called for policies for equalizing opportunities – placing emphasis on fair procedures – others have called for greater attention to outcomes that can reasonably be called just – placing emphasis on whether the results of these processes seemed fair.

There is little likelihood of resolving this debate once and for all. There are too many parties with different interests, even in an area as delimited and as closely linked by international trade as North America. Politics within nations in good measure involves continuing argumentation over these and other issues and continuing efforts to respond to, address, and balance the interests of diverse parties. The fundamental argument is that fairness exists within political systems if the various major social formations believe, however begrudgingly, that the balancing of procedural, distributive, and commutative perspectives is acceptable.

At the same time, as these political debates continue, we have argued that it would be useful to identify and acknowledge several considerations that might well serve as common points of reference. These include not only the need for flexibility and the importance of supporting both national and international trade supporting institutions. They also include the need to develop arrangements so that each country has the basic capacity to bargain for its own interests. They include as well the recognition that international trade ideally should act to support, complement, and extend local, national, and regional trade and that the possibility to debate how to balance these interests must remain open. Finally, we have argued that international system of trade will remain both fundamentally flawed and unjust until more concerted efforts are made to address the way the practices of abusive transfer pricing and false pricing distort international trading relations.

Acknowledgements Research for this essay was made possible in part by grants both from the Canadian Business Ethics Research Network and the University of Waterloo. We would like to thank Alex Caramento for help with some of the research.

References

Anderson, G. 2006, "Can Someone Please Settle This Dispute? Canadian Softwood Lumber and the Dispute Settlement Mechanisms of the NAFTA and the WTO," *The World Economy* 29 (6), 585–610.

Ayres, J. and Macdonald, L. 2007, "Deep Integration and Shallow Governance: The Limits of Civil Society Engagement across North America," *Policy and Society* 25 (6), 23–42.

Baker, R. 2005, *Capitalism's Achilles Heel* (John Wiley and Sons, Hobokan, N.J.).

Baldwin, D. 1980, "Interdependence and power: a conceptual analysis," *International Organization* 34 (4), 471–506.

Bernstein, W. 2008, *A Splendid Exchange: How Trade Shaped the World* (Atlantic Monthly Press, NY).

Bird, F. 1996, *The Muted Conscience: Moral Silence and the Practice of Ethics in Business* (Quorum Books, Westport, CT).

Bird, F. 2006, "Just Business Practice" *Just Business Practices in a Diverse and Developing World,* eds. Frederick Bird and Manuel Velasquez (Palgrave-Macmillan, NY), Chap. 2.

Byers, M. 2007, *Intent for a Nation* (Douglas & McIntyre, Vancouver).

Chang, Ha-Joon 2007, *The Bad Samaritans: Rich nations, Poor Policies, and the Threat to the Developing World* (Random House, London).

Clarkson, S. 2008, *Does North America Exist? Governing the Continent after NAFTA and 9/11* (University of Toronto Press, Toronto).

Clausing, K. A. 2006, "International Tax Avoidance and U.S. International Trade" *National Tax Journal* 59 (2), 269–287.

Coleman, W., Grant, W., and Josling, T. 2004, *Agriculture in the New Global Economy* (Edward Elgar, Cheltenham, UK).

Collier, P. 2007, *The Bottom Billion: Why the Poorest Countries Are Failing and What Can Be Done About It* (Oxford University Press, Oxford).

Congressional Research Reports, 2006, "WTO: Antidumping in the Doha Development Agenda" (Congressional Research Service, CRS).

Congressional Research Reports, 2008, "World Trade Organization Negotiations: The Doha Development Agenda" (Congressional Research Service, CRS).

Council on Foreign Relations, 2005, *Building a North American Community* (Council on Foreign Relations Press, New York).

Daly, H. E. and Cobb, J. Jr. 1989, *For the Common Good* (Beacon Press, Boston).

Dean, M., Feucht, F. J. and Smith, L. M. 2008, "International Transfer Pricing Issues and Strategies for the Global Firm," *Internal Auditing* January/February, 12–19

Deloitte 2007, *Strategy Matrix for Global Transfer Pricing: Planning for Methods, Documentation, Penalties and Other Issues* (Deloitte Development LLC).

Desai, M. A., Foley, C. F., and Hines, J. R. Jr. 2004, "A Multinational Perspective on Capital Structure Choice and Internal Capital Markets" *Journal of Finance* 59 (6), 2451–2487.

Desai, M. A., Foley, C. F., and Hines, J.R. Jr. (2006). "The Demand for Tax Haven Operations" *Journal of Public Economics* 90 (3), 513–531.

Ernst & Young 2008, *Precision Under Pressure: Global Transfer Pricing Survey 2007–2008* (Ernst & Young LLC).

Finn, D. K. 2006, *The Moral Ecology of Markets: Assessing Claims about Markets and Justice* (Cambridge University Press, Cambridge).

Friedman, M. 1970, "The Social Responsibility of Business is to Increase Its Profits" *New York Times Magazine* (September 13).

Froese, M. 2008, "Regulatory Frictions in the North American Marketplace: The Canadian-US Agriculture Disputes at the WTO," paper presented to the Annual Meeting of the Canadian Political Science Association, Vancouver, British Columbia, June.

Gagne, G. 2003, "The Canada-US softwood lumber dispute: a test case for the development of international trade rules," *International Journal* 58 (3), 335–368.

Garrison, R. H., Noreeen, E. W., and Brewer, P. C. 2006, *Managerial Accounting*, 11th edition (McGraw-Hill Irwin, New York, NY).

Gawande, K. and Hockman, B. 2006, "Lobbying and Agricultural Policy in the United States" *International Organization* 60 (3), 727–761.

Group of Lisbon 1995, *The Limits to Competition* (MIT Press, Cambridge, MA).

Hansen, D. R., Crosser, R. L., and Laufer, D. 1992, "Moral Ethics v. Tax Ethics: The Case of Transfer Pricing Among Multinational Corporations" *Journal of Business Ethics* 11, 679–686.

Hart, M. 2002, *A Trading Nation: Canadian Trade Policy from Colonialism to Globalization* (University of British Columbia Press, Vancouver) pp. 434–437.

International Monetary Fund 2008, *World Economic Outlook Database* (April, 2008).

Korton, D. 1996, *When Corporations Ruled the World* (Berrett-Koehler, San Francisco).

Kozlow, R. and Abaroa, P. 2006, *U.S. Multinational Companies, Dividends and Taxes* (U.S. Bureau of Economic Analysis).

KPMG International (2008) http://www.kpmg.com/Global/WhatWeDo/Tax/GlobalTransferPricing Services/Pages/default.aspx. Last accessed May 27, 2008.

Kuschnik, B. 2008. "Transfer Pricing in a Global Market" *Corporate Taxation* January/February, 17–24

Legrain, P. 2003, *Open World: The Truth About Globalization* (Abacus, London).

McDougall, J. N. 2006, *Drifting Together: The Political Economy of Canada-US integration* (Broadview Press, Peterborough, Ontario).

McMurtry, J. 1998, *Unequal Freedoms: The Global Market as an Ethical System* (Garamond Press, Toronto).

Neighbor, J. and Owen, J. 2002, "Transfer Pricing in the New Millennium: will the Arm's Length Principle survive?" *George Mason Law Review* 10, 951–958.

O'Brien, J. M. and Oates, M. A. 2008, "Covering your Backside in a Foreign Transfer Pricing Audit" *International Tax Journal* (March–April) 13–22.

Organisation for Economic Cooperation and Development 2008, http://www.oecd.org/pages/0,3417,en_36734052_36734103_1_1_1_1,00.html. Last accessed May 27, 2008.

OECD Statistical Extracts, International Trade, (2008)

Pastor, R. 2001, *Toward A North American Community* (Institute for International Economics, Washington, D.C.).

PricewaterhouseCoopers 2006, "Transfer Pricing Perspectives" http://www.pwc.com/extweb/pwcpublications.nsf/docid/EDB05418E3A09313852573A900672290. Last accessed May 31, 2008.

PricewaterhouseCoopers 2007, http://www.pwc.com/Extweb/service.nsf/docid/92E194F427FBD 3E485256FBE0073DCBD. Last accessed May 27, 2008.

Ramos, J. 2007, "A Place in the Sun: A Special Report on Offshore Finance" *The Economist* (February 24, 2007).

Rawls, J. 1970. *A Theory of Justice* (Harvard University Press, Cambridge).

Rodrik, D. 2007, *One Economics Many Recipes: Globalization, Institutions, and Economic Growth* (Princeton University Press, Princeton).

Roy, A. 2010, "Letting or Making Collaboration Happen: An exploration of global collaborative efforts among social movements" in Frederick Bird and Frances Westley (eds.) *Voices from the Voluntary Sector*, (University of Toronto Press) forthcoming.

Saul, J. R. 2005, *The Collapse of Globalism: and the Reinvention of the World* (Viking Canada, Toronto).

Staples, S. 2007, "Fortress North America: The Drive Towards Military and Security Integration and Its Impact on Canadian Democratic Sovereignty," in Ricardo Grispin and Y. Shamsie (eds.), *Whose Canada? Continental Integration, Fortress North America and the Corporate Agenda* (McGill-Queens University Press, Montreal).

Stiglitz, J. E. 2007, 2006, *Making Globalization Work* (W. W. Norton and Company, New York).

Stiglitz, J. E. and Charlton, A. 2004, "Common Values for the Development Round" *World Trade Review* 3, 495–506.

Stiglitz, J. E. and Charlton, A. 2005, *Fair Trade for All: How Trade Can Promote Development* (Oxford University Press, Oxford).

Stolper, W and Samuelson, P. 1941, "Protection and Real Wages" *The Review of Economic Studies* 9 (1), 58–73.

Swenson, D. L. 2001, "Tax Reforms and Evidence of Transfer Pricing" *National Tax Journal* 54 (1), 7–25.

Taylor, W. B. 2008, "Who Ate the Homework? The Treasury Department Report to Congress on Earnings Stripping, Transfer Pricing, and U.S. Income Tax Treaties. http://www.bna.com/tm/insights_taylor3.htm.

Van Hilten, J. P. 2002, "Transfer Pricing Policy in the International Tax System – Past and Present and a Quick Look in the Fiscal Crystal Ball" *George Mason Law Review* 10, 709–724.

Wade, R. 1990, *Governing the Market* (Princeton University Press, Princeton).

Williams, R. A. 2008, "Managing North American Trade Disputes: The Role of the World Trade Organization," paper presented to the "New North America" conference, Mount Allison University, New Brunswick, February 15, 2008.

Wolfe, R. 2008, "Arguing and bargaining in the WTO: Does the Single Undertaking make a difference?", paper presented to the Annual Meeting of the Canadian Political Science Association (University of British Columbia, Vancouver).

World Trade Organisation 2008, http://www.wto.org/english/thewto_e/whatis_e/tif_e/org6_e.htm. Last accessed on May 26, 2008.

Wundisch, K. 2007, "Rampant Globalisation – Yet a Dearth of Professionals to Lead the Way in Transfer Pricing" *Tax Management Transfer Pricing Report* 16 (8), 1–9.

Zampetti, A. B. 2006, *Fairness in World Trade: US Perspectives on International Trade* (Edward Elgar Publishing, Northampton, MA).

Chapter 10
Fairness in International Trade: The Case of Economic Partnership Agreements

Geoff Moore

> *Any attempt to define fairness in global trade relations should teach humility.* Brown & Stern (2007: 316)

10.1 Introduction

There are, perhaps, three reasons why humility is both required and will be learned from studying fairness in international trade. The first is due to the inherent complexity of international trade relations, which makes any attempt to grasp them difficult and the danger of over-simplification rife. The second is that, if it were possible to adequately summarise even a particular aspect of such relations, the application of fairness principles is by no means straightforward. While there have been numerous attempts to apply such principles, so that in one sense the ground is well-trodden, the judgements that emerge do not necessarily bring the kind of clarity that might be desired – in other words, judgments that such and such a practice is unfair and should be changed, or otherwise, are few and far between. Brown & Stern, cited above, continue: "even if we could transcend the self-serving bias inherent in the judgment of all interested parties, there is still no conclusive and incontrovertible way of assessing fairness" (2007: 316). And this leads to the third reason why humility will be required and learned, which is that fairness judgements on particular aspects of international trade relations, even if they were to be clear and unequivocal, may not lead to any change by those deemed to have infringed fairness towards those who are on the receiving end of such acts. Humility is involved in finding that one's work may lead to nothing substantive by way of change "on the ground" – where it really matters.

Despite these three reasons, any one of which might seem to be enough to persuade one not to embark on this particular journey, this chapter sets out to explore the case of Economic Partnership Agreements (EPAs). These are bilateral trade agreements between the European Commission (EC) and various groupings of African,

G. Moore (✉)
Professor of Business Ethics, Durham Business School, Durham University, Durham, UK
e-mail: geoff.moore@durham.ac.uk

G. Moore (ed.), *Fairness in International Trade*, The International Society
of Business, Economics, and Ethics Book Series 1, DOI 10.1007/978-90-481-8840-6_10,
© Springer Science+Business Media B.V. 2010

Caribbean and Pacific (ACP) countries, which have been the subject of intense negotiations leading up to and beyond the deadline of 31 December 2007 by which all such agreements were due to be set in place. The case of EPAs, therefore, provides both a timely and an excellent test case for exploring the fairness or otherwise of trade relations between developed and developing countries.

The chapter begins by setting out the background to international trade relations between the EC and developing countries before turning to look at EPAs themselves in more detail and the effects that have been predicted on the developing countries if EPAs were to be introduced in the way envisaged, together with a number of associated issues related to the introduction of EPAs. The chapter then comments briefly on a "Stop EPAs" campaign that has been run by NGOs for a number of years, before presenting and commenting on the current position showing which EPAs have been signed. The literature on fairness in international trade is then reviewed and, to some extent, extended and applied to the case of EPAs. Conclusions which, as might already be predicted, are somewhat tentative, but do raise some new issues are then drawn.

10.2 The Background to EU–ACP International Trade Relations

When the European Communities, as they were originally known, were founded in 1957 by the Treaty of Rome they rapidly established preferential relations with the ACP countries that had recently gained independence from their former colonial masters (Lang 2006: 1). From 1975 until 2001 trade relations between what became the European Union (EU) and the ACP countries were governed by the four Lomé Conventions. These represented a form of the EU's Generalized System of Preferences (GSP) which "put ACP countries at the top of the pyramid of preferences granted by the EU to developing countries" (Ochieng 2007: 367). These have provided ACP countries with "a very favourable trade regime, a substantial aid budget, and a set of joint institutions" which has meant that "ACP exporters have generally enjoyed a tax advantage over some of their competitors when selling products facing tariffs into the European market" (Stevens 2006: 442). These trade relations have been non-reciprocal in the sense that ACP countries have not been required to assume corresponding obligations to allow tax advantages to imports originating in EU countries (Ochieng 2007: 367).[1]

---

[1] Such preferential treatment is allowable under what is known as the "Enabling Clause", but is officially the "Decision on differential and more favourable treatment, reciprocity and fuller participation of developing countries" that was adopted by the General Agreement on Tariffs and Trade (GATT) in 1979. The Enabling Clause provides the legal basis for the World Trade Organisation's (WTO) GSP by which developed countries offer non-reciprocal preferential treatment (e.g. zero or low duties on imports) to products which originate in developing countries. Preference-giving countries can unilaterally decide which countries and which products to include. See www.wto.org/english/tratop_e/devel_e/dev_special_differential_provisions_e.htm, accessed 12/12/08.

However, such non-reciprocal arrangements have become increasingly open to challenge in the World Trade Organisation (WTO) because they were seen to discriminate against other developing countries (Powell 2007: 8). There is, therefore, immediately an issue of fairness between one set of developing countries and another set, as well as the possibility that such other developing countries might mount a legal challenge based on the General Agreement on Tariffs and Trade (GATT) Article XXIV (see further below). Indeed Peter Mandelson, the former European Commissioner for Trade since 2004, has claimed that "other developing countries are watching these final stages of our negotiations [over EPAs] like hawks" (Mandelson 2007), precisely to ensure fair treatment between all parties and the end of preferential treatment to ACPs. Despite this, there are a number of "special and differential treatment" (SDT) provisions, most notably the notion of non-reciprocity, that are enshrined in GATT articles and the Enabling Clause (Ochieng 2007: 391 and see Ochieng 2007: 367 and Footnote 1) which might allow more flexibility.

The successor to the Lomé Conventions between the EU and ACP countries was the Cotonou Agreement which was signed in 2000 for a period of 20 years. This Agreement "aims to promote economic growth and development as well as the smooth and gradual integration of ACP states into the world economy" (Borrmann & Busse 2007: 403). Although a 20 year Agreement, from a trade perspective the time period is shorter because of the WTO-compatibility issue identified above. Thus, at the WTO Doha conference in November 2001 a temporary waiver was granted giving a deadline by which WTO-compatible reciprocal trade agreements had to be signed of 31 December 2007. It has been the prospect of the end of this temporary waiver that has led to the negotiation of the EPAs which are the subject of this chapter.

The Cotonou Agreement placed these new arrangements under the jurisdiction of GATT Article XXIV whereas previously under the Lomé Conventions the arrangements were under the jurisdiction of the Enabling Clause. Article XXIV governs Free Trade Agreements (FTAs) between states or groupings of states, and includes the requirement that FTAs must eliminate tariff barriers on "substantially all trade" (SAT) within a "reasonable length of time" (see Lang 2006, Ochieng 2007, Powell 2007). Article XXIV defines the time period stating that it should exceed 10 years only in exceptional cases, such exceptions requiring specific justification. The exact definition of "substantially all trade", however, is not provided for within the Article but is usually taken to mean a minimum of 80% (Busse & Grossmann 2007: 808) allowing flexibility both over which 20% is omitted and whether this is divided equally. Lang (2006: 12–13), however, states that the EU has traditionally argued that liberalisation should extend to 90% of existing trade, but that this might be split unevenly so that, for example, the EU could accept full liberalisation of 100% with ACP countries committing to 80%. We will return to both these issues – of how much liberalisation and over what period – when considering EPAs in more detail below.

Despite the requirement to negotiate revised and reciprocal trade agreements, the Cotonou Agreement, as noted above, is more broadly based and includes specific provisions for development strategies and priority for the objective of poverty reduction, and a special focus on the Millennium Development Goals.[2] There is also a provision for a transitional period of up to at least 12 years on the new trade agreements, apparently in contradiction of the 10 year maximum under Article XXIV,[3] although the U.K.'s Department for International Development (DFID) suggests such periods may be as much as 25 years.[4] Both Powell (2007: 8) and Ochieng (2007: 382–3) draw attention to the objective of EPAs within the Cotonou Agreement as follows: "Economic and trade cooperation shall aim at fostering the smooth and gradual integration of the ACP states into the world economy, with due regard for their political choices and development priorities, thereby promoting sustainable development and contributing to poverty eradication in the ACP countries".

This leads us on to consider two other aspects of the context within which EPAs have been negotiated. The first is the WTO itself which has become the subject of bitter dispute and anti-globalization protests such as those at Seattle (Elsig 2007: 75). While providing, as we have seen, the overall legal context within which trade agreements such as FTAs are to be negotiated by those countries which have chosen to become WTO members (such that GATT Article XXIV, for example, forms part of WTO Law – Ochieng 2007: 365), there remains a dispute over whether the WTO is a trade rather than development organisation, and so whether it should or should not "be burdened by broad development concerns of which it has no comparative institutional advantage" (Ochieng 2007: 383). Not surprisingly the EU takes a pro-trade stance in which trade liberalisation, greater integration of the world economy, the increasing role of the market and a correspondingly diminishing role of the state all form key elements. However, "ACP countries and a number of scholars object to this conception of the objects and purposes of both EPAs and the WTO" (*ibid.*: 384, and see also Griffith & Powell 2007: 7–11).

The Doha Development Round of the WTO which began in 2001, was suspended in July 2006 and resumed in February 2007, had, as its name suggests, a fundamental focus on the needs of developing countries and has foundered on the issues of market access and agricultural subsidies (IDC 2007: 10). Negotiations may, however, now be moving towards some form of resolution.[5] The point in relation to EPAs, however, is that their WTO-compatibility, while not in dispute in itself and, indeed, part of the Cotonou Agreement (Lang 2006: 2), is subject to disagreement over what precisely such compatibility entails. Ochieng, for example, argues that the

---

[2] See http://ec.europa.eu/development/geographical/cotonouintro_en.cfm?CFID=2311138&CFTO KEN=de5549ec566e53bc-44BE1EAC-BCAD-6AE3-85FE869240E498A7&jsessionid=243062 fb88384a375d62, accessed 12/12/08.

[3] See http://ec.europa.eu/development/geographical/cotonouintro_en.cfm?CFID=2311138&CFTO KEN=de5549ec566e53bc-44BE1EAC-BCAD-6AE3-85FE869240E498A7&jsessionid=243062 fb88384a375d62, accessed 12/12/08.

[4] See, www.dfid.gov.uk/aboutdfid/organisation/economic-partnership-agreements.asp, accessed 12/12/08.

[5] See http://www.wto.org/english/tratop_e/dda_e/dda_e.htm, accessed 12/12/08.

EU takes a literal (textual) approach to the interpretation of WTO laws, an approach described as "legally problematic and relatively developmentally restrictive compared to the ACP's teleological approach to interpretation – a holistic examination involving textual, contextual and case law analyses of specific WTO Agreements, and assessment of the objects and purposes of the WTO" (Ochieng 2007: 364). Thus, not only are specific issues such as GATT Article XXIV open to renegotiation (Lang 2006), but the purpose of the WTO itself continues to be the subject of contention.

The final contextual issue that we need to take account of is the economic situation and trade objectives of the ACP countries. In 1976, just after the first Lomé Convention was introduced, the ACP states accounted for 6.7% of the EU market, while by 2005 it accounted for only 3% (see Borrmann & Busse 2007: 403). ACP's trade with the rest of the world has also fallen over the same period (Ochieng 2007: 377–8). In addition, about 68% of total ACP exports to the EU consists of agricultural goods and raw materials, with ten products accounting for some 74% of this (Borrmann & Busse 2007: 404). This is, of course, despite the trade preferences that the ACP countries have enjoyed over many decades. Thus, while trade with the EU continues to be important to ACP countries, there is evidence that it is in decline, at least proportionately, and that primary commodities continue to form a substantial part with little apparent progression to added value processed goods. Additional preferences on market access are, therefore, unlikely to benefit ACP countries in the future (*ibid.*: 404).

Perhaps associated with the decline in international trade, the African countries within the ACP have long held the view that regional integration leading eventually to full continental integration is a desirable objective (see Powell 2007: 18–23). Thus, there have been various regional groupings involving more than 20 economic co-operation arrangements and, while the success of these groupings is not proven and their considerable overlapping membership remain problematic (Powell 2007: 22, Stevens 2006: 445), the vision of regional integration remains and has recently been reinforced by the establishment of the African Union (succeeding the Organisation of African Unity) and the founding of the New Partnership for Africa's Development (NEPAD) (Powell 2007: 23).

Associated with this, the negotiations between the EC and ACP countries have been conducted not on a country-by-country basis, but between the EC and six regional groupings – four in Africa and one each in the Caribbean and Pacific. The groupings and countries within each group are shown in Appendix 1. Within each of these groupings it will be noted that there is a mixture of Least Developed Countries (LDCs) and others generally known as developing countries. While the United Nations maintains a precise definition and listing of the 50 LDCs in the world,[6] no official definition and listing of developing countries exists. In relation to EPAs the fact that each grouping contains a mixture is important, for under WTO

---

[6] See www.un.org/special-rep/ohrlls/ldc/list.htm, accessed 12/12/08.

rules developed countries can give non-reciprocal access to only two groups – either to LDCs only or to all developing countries.[7] Thus, it would be possible to negotiate different agreements with the two different types of countries within a regional grouping but potentially problematic to negotiate one overall regional agreement – a point to which we will return.

Given that negotiations were always likely, and have proven, to be problematic, one obvious question has to do with the fall-back position should such negotiations fail. Here, a further reason for difficulties associated with combinations of LDC and other developing countries within one regional grouping emerges. For LDCs a system known as "Everything But Arms" (EBA) exists. This was adopted by the EC in February 2001, granting duty-free access to imports of all products from all LDCs without any quantitative restrictions, except to arms and munitions. The EBA Regulation foresees that the special arrangements for LDCs should be maintained for an unlimited period of time and not be subject to the periodic renewal of the EC's scheme of generalised preferences.[8]

However, for non-LDCs a more restrictive GSP+ scheme, approved in June 2005, exists. To qualify for this a large number of good governance and economic conventions have to be implemented, which most ACP countries have not ratified,[9] and even then "this would mean less-favourable access to the EU market than the one granted under ... the Cotonou Agreement and thus a decline in their export earnings from the EU market" (Busse & Grossman 2007: 788). For this reason non-LDCs have been keener to sign up to EPAs than their LDC regional partners which have less to lose – a source of tension within some of the regional groups (see Borrmann & Busse 2007: 408). An illustration of the effects on non-LDCs is given in Ross (2007) citing the case of a Ghanaian pineapple producer with a turnover around $50 million supplying to the U.K. supermarket chain Marks and Spencer. Once the tariff-free status is removed, the juice products would become immediately unviable. If prices with European supermarkets could not be renegotiated, the company might be forced to consider relocating – presumably to a LDC where the tariff-free status would remain.

10.3 Economic Partnership Agreements and Their Predicted Effects and Associated Issues

With this as background, we are now in a position to look in more detail at EPAs themselves, their predicted effects and a number of associated issues. Given the requirement to have new trade agreements in place by the end of 2007, negotiations

---

[7]See, for example, www.dfid.gov.uk/aboutdfid/organisation/economic-partnership-agreements. asp, accessed 12/12/08.

[8]See http://ec.europa.eu/trade/issues/global/gsp/eba/index_en.htm, accessed 12/12/08.

[9]See www.dfid.gov.uk/aboutdfid/organisation/economic-partnership-agreements-myths.asp, accessed 12/12/08.

started in September 2002 but, as might be expected from the discussion above, have not progressed smoothly. This is despite the fact that, at least according to DFID, EPAs "are intended to be instruments for development, as opposed to standard trade agreements" with the aim being that ACPs "gradually build their capacity to compete in world markets".[10] This was expected to be a three-stage process first with regional integration within ACP regions, then with integration with the EU so that the EU market is slowly opened up, and finally integration as a whole with the world economy. At first sight, therefore, EPAs seem to be simple replacements for the WTO-incompatible agreements and to be beneficial to ACP countries, preserving the preferential treatment that has long been afforded to these countries and leading to regional and world integration.

What, then, are the concerns that have meant that EPAs have become the subject of such concern within ACP countries themselves and have led to a campaign by various NGOs against the EC? The main point of concern, as we noted above, is that these new agreements must be reciprocal if they are to be WTO-compatible, and this therefore involves liberalising substantially all trade and within a reasonable period. But, while such liberalisation has been the main source of concern, there have been a number of other associated issues. All in all, we can identify five such issues.

The first is the effects of EPAs on regional integration which, as we saw above, is a key objective particularly of African countries. There is a potentially negative effect on African regional integration with regional groups splintering between those countries which are willing to liberalise and those which are not (Stevens 2006: 446). This could cause regional realignments and, because of the possibility of differential liberalisation schedules, make regional partners reluctant to open their borders to trade with each other – making smuggling across borders a possibility (*ibid.*: 451). Powell (2007: 5–6) cites United Nations research estimating that West African countries would experience net trade diversion amounting to US$365 million of which US$35.6 million represents foregone exports from the Economic Community of West African States (ECOWAS) to the rest of the region. Stevens concludes, "All in all, the outlook for EPAs to support regional integration is not good" (2006: 455).

The second issue is an associated argument against EPAs put forward by Borrmann & Busse (2007). Their concern is with the quality of institutions and in particular market entry regulations for starting a business, the efficiency of the tax system and labour market regulation (Borrmann & Busse 2007: 406). Where these are in place and not excessive there is a positive relationship between trade liberalisation and growth, whereas the opposite is true where the institutional arrangements are poor. Analysing the ACP countries on this basis they find that there is limited concern in the Caribbean and Pacific countries due to the stage of institutional development already achieved. For the four African regions, however, the story is

---

[10]See www.dfid.gov.uk/aboutdfid/organisation/economic-partnership-agreements.asp, accessed 12/12/08.

very different: "the large majority of African countries [33 out of 46][11] ... are not likely to benefit from an increase in trade due to EPAs" (*ibid*.: 407). Hence, they argue that "reform of the institutional frameworks should be an important topic on the EPA agenda" (*ibid*.: 407), but are not convinced that even then, and even with appropriate aid assistance, sufficient time exists for such reforms to be introduced – a further point in relation to the "within a reasonable length of time" issue noted above. Borrmann & Busse (2007: 414) also note that larger or more powerful countries with good institutions may then force weaker countries into EPAs when the effects on the weaker countries may be for them to suffer rather than benefit. The alternative is the undermining of regional integration if they opt out of the EPA process – as we have already noted above.

The third issue, which follows from the first two, is the trade and fiscal impact of EPAs. As might be expected, various assessments of such effects have been made. Lang (2006: 13) compares the impact of EPAs under three scenarios – full reciprocal liberalisation; asymmetrical liberalisation (EU 100%, ACP 80%, SAT = 90%) under the EU's classic interpretation; and a larger degree of asymmetry (EU 100%, ACP 60%, SAT = 80%). The most favourable, of course, is the last scenario and only here does GDP increase for ACP countries though there are still fiscal losses due to reduced tariff income. The effect of reciprocity on the consequent reduction in revenues from tariffs is illustrated by the case of Zambia which would lose $15.8 m per year – the equivalent of its annual HIV/Aids budget (Bunting 2007).

Busse & Grossmann (2007) look specifically at the trade and fiscal impact on West African countries. While the detailed results that they present are beyond the scope of this chapter, their conclusions are instructive. Assuming complete tariff liberalisation, trade creation would exceed trade diversion in all West African countries, with total imports from EU countries also increasing in all countries (*ibid*.: 795). The effect on government revenues, however, is a decline of between 4% and 9% in most West African countries, although Cape Verde and Gambia would be more seriously affected (*ibid*.: 808). Since full liberalisation is unlikely the actual effects would be smaller, but nonetheless Busse & Grossman conclude that since "tariff revenue is a significant source of financing government expenditures in most of the West African countries ... the most urgent task ... will be to take measures to offset the decline..." (*ibid*.: 809), though they note the difficulties inherent in replacing this funding with domestic taxation. "To sum up", they say, "negotiations on EPAs pose a major challenge to West African countries. While there is little doubt that West African countries would benefit from improved or more secure access to EU markets, it is not clear whether it is in the interest of West African countries to eliminate customs duties for almost all EU products by 2020" and they call for the well-designed opening up of domestic markets "with specific attention given to country specifics and capabilities" (*ibid*.: 809). This echoes the call by Borrmann & Busse (2007: 414) for a high degree of flexibility in the EPA process if pro-development outcomes are to be achieved.

---

[11] Countries included in the analysis differ very slightly from those in Appendix 1.

Anderson & van der Mensbrugghe (2007) studied the specific case of Uganda. They compare full mutual liberalisation (including the removal of developed countries' agricultural subsidies) with two alternative scenarios. The first is a multilateral partial reform under the WTO's Doha round and the second is under EPAs. Again, the details of the findings need not concern us, but the conclusions are that "Uganda is not likely to gain a lot – and may even lose very slightly – from further reducing its tariffs, and likewise from the EU waiving the remaining tariffs on imports from Uganda and other ACP countries" (*ibid.*: 548). They stress that this does not mean that there is no need for Uganda and its ACP partners to undertake further trade reform, but again it seems that the conditions need to be right for Uganda to benefit significantly from trade liberalisation.

More anecdotal evidence from NGOs indicates the actual effects of rapid trade liberalisation "on the ground". A Traidcraft report showed that Jamaica's dairy market liberalisation "decimated small farmers, left local milk production with barely a tenth of the market, and led to the EU supplying two-thirds of the island's milk powder", while a "Christian Aid assessment of tomato liberalisation in Senegal showed that the local price halved, while imports of EU paste increased twenty-fold" (Cobham & Powell: 2007). These may be anecdotal but the effects on actual people in ACP countries reminds us that statistics ultimately mean people and communities.

This collection of evidence then, albeit based mainly and necessarily on a forecasting of the effects, indicates that ACP countries are unlikely to benefit directly from EPAs. Nor should this surprise us, given the evidence that exists generally on trade liberalisation. Ochieng (2007: 377–8) summarises this well:

> The relationship between trade and growth has been shown to be complex, if not ambiguous ... there is little evidence that trade liberalization is correlated with economic growth, poverty reduction, or economic development. Whilst no country has developed successfully by turning its back on international trade, none has developed by simply liberalizing its trade. The critical balance lies in each country adopting its own trade and investment policies and strategies, in line with its development needs ... [A]nalysis of trade, economic growth and poverty reduction needs to go beyond trade liberalization to include *inter alia*: the relationships between trade and inequality, trade and employment, bargaining power in global production chains and the distribution of gains from trade, the effects of trends in, and variability of terms of trade on poverty, the effects of primary commodity dependence, and the relationship between export and import instability and vulnerability.

Again the evidence in favour of the flexibility of individual countries to determine their own development needs is clear.

This brings us to the fourth issue of concern and one which is also related to the issue of flexibility. This is that the EC has attempted to include what are known as the "Singapore Issues" on the agenda within the negotiations on EPAs. These relate to investment, competition, government procurement and services, and the EC's position is that these should also be subject to negotiation within EPAs apparently "in order to achieve ACP development objectives" (Griffith & Powell 2007: 8). ACP countries, by contrast, have generally indicated that they do not wish these issues to be part of EPAs negotiations and, apart from services, these issues remain outside the ambit of the WTO. Within the Cotonou Agreement there is only an agreement to discuss co-operation not to agree binding rules (*ibid.*: 8–9). Again, there seems to be a lack of flexibility here on the EC's part, and an unwillingness to allow ACP countries the flexibility to negotiate on these issues at their choice and speed. This is exactly the concern of the U.K.'s International Development Committee which has expressed its view that the EU is abusing its position on this issue (IDC 2007: 14), and DFID in the U.K. is similarly concerned.[12]

The fifth and final issue is to do with aid. Given that there are, as already noted above, a series of supply side constraints such as poor infrastructure, weak production capacity and low levels of human resources (Powell 2007: 4) that need to be addressed in any case to enable development in ACP countries, together with the adjustment costs that EPAs themselves would entail, aid has always been a part of the negotiations (Griffiths & Powell 2007: 19). The core funding for supply side issues comes from the European Development Fund (EDF) but there is evidence that the tenth EDF, from which such funds would come, is both under-funded and will suffer a delayed start in 2010 leaving a 2 year gap between it and the ninth EDF (Powell 2007: 45). The EU has also promised further aid targeted specifically as "aid for trade", planned to reach €2 billion by 2010.[13] However, the issue of contention has been the extent to which such aid is being made conditional on signing EPAs. Not surprisingly, the two sides differ – DFID is explicit in stating that the EC's position is that "aid for trade is not conditional on EPAs",[14] while those reporting the ACP position are equally unequivocal in stating that, "aid is clearly being offered on condition of commitments made in EPAs" (Powell 2007: 45).

Whatever the rights and wrongs of this particular issue, there remains the fact that negotiations over EPAs have become highly contentious and politicised. The effects on regional integration, the need for reform in institutional frameworks, the estimated direct trade and fiscal effects of EPAs, together with the introduction or otherwise of the Singapore issues and the amount and conditionality of aid, all make for a complex situation where any assessments of fairness or unfairness are clearly not straightforward. However, NGOs have traditionally seen their role as cutting through the complexities and running campaigns to highlight what they perceive to be gross injustices. Before turning to issues of fairness, a brief look at the campaign against EPAs is worthwhile.

10.4 The "Stop EPAs" Campaign

Once negotiations on EPAs had begun in September 2002 African organisations became concerned at the potential effects of these new agreements and contacted

---

[12] See www.dfid.gov.uk/aboutdfid/organisation/economic-partnership-agreements-myths.asp, accessed 12/12/08.

[13] See http://europa.eu/scadplus/leg/en/lvb/r13002.htm, accessed 12/12/08.

[14] See www.dfid.gov.uk/aboutdfid/organisation/economic-partnership-agreements-myths.asp, accessed 12/12/08.

European charities to help. In 2004, after 2 years of detailed analysis, the "Stop EPAs" campaign was born (Traidcraft 2008). Since then an orchestrated campaign involving many organisations linked to the Trade Justice Movement (TJM),[15] has attempted at the very least to ensure that "fair" EPAs were negotiated or that alternatives such as EBAs and GSP+ were introduced to allow more time for the negotiations over EPAs themselves. It is not clear that the campaign ever had the objective or thought that it might actually "stop EPAs" from occurring, but in the nature of NGOs and campaigning a snappy title is more important than accuracy. Similarly, the content of some of the campaigning material expresses the enormous complexity of the issue in rather more bite-sized language. A briefing for U.K. MP's by the TJM issued in September 2007, for example, stated that "If [EPAs] are not changed dramatically in the next few months, they will threaten the futures of up to 750 million people" – quite what "threaten the futures" means in practice is far from clear.

This is not to say that the campaign has not had the intellectual weight behind it that such campaigns deserve – two extensive reports (Griffiths & Powell 2007, Powell 2007) have already been cited from above. One of these reports had as its focus not so much the content of the EPA negotiations but the manner in which they have been conducted – an approach that is described as "undermining partnership" (Griffiths & Powell 2007: 13). The claim is that in the dismissive approach to ACP proposals, the disregard for ACP institutions and processes, the forcing of negotiation on the Singapore issues, the manipulation of the prospect of aid, the threat of loss of market access, the refusal to consider alternatives, the exclusion of dissenting voices and the imposition of deadlines before development, the EC's conduct has been far from exemplary. This is an interesting and unusual "process" report which ends by placing the onus on EU states "to rein in the [European] Commission and insist upon a fundamentally different approach, based on non-reciprocity" (*ibid.*: 31). The issue of process is one that we will return to below.

10.5 EPAs – The Current Situation

The situation with regard to which EPAs had been signed was, of course, changing rapidly as the 31 December 2007 deadline came and passed. The position as of the date of writing in December 2008 (1 year after the supposed deadline), is shown in Appendix 2 where it may be seen that 35 countries in total out of 76 (46%) have signed EPAs. Of these, however, only 9 out of 39 (23%) are LDCs, whereas 26 out of 37 (70%) non-LDCs have signed. Given the option for LDCs to use EBA, making essentially no difference to their previous position under the Cotonou Agreement, it is not surprising that many have opted not to sign. Equally predictable is the

---

[15] See http://www.tjm.org.uk, accessed 12/12/08.

number of non-LDCs which have signed given that their alternative GSP+ gives less favourable access to the EU market and would thus lead to a decline in their export earnings. In terms of regional groupings, only the Caribbean has signed in its entirety, but given the presence of only one LDC (Haiti) in a group of 15 countries this is equally not surprising.

As noted in Appendix 2, the regional groupings that have signed EPAs are slightly different from the original groupings with which the EC was negotiating. Thus, seven EPAs have been signed in total.[16] Of these, only one – the Caribbean EPA – is considered to be a full or comprehensive EPA by the EC. The Caribbean EPA includes not just provisions for trade in goods, which were, of course, essential to comply with WTO rules, but services, investment, competition and public procurement aspects – in other words the contentious "Singapore" issues. The remaining six EPAs are regarded as "interim" in that they focus on goods only, but mostly include clauses to allow negotiations to continue on these other areas.[17] These Interim EPAs (IEPAs) have only been initialled rather than signed – an important difference since although the negotiations have come to a conclusion there is still a formal ratification process to be undertaken.

In a recent assessment of the legal texts of the EPAs that have been signed or initialled (Oxfam 2008), it is claimed that these are not development friendly. While the actual impact on those countries which have not signed EPAs at present has been small (*ibid.*: 8), the projected effects of EPAs themselves are generally felt to be against the interests of ACP countries. The liberalisation of goods is higher than Europe originally proposed, at between 67% and 83% of trade, although the timescales vary between 0 and 25 years (*ibid.*: 14). Regional disintegration is predicted (*ibid.*: 17), and ACP countries will be left worse off financially with a need for significant aid to upgrade basic infrastructure (*ibid.*: 19). The conclusion is that the initialled EPA deals "fail the 'development test'. Far from restructuring economic relationships to stimulate development, they risk locking ACP countries into current patterns of inequality and marginalisation, and further bias the multilateral trading system against the interests of developing countries" (*ibid.*: 34). While much of this is familiar from the earlier discussions, it is of note that Oxfam calls for "renegotiation of any aspect of the initialled EPAs … to reduce the deals to the minimum needed for WTO compliance" (*ibid.*: 38). Despite the 31 December 2007 deadline, the initialling process seems to have

---

[16]The seven are: West Africa (Ghana, Ivory Coast); Central African Economic and Monetary Community (Cameroon); East African Community (Burundi, Kenya, Rwanda, Tanzania and Uganda); East and Southern Africa (Comoros, Madagascar, Mauritius, Seychelles and Zimbabwe); Southern African Development Community (Botswana, Lesotho, Mozambique, Namibia and Swaziland); Caribbean (all countries – see Appendix 1); Pacific (Fiji and Papua New Guinea), www.dfid.gov.uk/aboutdfid/organisation/epas-progress-update.asp, accessed 12/12/08.

[17]See www.dfid.gov.uk/aboutdfid/organisation/epas-progress-update.asp, accessed 12/12/08. An alternative web-site for regular up-dates can be found at www.acp-eu-trade.org. See also http://ec.europa.eu/trade/issues/bilateral/regions/acp/regneg_en.htm.

bought time with the WTO, and may now allow the opportunity for further negotiations.

10.6 Assessing Fairness in International Trade

As noted at the outset, the inherent complexity of the situation described above rules out any simplistic application of fairness principles. So, we begin by looking at fairness principles themselves to see what light might be shed by such a review, before turning to their application. And while fairness has, of course, been the subject of much philosophical debate in general, it has also been the subject of discussion specifically in relation to international trade (Brown & Stern 2007, Davidson et al. 2006, de Jasay 2006, Franck 1995, Maseland & de Vaal 2002, 2003, Narlikar 2006, Ochieng 2007, Suranovic 2000). Much of this originates in the economics literature, from which three points are worth noting immediately. The first is that economists frequently "dismiss notions of rights, justice and fairness as, at best, muddled, and more likely welfare worsening" and that the most characteristic normative method adopted by economists is "straightforward individualistic utilitarian consequentialism" (Davidson *et al.* 2006: 989). This 'free market' position, of course, lends strong support to trade liberalisation and opposes protectionism in all its forms. And protectionism is the second point worthy of note, for 'fair trade' is often contrasted with 'free trade' to denote protectionism which seeks to mitigate the effects of international competitors on domestic industries (see, for example, Bhagwati 1995, Maseland & de Vaal 2002, Howse & Trebilcock 1996). This understanding of fair trade gives rise to the view that fair traders are "charlatans (protectionists masquerading as moralists)" (Howse & Trebilcock 1996: 61).

However, while we can dismiss this particular use of the term fairness, it is clear that issues of fairness do play "a non-trivial role in the politics of trade policy" (Davidson *et al.* 2006: 990) so that questions such as, "Is it fair for all countries to be held to the same set of standards when these countries are at different levels of economic development?", or "What are fair responses to the imminent changes in world trading patterns?" (Suranovic 2000: 283), or of direct relevance to this chapter, "Are EPAs fair?", are entirely legitimate. And the third point to note stems from this. As Franck (1995) has observed, for any discourse on fairness to take place, two preconditions must exist. The first is moderate scarcity: "Discussion about fairness ... is most likely to be productive when the allocation of rights and duties occurs in circumstances which make allocation both necessary and possible. This circumstance ... John Rawls has aptly called a condition of 'moderate scarcity'" (*ibid.*: 9). The second precondition is community: "It is only in community that the bedrock of shared values and developed principles necessary to any assessment of fairness is found" (*ibid.*: 10). And in Franck's view "we are witnessing the dawn of a new era, defined both by moderate scarcity and by an emerging sense of global community" (*ibid.*: 11). In other words, the preconditions are now met and the time is right for substantive discussion about fairness in international trade.

With this as background, we can turn to fairness principles themselves. And we find, not surprisingly, that these divide into the conventional distinction between procedural and distributive fairness – although "justice" is often used instead of fairness, a point to which we will return. That fairness has two dimensions – the process by which outcomes are derived and the outcomes themselves – is, of course, a common-place, but it is worth exploring some of the nuances that emerge within this distinction.

On the procedural side, Suranovic (2000), amongst the seven fairness principles that he derives,[18] gives four that relate to procedural fairness. These are non-discrimination fairness (where, if one group is allowed to take some action, then all other groups deemed to be equal should be similarly allowed – *ibid.*: 288); Golden Rule fairness (based on Kant's categorical imperative, where an agent should take some action which has an effect on another only if that agent is willing to have another agent take a comparable action with the identical effect on himself – *ibid.*: 291); and positive and negative reciprocity fairness (where agents exchange either positive "you scratch my back and I'll scratch yours", or negative "tit for tat" actions – *ibid.*: 295, 299). Brown & Stern (2007: 299–302) also discuss reciprocity noting that, understood as "rough equivalence", it remains an important criterion for negotiations in international trade.

Maseland & de Vaal (2002) make a distinction of fairness along deontological versus consequentialist grounds, the latter of which we will return to under distributive fairness, but the former of which is worth noting now. Essentially it is to do with the "conditions under which trade, and the production of traded goods, should minimally take place" (*ibid.*: 254). In a later paper they refer to this as "principle" fairness (Maseland & de Vaal 2003) and identify it as being trade conducted in compliance with designated basic prohibitions such as the absence of child labour or environmentally harmful production methods. They note that, while free trade can lead to the absence of such conditions, for instance because it raises incomes, it lacks a self-regulating mechanism to ensure such conditions are met. It therefore seems appropriate to categorise it here, under procedural fairness, because of the procedural requirements to enforce such compliance and because the overall outcome that follows may not necessarily be efficient – a distributive matter.

Legitimacy fairness is another way of describing procedural fairness (Franck 1995: 7–8, Narlikar 2006: 1007–8), a point that Elsig (2007: 81) using the term "input legitimacy" makes in relation to the WTO, and to which we will also

---

[18] Suranovic (2000) divides these seven into two categories: equality fairness and reciprocity fairness. I will cover six of the seven here, the seventh being privacy fairness – "an agent should be free to take any action which has effects only on himself" (*ibid.*: 301)

return. Meanwhile, Brown & Stern refer to "equality of opportunity" as a procedural issue noting, however, that they do not advance it as a high moral principle
but merely an "instrumental criterion to be valued for its consequences, namely
that it facilitates the reaching of inter-governmental agreements that protect and
enhance the mutually advantageous trading system" (2007: 295). This relationship
between the two forms of fairness is also something to which we will need to
return.

On the distributive side many of the authors already cited note the importance
of outcomes for fairness assessments (Brown & Stern 2007, Maseland & de Vaal
2002, 2003, Narlikar 2006, Ochieng 2007, Suranovic 2000) and it is in relation to
this discussion that economists refer to the concepts of welfare efficiency and Pareto
optimality:

> "For many economists – borrowing from welfare theory – a practically acceptable cri-
> terion of fairness would be that the trade negotiations result in a more efficient global
> economy. Greater efficiency is defined as a movement towards Pareto optimality and, in
> the context of international trade, such a state would be reached when no country can
> be made better off without some other country being made worse off" (Brown & Stern
> 2007: 296).

An alternative expression of this is to refer to "maximum benefit fairness"
(Suranovic 2000: 302–4), in which the utilitarian rhetorical device of "the greatest
good for the greatest number" is, in effect, applied irrespective of the consequences
for affected minorities.

However, another distributional principle that is included in the literature is perhaps best termed "poverty alleviation fairness" (Maseland & de Vaal 2003) and
is one in which "beneficial consequences for the poorest groups in the world"
(Maseland & de Vaal 2002: 256) are to be taken into account. As Maseland & de
Vaal note, this concept draws on Rawlsian thinking and attempts to combine Pareto
optimality with the idea that "the only inequality a rational individual would accept
is the minimum inequality necessary to improve the situation of the least well off in
society" (*ibid.*: 256). Franck refers to this as the 'maximin' principle (1995: 18–19)
and notes that it is a neo-egalitarian principle of distributive fairness. In relation to
the fairness of EPAs this will clearly be an important concept, but is also one that
acknowledges the "unequal starting positions" (Maseland & de Vaal 2003) of different countries. While a Nozickian approach would ignore such inequalities, it would
seem to be very much to the point that they be included in any consideration of
the fairness of international trade. This is not to argue for a socialist redistribution
of input factors (even were that to be possible), but for negative consequences of
inequalities to be at least taken into account (see Maseland & de Vaal 2002: 255–6).

An attempt at resolving the terminological issue that we noted above between
fairness and justice is made by de Jasay (2006). He argues, in effect, that justice
refers to procedural issues, while fairness refers to outcomes. On this basis (one
that is by no means universal) he is able to argue that trade made fair by regulation violates freedom of contract and as such is an injustice (*ibid.*: 175–6). In other

words, fair is not, or is not necessarily, just (and *vice-versa*). While we do not particularly need to follow the terminology here, the point is important – that procedural and distributive fairness do not necessarily follow one another with one leading automatically to the other, but are different aspects of fairness which may not coincide (Franck 1995: 22). Franck makes the further point that they may not even pull in the same direction, since distributive fairness is likely to lead to change, whereas procedural fairness tends towards stability (*ibid.*: 7).

However, it is often the case that both forms of fairness are needed if true fairness is to result – Elsig (2007), for example, refers to the need to balance what he calls input and output legitimacy in the WTO. Stiglitz & Charlton's set of principles (cited in Brown & Stern 2007: 312–3), in relation to the Doha Development round of the WTO, provide a further example. It is clear that the first two are to do with distributive fairness while the last two are procedural in nature:

1. Any agreement should be assessed in terms of its impact on development; items with a negative effect on development should not be on the agenda;
2. Any agreement should be fair (i.e. that the outcome should provide a larger share of aggregate benefits to the poorer countries);
3. Any agreement should be fairly arrived at;
4. Any agreement should be limited in scope (i.e. preventing unwarranted intrusions into national sovereignty).

While this completes a brief summary of fairness principles as covered in the relevant literature, there is one further and important area that we need to consider before we turn to an assessment of the fairness of EPAs. In some ways this takes us back to one of the two preconditions that Franck identified – that it is "only in community that the bedrock of shared values and developed principles necessary to any assessment of fairness is found" (Franck 1995: 10). The question that this raises is really an Aristotelian one, and so differs from the Enlightenment concepts of fairness discussed so far, and over which perhaps limited agreement can be reached.

The Aristotelian question is always to do with what makes for the flourishing of life as a whole both individually and in community. It therefore asks questions of purpose and relationship and is, in that sense, essentially *teleological*. Modern work on virtue ethics, as it is known (MacIntyre 2007), and as applied at the level of business organisations rather than trade *per se* (Moore & Beadle 2006, Moore 2009) focuses on such a teleological approach and encourages the pursuit of excellence rather than the "levelling tendency" that deontological ethics has been charged with (Koehn 1995: 537). In terms of something essentially practical like the negotiation of EPAs this will encourage us to ask what the purpose of such agreements are, how they support and benefit community both within developing countries and between developing and developed countries, and what excellence means in this context. It is probably apparent that questions such as these take us beyond the conventional approaches to ethics via the fairness discourse, but also that they have something in common with the teleological approach to interpretation of WTO laws taken by ACP countries, as noted above.

10.7 An Assessment of the Fairness of EPAs

From all that has been said above, it will come as no surprise that the fairness assessments that can be made are somewhat tentative. But the reasons for such tentativeness will be become clearer as we proceed, so we begin by considering issues of procedural fairness. The most extensive consideration of this is given in Griffith & Powell (2007), covered above in the "Stop EPAs" section. In "undermining partnership" through the eight procedural issues that were identified, in all of which the EC was regarded as being at fault, procedural fairness seems to have been compromised by the EC. That, at first sight, might seem a straightforward and incontrovertible judgment.

However, in considering WTO negotiations in general (of which EPAs can be viewed in this context as a separate but inter-related part), the situation becomes less clear-cut. Narlikar (2006: 1009) argues that the WTO has, in general, paid limited homage to the fairness discourse but "particularly its distributive justice component". In other words, the WTO, where it has included fairness considerations, has focused on procedural fairness, and has done so partly because any notion of *redistributive* justice through global trade has sat uneasily with "more liberal trade principles" and "with the national interests of already institutionalised countries" (Ochieng 2007: 389). Narlikar reinforces this point: "even if provisions in the WTO on distributional fairness are few, ... its dedication to fair process, order and legitimacy is borne out in its rules of non-discrimination and reciprocity" (2006: 1009). The concerns of the EC in ensuring that EPAs were WTO-compatible, and awareness of the procedural unfairness associated with the fact that such non-reciprocal agreements discriminated against non-ACP states, are further evidence of this approach.

Ochieng notes that even by the early 1990s "developing countries had been forced to change tack, toning down on the notion of *fairness of outcomes* and moving towards accommodating the *fairness of process* concept (even whilst complaining that WTO processes were not fair to them)" (Ochieng 2007: 389, emphasis in original). It seems, therefore, that developing countries might have been better prepared for negotiating on EPAs, having accepted that this would be the focus of the EC in such negotiations. Being better prepared might have helped the ACP countries to negotiate more forcefully and within the reasonable time periods laid down in the Cotonou Agreement.

Accepting that ACP countries might have expected the EC to focus on procedural issues does not, however, mean that they would or should have abandoned their interest in distributive fairness. Narlikar (2006: 1028), indeed, suggests that developing countries generally have had some success in maintaining a focus on distributive fairness and that this may lead to the reintroduction of the fairness-as-equity discourse into the WTO, with the Doha *Development* Agenda as an indicator of this.

Elsig, however, recognises the link between the two forms of fairness arguing that "the input side should not be neglected as the belief in fair processes potentially increases the rate of compliance with negotiated treaties, thus increasing output legitimacy" (2007: 89).

However, allowing for the continuing asymmetries in the WTO and the continuing complaints of the developing countries over equity of process (Narlikar 2006: 1024–5), and therefore their likely extension into negotiations over EPAs, it seems probable that procedural fairness has been compromised during the process. The attempt (and success with the Caribbean grouping) to bring the Singapore issues onto the agenda, and the attempt to introduce conditionality on aid strengthens the suspicion that EPAs have not been fairly negotiated.

What, then, of distributive fairness? While, of course, the judgment in this case has to be tentative until actual outcomes are known, the evidence cited above in relation to the likely negative impact on regional integration especially in Africa; on the timing of the introduction of EPAs in relation to the poor institutional quality which is likely to mean, again, that African countries are not in a position to benefit from trade liberalisation; and the more general trade and fiscal effects, all suggest that the distributive outcomes will not benefit ACP countries.

The counter argument to this, however, is the potential distributive unfairness that non-ACP, non-LDC countries have been experiencing (following the procedural unfairness noted above) – and hence the reason that they have been watching the EPA negotiations "like hawks" (Mandelson 2007, cited above) and might mount a legal challenge under Article XXIV. The EU countries, and on their behalf the EC, have, they would argue, been negotiating on EPAs in order to ensure that a WTO-compatible legal basis on which continuing preferential treatment of ACP countries could be provided. It is not their fault, they can argue, that the WTO requires reciprocity on substantially all trade within a reasonable period. In addition, the extended time periods (at least 10 years and possibly up to 25 – see above) allowable within EPAs for SAT to be realised would, the EU states might well argue, give both sufficient time and incentive to resolve the institutional development and other issues.

That it is in both the developing and developed countries' interests ultimately to make significant progress on trade liberalisation is something both sides can probably agree on. That EPAs are necessary in this is something developing countries, with the exception of the Caribbean grouping, are clearly more reluctant to agree on. That EPAs are likely to lead to appropriate and substantive development, and therefore to distributive fairness, is something that the two sides are, again with the possible exception of the Caribbean grouping, at odds over and only time will tell which side is right.

Within this debate, however, the issues of community and purpose, the Aristotelian questions, seem rarely to get asked, with sides being taken and personal advantage being sought. This takes us back to the different interpretations of WTO laws discussed in the background section above. Here, it would seem that the ACP's teleological approach is the more appropriate. The ACP states see the

WTO as developmentally oriented while the EC and other developed countries see it as solely a trade organisation. Although not explicit, it could be argued that the ACP countries see the "dawn of a new era" characterised by "an emerging sense of global community" (Franck 1995: 11, cited above), and would argue for notions of excellence in international trade to emerge. Such excellence might well include the flexibility necessary to recognise the different starting positions and speed of development that developing countries in general, and LDCs in particular, are capable of, and to design processes that would allow such flexibility – a key point of concern noted on a number of occasions above. To achieve this flexibility, while still enabling regional integration, is obviously no simple task, but one that excellent trade negotiations and outcomes ought to seek.

Perhaps, a more genuine attempt by the EC to take a developing country perspective, to seek to realise the purpose of EPAs and the Doha Development Round more generally as to do with sustainable development as we try to learn to live together on one earth, and to effect that through more community-minded initiatives that extend, if necessary, to other non-ACP countries, might have led not only to a process that was more acceptable to ACP countries but one in which the outcomes are more likely to be developmentally good. The opportunity for further negotiations may yet lead to such an outcome.

10.8 Conclusion

I indicated at the outset that the conclusions that could be drawn would necessarily be somewhat tentative. It is difficult to be conclusive in such a fast-moving and complex area. However, while the evidence is generally against the EC and, behind it, the EU states, it does seem that both "sides" may have lessons to learn from EPAs over both the process of negotiating and the outcomes that are sought, even though the actual outcomes may in some cases be many years away from being realised. The existing conceptualisations of fairness, based on Enlightenment principles, provide a basic mechanism by which such fairness claims can be examined, but they do not take sufficient account of the purposive and community aspects of international trade negotiations. Perhaps here, as EPAs continue to be negotiated and these agreements are implemented, there is a chance for something developmentally beneficial to emerge. This will require the EC to focus more on distributive fairness, and accept the changes that will necessarily accompany this, rather than rely upon the stability that arises from procedural fairness considerations.

Within this, there is a potential knock-on effect on the WTO itself. As Ochieng concludes, "development-oriented EPAs will require not only innovations in their design and scope but also innovative interpretation of existing WTO rules or innovations to some of the existing WTO rules, most notably, Article XXIV and a wide array of other SDT provisions" (2007: 395). Hence, one of the benefits of EPAs may be to challenge the WTO and the EU's conservative interpretation of its purpose, and lead to international trade that is, indeed, not just procedurally fair in its negotiation and distributively fair in its implementation, but also genuinely develops the global community.

Appendix 1

ACP countries by regional groupings

	ECOWAS	CEMAC	ESA	SADC	Caribbean	Pacific
1	*Benin*	Cameroon	*Burundi*	*Angola*	Antigua & Barbuda	Cook Is.
2	*Burkina Faso*	*Central African Republic*	*Comoros*	Botswana	Bahamas	Fed. Micron.
3	*Cape Verde*	Chad	*Djibouti*	*Lesotho*	Barbados	Fiji
4	Gambia	Congo (Brazzaville)	*Eritrea*	*Mozambique*	Belize	*Kiribati*
5	Ghana	*Congo (Dem. Rep.-Kinshasa)*	*Ethiopia*	Namibia	Dominica	Marshall Is.
6	*Guinea*	Equatorial Guinea	Kenya	Swaziland	Dominican Rep.	Nauru
7	*Guinea-Bissau*	Gabon	*Malawi*	*Tanzania*	Grenada	Niue
8	Ivory Coast	*Sao Tome & Principe*	Mauritius	South Africa	Guyana	Palau
9	*Liberia*		*Madagascar*		*Haiti*	Papua New Guinea
10	*Mali*		*Rwanda*		Jamaica	*Samoa*
11	*Mauritania*		Seychelles		St. Kitts & Nevis	*Solomon Is.*
12	*Niger*		*Sudan*		St Lucia	Tonga
13	Nigeria		*Uganda*		St Vincent & the Grenadines	*Tuvalu*
14	*Senegal*		*Zambia*		Surinam	*Vanuatu*
15	*Sierra Leone*		Zimbabwe		Trinidad & Tobago	
16	*Togo*					
No. LDCs	13	5	11	4	1	5

Sources: http://ec.europa.eu/trade/issues/bilateral/regions/acp/plcg_en.htm, accessed 12/12/08; www.dfid.gov.uk/aboutdfid/organisation/epas-progress-update.asp, accessed 12/12/08, and Lang 2006: 36–38

Note: Countries in italics are Least Developed Countries (LDCs) – 39 out of a total of 76

Key:

ECOWAS Economic Community of West African States

CEMAC   Economic and Monetary Community of Central Africa

ESA   Eastern and Southern Africa

SADC   Southern African Development Community

Appendix 2

Signatories to economic partnership agreements

	ECOWAS	CEMAC	ESA	SADC	Caribbean	Pacific
1	Ghana	Cameroon	*Burundi*	Botswana	Antigua & Barbuda	Fiji
2	Ivory Coast		*Comoros*	*Lesotho*	Bahamas	Papua New Guinea
3			Kenya	*Mozambique*	Barbados	
4			Mauritius	Namibia	Belize	
5			*Madagascar*	*Swaziland*	Dominica	
6			*Rwanda*	*Tanzania*	Dominican Rep.	
7			Seychelles		Grenada	
8			*Uganda*		Guyana	
9			Zimbabwe		*Haiti*	
10					Jamaica	
11					St Kitts & Nevis	
12					St Lucia	
13					St Vincent & the Grenadines	
14					Surinam	
15					Trinidad & Tobago	
16						
No. LDCs	0	0	5	3	1	0

Source: http://ec.europa.eu/trade/issues/bilateral/regions/acp/regneg_en.htm, accessed 12/12/08. The web-site gives slightly different groupings from those shown in Appendix 1. For ease of comparison, the same groupings are maintained

Note: Countries in italics are Least Developed Countries (LDCs). Only 9 from a possible 39 LDCs have signed EPAs; for non-LDCs the number is 26 from 37

References

Anderson, K. and van der Mensbrugghe, D. 2007, Effects of multilateral and preferential trade policy reform in Africa: the case of Uganda. *Journal of International Trade & Economic Development* 16 (4), 529–550.

Bhagwati, J. 1995, Trade liberalisation and 'Fair Trade' demands: addressing the environmental and labour standards issues. *World Economy* 18 (6), 745–759.

Borrmann, A. and Busse, M. 2007, The institutional challenge of the ACP/EU Economic Partnership Agreements. *Development Policy Review* 25 (4), 403–416.

Brown, A. G. and. Stern, R. M. 2007, Concepts of Fairness in the Global Trading System. *Pacific Economic Review* 12 (3), 293–318.

Bunting, M. 2007, The EU is bullying the world's poor to rush into a dubious deal on trade. *The Guardian*, 19/11/07.

Busse, M. and Grossmann, H. 2007, The trade and fiscal impact of EU/ACP Economic Partnership Agreements on West African countries. *Journal of Development Studies* 43 (5), 787–811.

Cobham, A. and Powell, S. 2007, The EU is trying to trick developing countries into poor trade deals. *The Guardian*, 8/11/07.

Davidson, C., Matusz, S., & Nelson, D. 2006, Fairness and the political economy of trade. *World Economy* 29 (8), 989–1004.

De Jasay, A. 2006, When fair is not just and just is not fair. *The Independent Review* 11 (2), 165–176.

Elsig, M. 2007, The World Trade Organization's legitimacy crisis: what does the beast look like? *Journal of World Trade* 41 (1), 75–98.

Franck, T. 1995, *Fairness in International Law and Institutions* (Clarendon Press, Oxford).

Griffith, M. and Powell, S. 2007, *Partnership under pressure. An assessment of the European Commission's conduct in the EPA negotiations.* London: ActionAid, CAFOD, Christian Aid, Tearfund, Traidcraft Exchange.

Howse, R. and Trebilcock, M. 1996, The Fair Trade – Free Trade debate: trade, labour and the environment. *International Review of Law and Economics* 16 (1), 61–79.

IDC 2007, *EU Development and Trade Policies: An Update, International Development Committee* (House of Commons, London).

Koehn, D. 1995, A role for virtue ethics in the analysis of business practice. *Business Ethics Quarterly* 5 (3), 533–539.

Lang, R. 2006, Renegotiating GATT Article XXIV – a priority for African countries engaged in North-South trade agreements, Work in Progress No. 33, Africa Trade Policy Centre, Economic Commission for Africa.

MacIntyre, A. 2007 [1981], *After Virtue*, 3rd edn. (Duckworth, London).

Mandelson, P. 2007, Comments by Peter Mandelson to the European Parliament Development Committee on EPAs, Doha trade talks, Brussels, 5 November, http://ec.europa.eu/ commission_barroso/mandelson/speeches_articles/sppm177_en.htm, accessed 12/12/08.

Maseland, R. and de Vaal, A. 2002, How fair is Fair Trade? *De Economist* 150, 251–272.

Maseland, R. and de Vaal, A. 2003, Fairness in International Trade. Paper presented at the International Conference "Managing on the Edge" (University of Nijmegen, Nijmegen).

Moore, G. 2009, 'Virtue ethics and business organizations'. In J. Smith (ed.) *Normative Theory and Business* (Rowman and Littlefield, Lanham, MD).

Moore, G. and Beadle, R. 2006, In search of organizational virtue in business: agents, goods, practices, institutions and environments. *Organization Studies* 27 (3), 369–389.

Narlikar, A. 2006, Fairness in international trade negotiations: developing countries in the GATT and WTO. *World Economy* 29 (8), 1005–1029.

Ochieng, C. 2007, The EU-ACP Economic Partnership Agreements and the 'Development Question': constraints and opportunities posed by Article XXIV and Special and Differential Treatment provisions of the WTO. *Journal of International Economic Law* 10 (2), 363–395.

Oxfam 2008, *Partnership or Power Play? How Europe should bring development into its trade deals with African, Caribbean and Pacific countries* (Oxfam International, Oxford).

Powell, S. 2007, *Economic Partnership Agreements: Building or Shattering African Regional Integration?* (EcoNews Africa, Seatini, Traidcraft Exchange, London).

Ross, W. 2007, Africans wary of Europe's trade offer, BBC News, 8/12/07, http://news.bbc.co.uk/1/hi/world/africa/7134407.stm, accessed 10/12/07.

Stevens, C. 2006, The EU, Africa and Economic Partnership Agreements: unintended consequences of policy leverage. *Journal of Modern African Studies* 44 (3), 441–458.

Suranovic, S. M. 2000, A positive analysis of fairness with applications to international trade. *World Economy* 23 (3), 283–307.

Traidcraft 2008, Economic Partnership Agreements; the fight for trade justice goes on. The Magazine, Spring 2008, Traidcraft, Gateshead, pp. 10–11.

Index

Note: Locators followed by 'f', 'n' and 't' refers to figures, note numbers and tables cited in the text

G. Moore (ed.), *Fairness in International Trade,* The International Society
of Business, Economics, and Ethics Book Series 1, DOI 10.1007/978-90-481-8840-6,
© Springer Science+Business Media B.V. 2010